BY STEVEN RINELLA

The MeatEater Fish and Game Cookbook

The Complete Guide to Hunting, Butchering, and Cooking Wild Game:
Volume 2, Small Game and Fowl

The Complete Guide to Hunting, Butchering, and Cooking Wild Game:
Volume 1, Big Game

Meat Eater: Adventures from the Life of an American Hunter

American Buffalo: In Search of a Lost Icon

The Scavenger's Guide to Haute Cuisine

The
MEATEATER
FISH & GAME
COOKBOOK

RECIPES AND TECHNIQUES FOR EVERY HUNTER AND ANGLER

Steven Rinella

WITH KRISTA RUANE

Photography by John Hafner
Additional photography by Garret Smith

Spiegel & Grau
New York

Published in the United States by Spiegel & Grau,
an imprint of Random House, a division of
Penguin Random House LLC, New York.

SPIEGEL & GRAU and colophon is a registered
trademark of Penguin Random House LLC.

LIBRARY OF CONGRESS CATALOGING-IN-PUBLICATION DATA
Names: Rinella, Steven, author.
Title: The MeatEater fish and game cookbook : recipes
and techniques for every hunter and angler / by
Steven Rinella.
Other titles: Meat eater fish and game cookbook |
MeatEater fish & game cookbook
Description: New York : Spiegel & Grau, [2018] |
Includes index.
Identifiers: LCCN 2018002015 | ISBN 9780399590078 |
ISBN 9780399590085 (ebook)
Subjects: LCSH: Cooking (Meat) | Cooking (Game) |
MeatEater (Television program) | LCGFT: Cookbooks.
Classification: LCC TX749 .R624 2018 |
DDC 641.6/6—dc23
LC record available at https://lccn.loc.gov/2018002015

Printed in China on acid-free paper

randomhousebooks.com
spiegelandgrau.com

9 8 7 6 5 4 3 2 1

First Edition

Project editor and producer: Krista Ruane

Food styling: Krista Ruane

Prop styling: Krista Ruane

Book design: Debbie Glasserman

FOR JAMES,
ROSEMARY,
AND MATTHEW.
MAY YOU LIVE IN A
WORLD FULL OF
WILD PLACES.

CONTENTS

INTRODUCTION

Wild game represents both the first and final frontier in cooking. While scholars like to argue over exactly how long anatomically modern humans have been here on Earth, there's no denying that we were eating strict wild game diets for well over 90 percent of the time. From our earliest days our dietary habits have fallen a long ways, to a point where in many circles the consumption of wild game is perceived as exotic, anachronistic, or even cruel. But in recent years, we've witnessed a great awakening around the subject of wild game in popular culture. Across the spectrum, from our most celebrated chefs to our most innovative tech executives to some of our most admired actors, athletes, and comedians, we've seen an enthusiasm for wild game that hasn't been witnessed since Daniel Boone extolled the virtues of bear meat and elk liver. It's an exciting time to be living a wild game lifestyle.

What is it about wild game that's getting people so excited? At the top of the list, certainly, is a desire to forge a deeper and more hands-on relationship to food. Going to the local farmers' market doesn't cut it. At best, you're still an arm's reach away from a truly intimate food experience. If you want to close that gap and get downright cozy with your protein, you need to pick up farming or else learn to hunt and fish. And believe me, hunting and fishing are way more exciting. What's more, hunting and fishing for food can inspire an empowering sense of self-reliance. So many of the processes that support our daily life occur out of sight and, unfortunately, out of mind. It's refreshing to take responsibility for such an elemental function of one's existence.

There's also the matter of variety. While most folks will eat dozens of types of fruits, vegetables, and grains throughout the year, many consume just three or four kinds of meat and only a small handful of fish species. Meanwhile, a skilled hunter and angler, no matter where he or she lives, has access to literally dozens of species of wild game, including many that would be impossible to obtain through commercial transactions. Pursuing these food resources will radically transform your perspective on life and the world you live in. When you open your eyes to the bloody, beautiful, sharp-toothed, and sometimes scary world of wild game, nothing will ever be the same.

It's helpful for a wild game cook to stop and think about the term *wild game*. In this context, I consider the word *wild* to have two meanings. The first is obvious, in that the meat is coming from untamed creatures that have not been corrupted through domestication by man. The other, less obvious meaning pertains to the quality of the meat itself. Dictionaries describe wild as "unrestrained" and "out of control," and those are pretty fitting descriptors for flesh that's been harvested from the natural world. Imagine for a moment the last time you were in a grocery store and saw a package of "Certified Angus Beef." Whether you saw that package in Tallahassee, Toledo, or Tacoma, you were looking at basically identical products. The animal was sent to a feedlot when it was about twelve months old, weighing about 700 pounds. It was then medicated and fed a diet of grain that added about 3.5 pounds of weight to its body every day. Ten to twelve months later, it was slaughtered at about 1,200 to 1,400 pounds in a mechanized, tightly regulated environment. The system is almost unerring in its consistency.

Wild game doesn't work that way. A pair of white-tail bucks coming at you on a trail in the woods could have two radically different histories. One might be a robust eighteen-month-old deer weighing 110 pounds that's been fattened beautifully on acorns. The other might be an emaciated six-year-old that recently lost thirty pounds while recovering from injuries sustained from coyotes when it got hung up on a barbed wire fence. That's an extreme example, but you get the point. Wild game is wildly variable. It's variable when it's alive, and variabilities are added on as you go through the processes of killing, butchering, and storing the meat. A salmon fillet taken from the left side of the fish and eaten raw on the day you caught it will be different from the right-hand fillet after it's been frozen for six months. Not that there's something wrong with a frozen salmon fillet. Handled properly, it will be a delicious reminder of your time spent on the water. But it might require some additional steps, such as the application of a dry brine followed by some applewood smoke, in order for it to reach its full and glorious potential. Such is the know-how that you'll find inside *The MeatEater Game and Fish Cookbook*.

The book is broken into eight chapters: Big Game, Small Game, Waterfowl, Upland Birds, Freshwater Fish, Saltwater Fish, Reptiles and Amphibians, and Shellfish and Crustaceans. The chapter breakdown is essential for imposing some discipline on the book and making it easy to use. But don't just hang out in whatever chapter seems to be the most relevant to the type of hunting or fishing you happen to do. No matter your personal interests, you'll find usable information in each and every chapter. For instance, a smallmouth bass fisherman who lives a thousand miles away from the nearest body of saltwater would be wise to check out the yelloweye rockfish processing photos in the saltwater chapter. (Hint: The pinbone removal cuts are the same on a smallmouth.) Also, pay close attention to the "Nature of the Beast" sections, where I share some general thoughts and guidelines about the rela-

tive qualities of a wide host of wild game species, and the "Also Works With" sections that are built into each individual recipe. At the back of the book (in the Basic and Not-So-Basic section), I have included a collection of some of my go-to recipes for stocks, sauces, sides, and accompaniments that you can use alongside the main recipes in the book or in other preparations you're making at home. The combined information from these portions of the book will prove invaluable for finding suitable substitutions for the wild game cook. A successful deer hunter who's interested in making some goose pastrami will be pleased to learn that their freezer already contains a reasonable facsimile of the necessary protein.

The recipes that follow are meant to encourage a nose-to-tail approach to wild game cooking. It's my personal belief that our wild game resources should be utilized to the fullest extent possible. I encourage deer hunters to experiment with tongue and liver; I encourage waterfowl hunters to grill their duck hearts; I encourage anglers to eat the cheeks and collars from their fish. There are practical implications to this approach—more food!—as well as benefits of a slightly more spiritual nature. To eat is to feed both your body *and* mind. Responsible use is a way of paying proper homage to the fish and animals you pursue, and it makes you a better, more thoughtful outdoorsman and wild game cook.

No matter how you rank yourself—newbie, awful, locally famous—I promise that your skill sets will grow as you apply these techniques and cook these recipes. I've been hunting and cooking for my entire life. Considering my own experiences and those of everyone else who aided in the production of this book, either directly through the contribution of recipes or indirectly by sharing with me their hard-earned tips and tricks, I can confidently say that it contains centuries' worth of wild game knowledge. It's with joy that I pass it along to you.

01 BIG GAME

INTRODUCTION

The big game section is in the front of this book because it is a fitting position for what I consider to be the pinnacle of the wild game world. While I regard myself as a hunting generalist (I'll chase anything that's good to eat, and at times my definition of good has been elastic enough to include everything from common carp to porcupines), big game hunting is my deepest passion. I killed my first deer when I was thirteen, after two unsuccessful seasons of misses and mistakes. I've kept at it, without ever missing a season, for the past thirty-three years. Every fall and winter, I put fifty days or more into pursuing big game. I believe that it's the most challenging form of hunting, both physically and mentally, and it pays off in the biggest way. Long ago, I committed to feeding my family a diet of wild meat. Big game is how I'm able to stay true to that commitment.

Most hunters share my fondness. According to statistics from the U.S. Fish and Wildlife Service, 80 percent of all hunters chase big game at some point during the year. Each of those hunters has his or her own particular set of motivations, but you can't argue with the seductive size of big game animals. A mature whitetail deer can yield anywhere from forty to eighty pounds of boneless, recipe-ready meat. An elk can yield well over two hundred pounds. A moose, well over three hundred pounds. In addition to abundance, big game also gives you variety. I break my deer down into a dozen different cuts, ranging from short ribs to sirloins to tongue. Each cut is suitable for an endless array of recipes and preparations. With just a single deer in your freezer, you can have months' worth of eating with no fear of redundancy or boredom.

This cut-based approach is the key to big game cooking. It remedies a problem that I have with wild game cookbooks in general, which tend to draw unnecessary distinctions among various species of antlered and horned game. To me, there is no fundamental difference between a recipe for a pronghorn antelope shank and a recipe for a whitetail deer shank beyond some minor adjustments in cooking times. In fact, I'd argue that it's more important to understand what part of the animal you're cooking than it is to understand what kind of big game animal it came from.

Keep this approach in mind as you work through this section. Virtually every recipe here is interchange-

able from one big game species to the next. Admittedly, the recipe for Kimchi Tacos with Wild Pig or Javelina shoulder on page 54 is especially suitable for the stringier meat and sometimes stronger flavors of those particular animals. But it could easily be applied to a venison shoulder or bear shoulder, as all three of these pieces of meat share in common a lot of sinews and connective tissue that will break down during the cooking process and yield a finished product that is rich, moist, and silky. This is just one example where substitutions are appropriate; I have called out many others in the following recipes. I'm hopeful that you'll make additional discoveries on your own as you apply these methods to whatever big game happens to turn up in your freezer over the coming years.

Finally, I'd like to throw in a few thoughts on the subject of big game meat that tastes "gamey," a term that drives me a little bit insane every time I hear it. As best as I can tell, *gamey* has no fixed definition. I've heard it used to describe a dozen or more different things. It's used to describe meat that was spoiled, meaning rotten, from improper handling in the field. I've heard it used to describe meat that hadn't been trimmed of tallow and blood clots. I've heard it used to describe meat that had been tainted by secretions from the tarsal gland on a deer's back leg. And I've heard it used by people who are trying to say that game meat doesn't taste like the flavorless beef that they're used to buying from fast-food restaurants.

Whatever it actually means to you or the people you're cooking for, most causes of gamey meat can be eliminated by taking a careful approach to your hunting techniques and field care. First off, don't let fly with an arrow or bullet unless you know exactly what's going to happen when you do it. There is no place for guesswork or surprises when it comes to marksmanship. You need to put your projectile cleanly through the lungs and/or heart of the animal for a quick, clean kill. Poor shot placement can lead to an animal being heavily stressed before it eventually dies. When that happens, there's a chance that the animal could indeed have tough meat with strong, off-putting flavors.

Gut the animal immediately. Big game animals have an internal body temperature of over one hundred degrees. Once the animal is dead, that heat will quickly spoil the meat. The area around the ball joints, at the base of the rear legs, is the first to go. Removing the guts helps cool things down. In this chapter you'll see how to properly do the job. After gutting, pack the chest cavity with ice or snow. If need be, quarter the animal and get the quarters into a walk-in meat locker, a household fridge, or even a cooler loaded with ice. Whatever it takes, keep the animal cold and dry until you're ready to butcher it. And when it comes to butchering, keep things cold and clean and follow the directions that are laid out here. You'll eliminate the majority of your gamey situations.

But no amount of careful shooting and trimming is going to change the minds of squeamish folks who think that anything other than domestically produced meat tastes different and, therefore, gamey. What will change their minds is repeated exposure to what real meat actually tastes like. It only helps when it's properly prepared and served. Getting a deer—or an elk, moose, caribou, or bear—in your freezer is the first step of the process. This chapter is the second step. Enjoy.

THE BIG BUCK/LITTLE BUCK MYTH

A lot of hunters have this idea that big bucks aren't that good to eat. This is nonsense. There are myriad factors that influence the palatability of a deer; age is hardly the defining one. We put this idea to the test on a Colorado mule deer hunt when we killed two bucks. The first was a three- to four-year-old giant; the second was a year-and-a-half-old forky. Served raw, the unanimous consensus was that the bigger and older ham was a better piece of meat. In all fairness, the older buck had been aged a day or so longer—which goes to show that factors beyond the animal's age are at play when it comes to quality meat.

THE NATURE OF THE BEAST

American Pronghorn (Antelope)

The meat of the American pronghorn, or antelope, tends to be rather polarizing. Critics often say that it tastes gamey or musky, while fans of antelope will say that the faint hint of sage is a welcome attribute that brings to mind the open landscapes of the American West. Unpleasant experiences with antelope meat can be avoided if the hunter practices good marksmanship and field care. If you follow all of the advice within this book, you'll find that antelope have an excellent flavor on par with the finest big game animals.

Black Bear

During the time of Daniel Boone, black bear was the preferred meat on the American frontier. Deer were good for buckskin clothes, bear was good for eating. There's no reason to think any differently about black bear meat today. Trimmed of fat, the meat is excellent and can be used for a wide variety of purposes. When slow-cooked or braised it resembles beef pot roast in texture and flavor. The quality of the meat does vary according to the animal's diet. Bears that have been feeding on fish or marine mammals can have an off-putting fishy taste. A bear that's been feeding heavily on rotten carrion can also taste bad. These occasions are rare, however, as most black bears derive the bulk of their diet from plant matter. Some of the best bear meat comes from animals feeding on berries or hardwood mast. When baiting bears, avoid using animal or fish matter so that you don't taint the flesh of the animals that you're hunting. Trichinosis is another consideration with bear meat. Unless you've had your animal tested, it's safe to assume that all bears are infected by microscopic Trichinella larvae—the same larvae that used to commonly infect domestic pork and is still present in wild hogs. Destroying the threat is simple: cook all bear meat to 160°F and you're safe.

Caribou

Complaints about the gamey qualities of caribou meat can often be attributed to bulls killed during the rut. Caribou flesh seems to be affected by the hormonal changes of the breeding season in a more dramatic way than any other big game animal. For most hunters, this isn't an issue, because caribou are typically hunted between late August and early October, before the rut begins. People accustomed to eating beef are likely to recognize caribou meat as being "different," though it is highly prized by hunters who live in caribou country. The meat is often more tender than other antlered game, to the point that some people have described it as "pasty." Its coloration is sometimes lighter, too, and it can lack the deep mahogany color that characterizes the flesh of other members of the deer family. Caribou meat can be used in any recipe calling for venison.

Elk

Elk are widely regarded as the best of the best among wild game meats and are often compared to grass-fed beef. There is no such thing as a bad-tasting elk, and rarely does anyone complain about gamey elk. Older animals can be tough, but aging and proper cooking methods can take care of that. Elk meat can be used for any recipe calling for venison.

Moose

In the north, moose meat is as popular among hunters as elk meat is in the Rockies. While it doesn't prompt as many comparisons to grass-fed beef, it is mild and easily approachable. The flesh is heavily grained and colored a deep, rich red. It is generally a tougher, chewier meat than whitetail deer. It's a good practice to age your moose meat for a week or so before butchering. If you can't do that, you can let your butchered cuts rest in the freezer for a few months. You'll find that the meat gets better and better as time goes by. Moose can be used in any preparation calling for venison.

Mule Deer

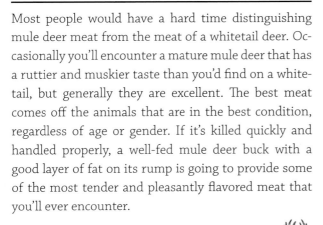

Most people would have a hard time distinguishing mule deer meat from the meat of a whitetail deer. Occasionally you'll encounter a mature mule deer that has a ruttier and muskier taste than you'd find on a whitetail, but generally they are excellent. The best meat comes off the animals that are in the best condition, regardless of age or gender. If it's killed quickly and handled properly, a well-fed mule deer buck with a good layer of fat on its rump is going to provide some of the most tender and pleasantly flavored meat that you'll ever encounter.

Whitetail Deer

Whitetail deer are by far the most widely consumed game meat in the United States. If care is taken to avoid contamination by the fluids produced by the tar-

sal glands on the animal's rear legs, the meat is exceptionally mild and usually quite tender. Most people who have a familiarity with both whitetails and elk will choose elk as their favorite, though whitetail meat is highly regarded by most hunters.

Wild Pigs

Wild pigs, or feral hogs, are the exact same species as the farm-raised varieties of pigs that you can find in a butcher shop or grocery store: *Sus scrofa*. The difference is that wild pigs are far leaner than domestic pigs, as they eat a lot less food and get a lot more exercise. For perspective, consider that it's virtually unheard of to find a wild pig that can be used to make a slab of bacon. Because of their leanness, wild pig flesh has more in common with venison than it does with commercially produced pork. It is generally regarded as more flavorful and complex than domestic pork. When cooking with it, you usually need to add fat and take measures to prevent it from drying out. Younger pigs generally have better meat than older pigs. Many hunters prefer the flesh of a pregnant sow above all others, as they have a lot of stored body fat. Most hunters regard sexually mature boars as the least desirable when it comes to eating. At times, their meat can be very tough, with an off-putting odor. Diet matters with wild pigs. Animals feeding on green grass or acorns, for instance, will likely have much better meat than animals that are ingesting lower-quality foods or animal matter. Wild pigs often carry microscopic Trichinella larvae in their flesh, which can cause the disease trichinosis. (The larvae used to be carried by domestic pigs as well, though it's been virtually eradicated from pigs raised in accordance to USDA guidelines.) Cook all wild pork to 160°F and you're safe.

GUTTING BIG GAME ANIMALS

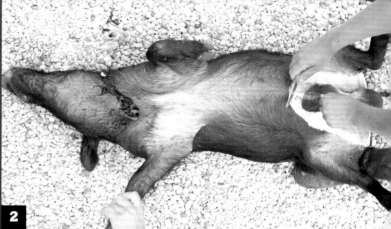

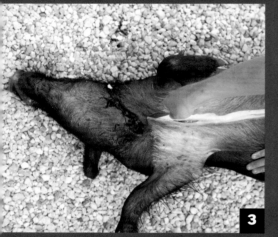

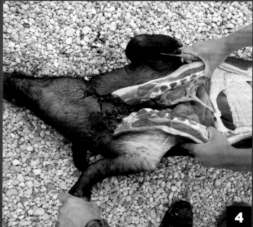

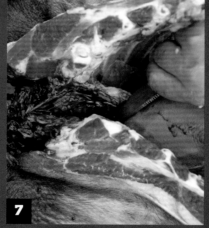

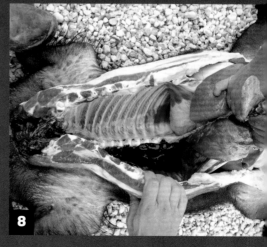

Wild hogs, like the one pictured here, share the same basic anatomy with all hooved big game animals. The process of skinning, gutting, and butchering any big game animal is basically the same, whether it's a wild pig or a whitetail deer. But there are different approaches to big game field care. Here Ben Binnion, a commercial wild hog trapper who has handled thousands of wild hogs, demonstrates a clean and efficient way to go about this process. For additional information on butchering big game animals check out *The Complete Guide to Hunting, Butchering, and Cooking Wild Game, Volume 1: Big Game.*

How to Gut Big Game Animals

1. Because this hog was trapped and shot in the head, it was necessary to bleed it out by cutting its throat immediately after the shot. Bleeding out a big game animal can give the meat a cleaner taste and better appearance, but it is unnecessary if the animal was shot in the vital heart/lung area with a rifle or bow.

2. Start by cutting through the skin around the genitals and down to the anus. Be extremely careful to cut only the hide without puncturing the gut cavity. Once this cut is made, use your knife to separate the skin and genitals from the carcass. This hog was trapped in Texas, where leaving evidence of sex on the carcass is not a legal requirement. However, some state game agencies do require that you leave evidence of sex naturally attached to the carcass of big game animals. (Read more on page 18.)

3. From the spot where the hide and genitals have been removed, make an incision through the skin extending forward to the throat. (Again, make adjustments if you need to leave evidence of sex attached.)

4. To open up the gut cavity, start at the anus and cut forward to the sternum. Point your knife toward the head of the animal with the blade facing up for this cut. With your fingers behind the knife, use them to spread and lift the abdominal wall as you cut. Make very shallow cuts through just the abdominal wall without touching the guts. On smaller big game animals, it's possible to extend this cut alongside the sternum all the way to the throat with just a knife. Bigger critters like elk may require the use of a bone saw.

5. Next, use a bone saw or stout knife to split the pelvis bone between the rear quarters just above the anus. Once the pelvis bone has been cut, the lower intestine will be exposed where it meets the anus. Make a circular cut around the anus and lower intestine to free it from the carcass.

6. Now look for the diaphragm, which divides the heart and lung area (the thoracic cavity) from the liver and digestive system (the peritoneal cavity). This thin wall of muscle needs to be cut free from the interior of the rib cage on both sides of the animal.

7. Reach forward into the chest cavity to locate the esophagus. You'll find this rigid tube above the heart and lungs in the throat of the animal. Hold the esophagus with your nondominant hand while you use your knife to sever it. You may be working by feel here, so be extremely careful not to cut yourself.

8. Now get a good grip on the esophagus with both hands and pull up and back. If you've done things right up until this point, the whole works will come out in one piece. This is the time to remove the heart, liver, kidneys, and caul fat from the rest of the gut pile. Before moving on to skinning, wash the interior of the animal to remove any blood, dirt, or digestive matter.

GAMBREL SKINNING BIG GAME

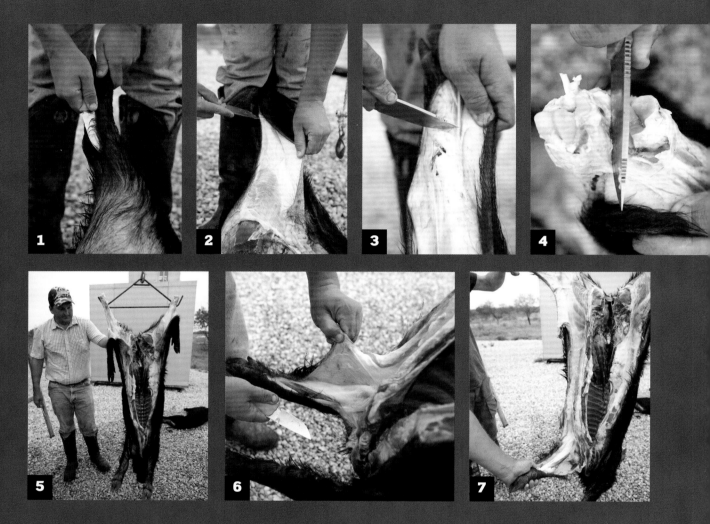

Once a big game animal has been gutted, the next butchering step is skinning. The easiest way to skin an animal is while it is hanging from a gambrel, which looks like a heavy-duty coat hanger. It is much easier to work on an animal that is suspended above the ground, and gambrels are ideal for deer-size game that hunters are able to get out of the woods in one piece.

Skinning

1. Begin by making an incision through the hide on the lower rear leg near the foot.

2. Extend this cut down along the inside of the ham until it meets your original gutting cut at the abdomen. Now begin skinning the rear leg by slicing between hide and flesh. Do your best to keep the meat clean and free of hair and dirt.

3. Skin around the ankle joint.

4. Next, you'll need to separate the meatless shin bones from the rear quarters. Find the knee joint at the top of the shin. Use your knife to cut the tendons around this joint. Continue cutting these tendons until the joint loosens enough to twist it. Twist the shin bone in a circular motion until it "pops." At this point, one or two more cuts will completely free the lower leg.

5. Each rear leg has a heavy tendon behind the knee. Cut a slit through the skin in the gap between the tendon and the leg. Lower the gambrel, or with the help of a buddy, lift your animal in order to place the hooks on each side of the gambrel through these slits. Try to hang the animal at a height that allows you to work comfortably.

6. On each front leg, make a cut from the foot to the gutting incision at the chest cavity. Now skin each front leg until the hide is hanging freely.

7. Next, move up to the rear legs. Continue skinning each rear leg downward to the rump. You should be able to separate portions of the hide from the carcass just by pulling on it. In other places, you'll need to use your knife.

8. Once each rear leg is completely skinned, continue skinning down and around the back, flank, and belly of the animal.

9. Skin the animal downward past the shoulder and front legs. At the neck, keep skinning until you reach the animal's head.

10. Now separate the head and hide from the carcass where the spine meets the base of the skull. Use a knife to do this the same way you popped the leg joints or you can quickly sever the spine with a bone saw.

11. Finally, take the time to pick any hair off the meat and then wash the carcass before moving on to breaking the animal down into individual cuts of meat.

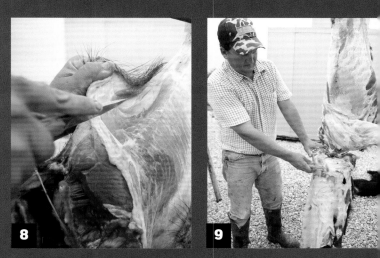

BUTCHERING BIG GAME ON THE GROUND

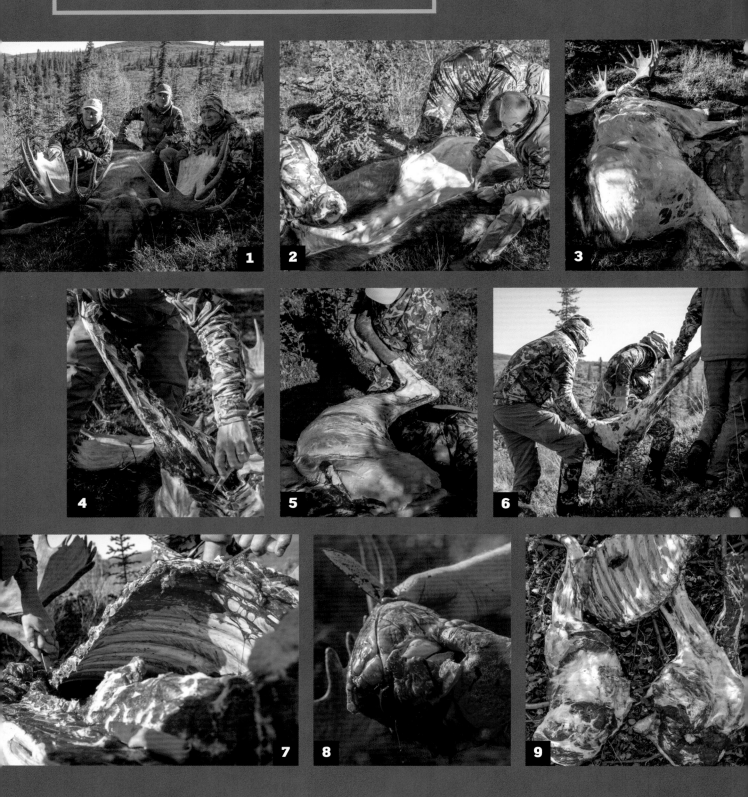

Some big game animals are much bigger than others. Bull moose can weigh more than 1,500 pounds. That's ten times the weight of the average whitetail deer. Hunters who kill large animals like elk and moose in the backcountry, or even a deer in a remote location, often use a field butchering method commonly referred to as the "gutless method." This means that the animal is butchered without removing the guts from the body cavity as a first step. It's particularly well suited for large animals that are difficult to maneuver. After butchering a large animal in the field, it's possible to pack manageable loads of meat back to camp or your vehicle.

Field Butchering Big Game

1. Field butchering large animals is a big job. If possible, it's good to have help from some friends.

2. Start by opening up the hide along the back from the neck to the tail. Then begin skinning the hide toward the belly and legs.

3. Skin one entire side of the animal first. Once the hide is removed, lay it out flat, hair-side down on the ground. This provides a relatively clean spot to place meat as it is removed from the animal.

4. The easiest piece of meat to remove is the backstrap. This tender, boneless piece of meat extends from the base of the neck to the hip bones.

5. Now remove the upward-facing rear and front legs.

6. Move your meat to the shade, where it can cool off. Hanging meat in a game bag from a tree limb is ideal, but you may need to lay large, heavy quarters on a bed of branches so they stay clean.

7. Bone saws are handy for large butchering jobs. Here, a saw is used to remove the entire rib rack in a single piece. You can reduce weight by deboning the rib meat, but you'll be missing out on grilled bone-in moose ribs.

8. With the ribs removed, you'll have easy access to all the good stuff inside the animal. The inner tenderloins rest along the spine, above the intestines, just in front of the hips. You'll also want to save the heart, liver, tongue, and perhaps the web of caul fat that surrounds the digestive system. See recipes using the heart (Skewered and Grilled Duck Hearts, page 124), liver (Venison Liver Mousse, page 30), and tongue (Seared Tongue Sandwich, page 36).

9. Here you have one side of a moose (front and rear quarters, rib rack, and backstrap) removed from the carcass. You'll also need to remove the brisket, neck meat, and other meat left on the upward side of the carcass. Now roll the animal over and repeat the process on the other side. (See pages 20–27 for information on breaking down an animal into individual cuts.)

EVIDENCE OF SEX

Most states require hunters to provide evidence of sex on big game animals until the animal has been processed and packaged. For horned or antlered big game, evidence of sex can include the head of the animal as long as it remains naturally attached to the carcass. Otherwise the reproductive organs must remain naturally attached to one or both hindquarters in order for a hunter to meet evidence of sex requirements.

Proof of Sex, Male

Carefully skin the penis and testicles during the gutting process. The skinned penis can then be cut and removed at its base near the anus. Each testicle is attached to the muscle of the corresponding hindquarter with a small amount of connective tissue. Leave the testicles attached, being careful while working in this area during field butchering.

Proof of Sex, Female

Where you see the teats, skin the hide away from the mammary glands during the gutting process. Under the skin is the actual mammary gland. Like the testicles, the mammary gland is attached only by fragile connective tissue. Leave the gland attached to the muscle of each hindquarter and cut carefully around this area during field butchering.

WANTON WASTE

Hunters who are interested in filling the freezer shouldn't need to be convinced that it's worth saving neck roasts, briskets, or flank meat. But hunters should be aware that most states have various laws mandating what portions of an animal must be retained. In Alaska, where the bull moose on page 16 was killed, strict wanton waste laws require hunters to pack out all edible meat.

BLACKTAIL BACKSTRAP

BLACKTAIL SHANK

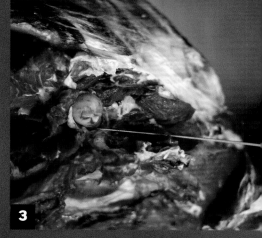

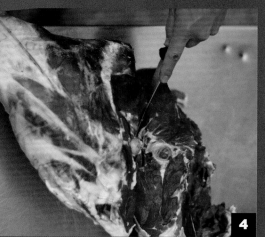

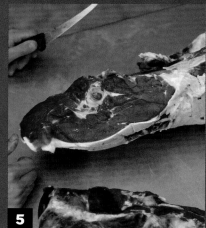

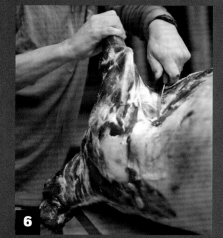

Breaking down a big game animal is easy with a few simple tools and some know-how. A stainless steel table makes for a clean workspace, but you can also use a kitchen counter or garage workbench. Just make sure you're starting out with a sanitized surface and sharp knives.

Removing Legs

1. Start out by inspecting the skinned and gutted carcass for hair, dirt, or blood-shot meat. Take the time to clean up the carcass before you begin cutting.

2. Begin with separating a rear leg. You'll want to start by cutting into the seam on the inner part of the hindquarter where the ham rests against the abdomen.

3. As you cut, try to run your knife between the hip bones and the meat. You'll run into bone at the hip's ball-and-socket joint. Separate this joint by cutting the tendons that surround it.

4. With the ball-and-socket joint separated, continue cutting the meat down to and around the pelvis bones.

5. After the hind leg is free, go back and trim up the hip bones around the socket. These small pieces of meat should be saved for grinding into burger or sausage.

6. Now move to the front leg. Pull the leg away from the body and begin cutting the muscle around the shoulder.

7. There are no bones or joints to worry about. Just cut between the shoulder muscle and the rib cage to separate the front leg from the carcass.

8. Next, flip the carcass over and remove the front and rear legs from the other side.

CHRONIC WASTING DISEASE

Chronic wasting disease (CWD) is a fatal degenerative disease similar to mad cow disease, which afflicts members of the deer family. CWD was first discovered in mule deer in Colorado and can also infect whitetails, elk, and moose. While there have been no known cases of humans developing CWD, there may be risks, however small, with eating CWD-infected animals. In states where CWD outbreaks have occurred, such as Colorado, Minnesota, and Missouri, hunters in certain parts of the state may be required to have their animals tested for CWD. Even where testing is not mandatory, if you kill an animal in an area where CWD is known to be present, it's a good idea to have that animal tested before consuming its meat. State fish and game agencies often conduct these tests free of charge. The prions that cause CWD are known to concentrate in the brain, spinal cord, spleen, and lymph nodes of infected deer, so it is recommended that hunters avoid cutting through the spine. Still, we enjoy bone-in neck roasts and we're comfortable preparing this meal from deer that have tested negative for CWD.

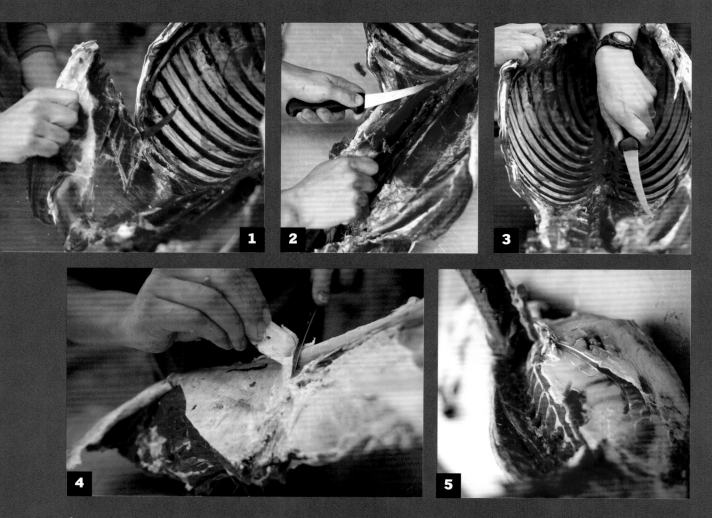

1. Start by removing the thin, flat section of belly muscle, commonly known as the paunch, which hangs behind the ribs.

2. The inner loins, or tenderloins, rest on either side of the spine just behind the ribs. Remove any fat and make a cut along each side of the tenderloin. Lift it up and cut the ends free.

3. Next, remove the paunch and tenderloin from the opposite side of the animal.

4. Position the carcass so the back faces up. Along either side of the spine are the two backstraps. Trim the tough, outer layer of fat away from the backstrap.

5. The long, tubular backstrap muscle rests between the bones of the spine and the ribs. To remove it cleanly without wasting meat, your knife should periodically scrape bone as you cut.

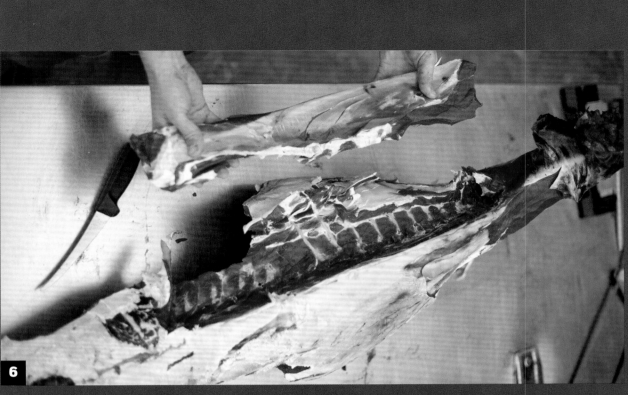

6. Here, the backstrap is completely removed. Repeat the process with the second one.

7. Each backstrap has a thick layer of tough silver skin and tendons on one side. Carefully cut it away from the meat. You can also freeze the backstrap without doing this and remove the silver skin later. It helps protect the meat from freezer burn.

8. Take the time to remove any meat attached to the silver skin. Little pieces of trimmed meat add up to a big pile of burger meat later.

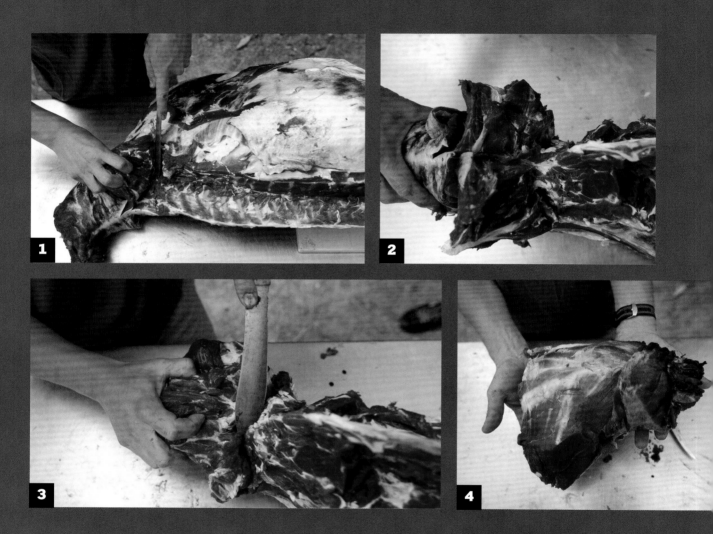

Neck Roast

1. To remove a bone-in neck roast, start at the base of the neck where it meets the chest.

2. Cut the lower neck muscles down to the spine around the entire circumference of the neck.

3. With the spine exposed, you'll be able to make a cut between the vertebrae at the base of the neck to separate it from the carcass. You can also use a bone saw to do the job. Before cutting or sawing through a deer's spine, make sure to consider the potential risks of chronic wasting disease (see sidebar on page 21).

4. Here you have a whole bone-in neck roast, which is great for slow-cooking recipes. The neck meat can also be cut away from the spine for boneless neck roasts or grinding into burger meat.

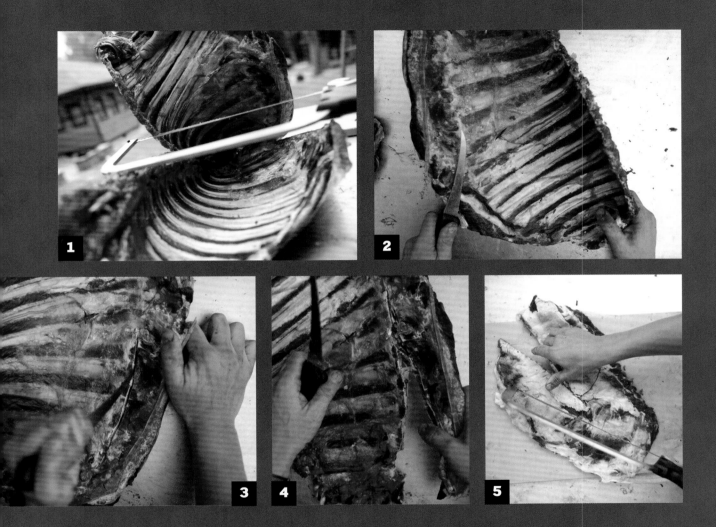

Ribs

1. Use a bone saw to separate each rib rack.

2. Now the rib rack is ready to be broken down into smaller pieces.

3. There's very little edible meat along the sternum bone of a deer. (On larger game, such as elk or moose, there's enough to warrant your attention.) Cut between the ends of the rib bones and the sternum to separate it from the rib rack.

4. Continue this cut until the sternum is removed. Trim any meat remaining on the sternum for making burgers and reserve the bone for making stock.

5. Now use your bone saw to cut the rib rack lengthwise into sections. You can then use a knife to divide these long sections into shorter, serving-size pieces of three or four ribs.

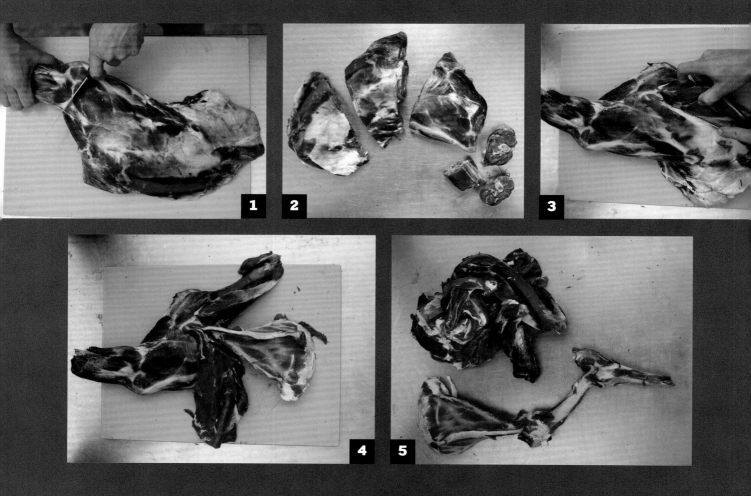

1. The front leg of a deer can be broken down into several bone-in roasts, all of which are great for braising recipes. Start by removing the shank at the joint where it joins the lower shoulder.

2. Next, use a bone saw to divide the shoulder into three bone-in blade roasts. Then saw the shank into three thick discs for making osso bucco. Check out the blade roast recipe in *The Complete Guide to Hunting, Butchering, and Cooking Wild Game, Volume 1,* and see page 60 for the Osso Bucco recipe.

3. You can also debone the front leg. Start by re-moving the roast along the rearward side of the nar-row, raised piece of bone that divides the shoulder blade. This roast is good for jerky and slow-cooking.

4. Next, remove the roast from the other side of the shoulder blade.

5. Continue deboning the entire shoulder and shank. You can use the larger deboned roasts and shank for the same bone-in recipes mentioned above. Use the smaller pieces for burgers and sau-sage. Reserve the leg bones for the stock recipe on page 305.

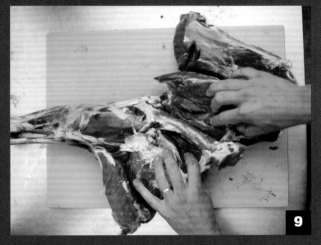

6. The rear leg can be deboned and divided into large roasts that are suitable for grilling whole or cutting into steaks.

7. Start by removing the lower, rear roast from the ham. It will separate easily if you cut between muscles rather than cutting through meat.

8. From here, it's easy to debone the rest of the rear leg.

9. Cut the large muscle groups above the shank away from the femur.

10. You'll be left with three large boneless roasts and the shank. They can be left whole or cut into smaller pieces.

APRIL BLOOMFIELD'S SCOTCH EGGS

SERVES 6

Chef April Bloomfield is always doing exciting stuff with meat and fish, and I've used her food as inspiration for my own experiments with wild game. The thing about April's Scotch egg, though, is that it's too perfect to mess with on my own. So I went straight to April and asked her what she'd do differently if she were working with wild venison rather than domestic pork. She suggested some tweaks to her original recipe, including the addition of nutmeg and juniper. The next time you have guests and want to do something truly memorable, try this. It's well worth the effort.

FOR THE SAGE PASTE: Mince the sage with the salt and oil on a cutting board using the side of a chef's knife until it's a uniform pesto-like paste. Alternately, use a mortar and pestle.

FOR THE VENISON MIXTURE: Combine the venison, fatback, sage paste, breadcrumbs, milk, salt, rosemary, nutmeg, and juniper in a medium bowl. Using your hands, portion the meat mixture into six 4-ounce balls. Carefully flatten out each portion into a pancake, making sure the thickness is even all around.

Fill a large bowl with ice and water and set aside. Bring a large saucepan of water to a boil. Slowly add the eggs to the water and cook for 5½ minutes, then remove the eggs with a slotted spoon and shock them in the ice-water bath. Remove the eggs from the ice-water bath and peel them.

Place one of the soft-boiled eggs on top of the sausage and wrap it around the egg. Repeat with the remaining eggs and sausage and refrigerate until cold, 30 minutes to 2 hours.

FOR THE BREADING: Place the breading ingredients in separate shallow bowls. Remove the meat-covered eggs from the refrigerator. Dredge them first in the flour, then coat them with the egg wash, then cover with a layer of the fine breadcrumbs. Repeat the egg wash and coat a second time with a layer of coarse breadcrumbs. Repeat with the remaining eggs.

FOR FRYING: Heat the oil in a large pot until it reaches 350°F on a deep-fry thermometer. Fry the eggs, two or three at a time, depending on your pot size, for 9 minutes, then let them rest for 1 minute. You're looking for the yolk to be runny but warm inside. Repeat with the remaining eggs. Serve immediately garnished with chopped parsley (if using).

SAGE PASTE

½ ounce fresh sage, finely chopped

½ teaspoon flaky salt

½ teaspoon extra virgin olive oil

VENISON MIXTURE

1 pound ground venison

7 ounces ground salted fatback

⅓ cup coarse filone breadcrumbs (see page 324)

⅓ cup milk

2 teaspoons kosher salt, or to taste

¼ teaspoon chopped fresh rosemary

⅛ teaspoon freshly grated nutmeg

2 juniper berries, grated on a Microplane

6 large eggs

BREADING

¼ cup all-purpose flour

2 large eggs, beaten

½ cup fine filone breadcrumbs (see page 324)

½ cup coarse filone breadcrumbs (see page 324)

5 cups peanut oil, for frying

Chopped parsley, for serving (optional)

ALSO WORKS WITH: Go ahead and make the venison mix with any ground meat. As mentioned above, April usually makes her Scotch eggs with pork, so this is particularly well suited to wild pigs. But I'd feel comfortable making it with anything from bear to caribou to javelina.

Tip: Filone is a rustic, crusty Italian bread. Any crusty rustic bread will work.

VENISON LIVER MOUSSE

MAKES ABOUT 3 CUPS

3 large eggs

1 pound wild game liver, fresh

¼ cup (½ stick) unsalted butter

1 large onion, finely chopped

1 clove garlic, minced

¼ cup red wine

2 tablespoons extra virgin olive oil, plus more as needed

2 tablespoons honey mustard

1 teaspoon kosher salt, plus more as needed

Freshly ground black pepper

French bread slices, rye toast points, or crackers, for serving

ALSO WORKS WITH: The age of the animal is more important than the species. The liver from any young specimen of horned or antlered game will work.

Most hunters who enjoy venison liver like to eat it as simply as possible: gently sautéed in butter or bacon grease alongside a sliced onion. There's no denying how delicious that preparation is, but it's helpful to have a few more tricks on hand for those years when you're lucky enough to kill multiple deer, or just when you're looking to try something fresh and new. This liver mousse recipe is based on one that was passed along by my friend Tim Collins, a Manhattan-based lawyer and avid deer hunter whose farm happens to produce some excellent honey and maple syrup along with a fair bit of wild venison. Be aware that the best and mildest livers come from young animals. It's really hard to beat a liver from a yearling whitetail, mule deer, or elk. All livers are best when eaten fresh. While it's possible to freeze liver, the quality quickly goes downhill.

Fill a large bowl with ice and water and set aside. Place the eggs in a small pot, add water to cover, and bring to a boil. Reduce the heat to maintain a simmer and simmer for 10 minutes. Remove the eggs with a slotted spoon and shock them in the ice-water bath. Remove the eggs from the ice-water bath and peel them, then coarsely chop them.

Slice the liver into ½-inch-thick strips. Melt the butter in a large skillet over medium-low heat. Working in two batches, gently fry the liver slices on each side for 4 to 5 minutes. Do not overcook the liver and avoid searing the surfaces. It should remain a little pinkish on the inside. Remove to a plate.

Add the onion and garlic to the same skillet, increase the heat to medium, and cook until the onion begins to caramelize. Cut the liver into ½-inch cubes and add them to the pan along with the wine, oil, honey mustard, salt, and 8 or 9 twists of black pepper. Stir to combine, bring to a simmer, and then remove the pan from the heat.

Once the mixture is cooled to a safe handling temperature, transfer to the bowl of a food processor along with the chopped eggs and process until smooth. Taste and adjust the seasoning with salt and pepper. Chill and serve with bread, toast, or crackers.

MARROW BONES
WITH CELERY AND PICKLED RAISINS

SERVES 2 TO 4

I first became interested in bone marrow while researching a writing project about a Paleo-Indian archaeological culture known as the Folsom Complex. There are a lot of mysteries surrounding the lifeways of these Ice Age hunters, but there's little doubt that they enjoyed bone marrow. Femurs and shin bones that have been shattered by stone tools are a common find during archaeological excavations of their encampments and kill-sites on the high plains of the American West. Nowadays, thanks to bandsaws and hacksaws, we don't need to bust our marrow bones apart in order to get at the meaty and buttery goods that lie inside. I like to cut mine into discs and then serve the marrow right inside these all-natural and visually stunning bowls of bone.

FOR THE CELERY AND PICKLED RAISIN SALAD: Combine the vinegar and sugar in a small saucepan and bring to a boil over high heat. Turn off the heat, add the raisins, steep for 10 minutes, and then stir in the red chile flakes. Let cool. Remove the raisins from the pickling liquid using a slotted spoon. Combine the celery, celery leaves, pickled raisins, onions, and oil in a small bowl, and season to taste with salt and black pepper.

FOR THE MARROW BONES: Saw the bones into 2-inch discs. (It works well to freeze them first, but it's not necessary.) A butcher's band saw is the easiest way to cut the bones, but a basic hacksaw fitted with a metal cutting blade will do the trick. Inspect each disc to make sure there's a usable amount of marrow inside. It will look like frozen butter. Discs cut from the ends of the bones might be partially or mostly filled with a honeycombed bone structure. Use these instead for making stock or bone broth.

Preheat the oven to 400°F. Line a baking sheet or any kind of ovenproof skillet or baking dish with foil.

Stand the discs upright on the prepared pan. Roast until the marrow is soft throughout and begins to pull away from the bone. Allow the surface to bubble and crisp a bit, but don't let the marrow spill over the top. Cooking time varies according to the size of bone, but they are typically ready within 10 to 12 minutes.

Sprinkle each bone with a pinch of coarse sea salt and garnish with a small sprig of thyme placed into the marrow. Serve with the celery salad alongside. Invite your guests to spread their hot marrow on top of toasted bread slices or a warmed baguette. While there is such a thing as an actual marrow spoon, meant for digging the marrow from the bones, the handle end of a small teaspoon works really well.

CELERY AND PICKLED RAISIN SALAD

1 cup white wine vinegar

¼ cup sugar

1 cup golden raisins

Pinch of red chile flakes

2 ribs celery, thinly sliced

⅓ cup celery leaves

2 tablespoons thinly sliced red onion

1 tablespoon extra virgin olive oil

Kosher salt

Freshly ground black pepper

MARROW BONES

1 (or more) femur or shin bone from large-bodied game (see list below)

Coarse sea salt

3 to 6 sprigs fresh thyme, separated into pieces (optional)

Baguette or toasted sliced bread, for serving

ALSO WORKS WITH: Femurs or shin bones from elk, moose, caribou, buffalo, or other large-bodied game. If using whitetail deer or mule deer, get bones from the biggest deer you can find.

SPECIAL EQUIPMENT: band saw or hacksaw fitted with a metal cutting blade

---

VENISON CARPACCIO
WITH BITTER GREENS SALAD

SERVES 4 AS AN APPETIZER

A traditional practice among some indigenous caribou hunters in the Arctic was to open the hide on a freshly killed caribou in the center of the family's lodge and then devour the entire thing raw. I've enjoyed enough raw game meat that this tradition doesn't seem entirely foreign to me, though I've met plenty of other hunters who are afraid to try wild game carpaccio. None have cited specific fears; rather, it's just a general apprehension about picking up some sort of unknown ailment. If you share these fears, by all means, do your own research and don't just take my word for it. But I have eaten many pounds of carpaccio from horned and antlered game with no ill effect. I should point out, too, that I'm very careful about proper field care and storage. I make sure that my meat is clean and well-trimmed, and I typically freeze it beforehand as an added precaution. I also recommend that you eat carpaccio in moderation, at least at first. If your system isn't used to raw or rare meat, a large meal of it can give you a stomachache, so start out with just a few slices. After some practice, you might end up craving that whole caribou.

¼ cup black peppercorns

8- to 10-ounce portion elk loin or round roast

8 ounces fresh bitter salad greens, such as mustard, dandelion, or arugula

Spicy Citrus Dressing (page 315)

Maldon or other flaky sea salt

ALSO WORKS WITH: You could theoretically prepare carpaccio using the loin or round roast from any horned or antlered game (deer, elk, and moose are all perfect), but if you want a truly positive experience, you need to be a bit pickier than that. There's little here to mask any strong flavors, and the lack of cooking means that a tough cut of meat is going to remain tough. I try to use only the highest-grade animals for my carpaccio, meaning that I select healthy, well-fed animals for this preparation. You don't need to be a wild game expert to make such a judgment call. When butchering an animal, just take a thin slice of the backstrap or round roast and give it a quick sear on a hot skillet. Add a touch of salt and pop it into your mouth. If it tastes great and it's tender, it'll be good carpaccio. If it's tough and doesn't taste good, move on to other recipes in this book. (Warning: wild pigs, bears, javelinas, or any other carnivores or omnivores are not suitable for carpaccio.)

FOR THE VENISON: Toast the peppercorns in a small dry skillet over medium-high heat until wisps of smoke start to rise, 3 to 4 minutes. Cool, then grind in a spice grinder.

Make sure all the silver skin is carefully trimmed away and the meat is clean and dry. On a large plate or baking sheet, sprinkle the pepper in a thin even layer. Roll the loin in the pepper to completely coat. Wrap tightly in plastic wrap and freeze until the loin firms, about 1 hour. When you are ready to serve it, remove the loin from the freezer and, using a sharp slicing knife, slice the meat as thinly as possible. Arrange the slices on a platter.

FOR THE SALAD: Place the greens in a large bowl and lightly toss with the dressing right before serving.

Sprinkle the carpaccio with the flaky salt and garnish with the dressed bitter salad. Serve immediately.

SEARED TONGUE SANDWICH
WITH SPICY PICKLED RED ONIONS

SERVES 4 TO 8, DEPENDING ON THE SIZE OF THE TONGUE

12 cups cold water, plus more as needed

1 cup kosher salt

1 cup brown sugar

1 tablespoon allspice berries

1 tablespoon black peppercorns

1 teaspoon coriander seeds

1 teaspoon yellow mustard seeds

2 whole cloves

1 bay leaf

2 carrots, cut into large pieces

2 ribs celery, cut into large pieces

1 head garlic, halved through the middle horizontally

1 large onion, quartered

1 game tongue, rinsed well

1 tablespoon olive oil

Sliced country bread or split rolls, lightly toasted

Grainy mustard (optional)

Spicy Pickled Red Onions (page 318)

ALSO WORKS WITH: I've eaten tongues from black bear, whitetail deer, mule deer, elk, buffalo, caribou, muskox, wild pigs, and moose. They're all good, and they're all worthwhile, but the bigger tongues from the bigger animals are a lot more exciting because you have a lot more to work with.

I became interested in cooking wild game tongue when I was researching my book *American Buffalo*. In the 1800s, pickled and smoked buffalo tongues were a popular food item in places like Chicago, Boston, and New York. The historic record is full of tales of Euro-American and Native American hunters killing herds of buffalo just to get some quick cash, or a quick meal, from the tongues. They are just as tasty today. I've served game tongue to dozens of people who'd never had it, and the typical response is a shocked disbelief that a tongue could be so damn good.

This preparation is a great addition to any wild game charcuterie platter. (See page 122 for mine.) For a wonderful sandwich combination, serve the tongue with the Walnut and Mint Pesto on page 320.

Combine 4 cups of the water, the salt, brown sugar, allspice, peppercorns, coriander seeds, mustard seeds, cloves, and bay leaf in a medium saucepan. Bring to a boil over high heat. Reduce the heat to maintain a simmer and simmer for about 5 minutes, stirring until the sugar and salt dissolve. Transfer the brine to a large heatproof bowl or pot. Add the carrots, celery, garlic, and onion and the remaining 8 cups water and let cool completely.

Add the tongue to the brine, putting a plate on top if necessary to keep it submerged, and cover. Alternatively, put it all into an extra-large resealable plastic bag. Refrigerate for 5 days.

Preheat the oven to 300°F. Strain the tongue, reserving the solids, and put the tongue and the solids into a medium heavy-bottomed saucepan or Dutch oven. Add enough cold water to cover. Bring to a boil over high heat, then reduce the heat to maintain a simmer, partially cover, and cook until the tongue is very tender, 4 to 5 hours. Transfer the tongue to a colander and rinse with cold water. Let it rest until it's cool enough to comfortably handle, then peel off the tongue's outer skin. The tongue can be used immediately, or wrapped tightly in plastic wrap and stored for a week in the refrigerator.

When ready to serve, thinly slice the tongue. Heat a large skillet over high heat. Add the oil and sear the bread slices until golden brown on both sides, 3 to 5 minutes. Assemble the sandwiches with a smear of the grainy mustard and some spicy pickled red onions.

HOW TO ROAST A HUNK OF MEAT TO PERFECTION

SERVES 4 OR MORE

ALSO WORKS WITH: This works with all horned and antlered game. If the meat is safe to eat rare, this is a good way to cook it. When dealing with stronger-flavored game such as antelope, finicky folks who are unaccustomed to game might appreciate a sauce or other accompaniment. It's totally unnecessary, in my opinion, but then everyone has their own tastes and preferences. See opposite for serving suggestions including sauces and compound butters from the Extras section of this book.

The name of this recipe is not hyperbolic. If I had to choose one way to handle wild game meat for the rest of my life, this would be it. It doesn't matter if you're making roast venison sandwiches, a simple appetizer, steak salads (my wife's favorite), or a full-on centerpiece to anchor a spread of roast vegetables and mashed potatoes, this is the single best way to go about it. This preparation works with whole or partial backstraps and tenderloins, plus any of the major muscles—sirloins, top and bottom rounds, eye rounds—from the back legs on horned or antlered game. I prefer to work with a two- to four-pound hunk of meat. When pulling a roast from your freezer, it's best if you can take it out a few days ahead of time and let it thaw gradually in your fridge. Once thawed, give it a very quick rinse under cold water and immediately pat it dry with paper towels. Then let it sit on a rack in your fridge, uncovered, for a day or so. Before cooking, pull the roast out of the fridge and let it come to room temperature. Finally, make sure you've got an accurate meat thermometer. A difference of ten degrees can be the difference between perfection and meat-flavored cardboard.

Position a rack in the middle of the oven and preheat the oven to 375°F.

Coat the roast with 1 tablespoon of the oil and sprinkle liberally with salt and pepper. Remember, you're seasoning the outside of the roast, which is a small percentage of the total meat. When you go to put a piece in your mouth, only a small portion of the outside seasoning will accompany each bite. The salt and pepper should be a visible coating on the meat.

Heat 1 tablespoon of the oil in a large heavy-bottomed pan, preferably cast-iron, over medium-high heat. When the oil shimmers, add the roast and sear for 4 minutes per side on all sides. If the pan begins to smoke, reduce the heat. Note: With a skinny roast like a tenderloin, eye round, or the skinny end of a backstrap, the pan searing might be all you need to reach the desired doneness. Once the meat is seared, check the internal temperature of the roast with a meat thermometer. I aim for 120 to 125°F in the middle, or fattest part, of the roast, to achieve a finished product that's medium-rare (130 to 135°F) in the middle, and getting toward medium on the ends. (Most of these roasts will be oblong in shape, making for uneven temperatures from end to middle.) When the roast has reached the desired internal temperature, remove it to a grooved cutting board and allow it to rest for 5 to 10 minutes. Then proceed to the serving instructions below.

If the roast has not reached 120 to 125°F, place the pan in the preheated oven. Roast for 10 minutes and then check the roast's internal temperature again. (This is the single most important step in the process: yanking the meat from the oven at a precise temperature produces a delicious, consistent, and repeatable product.) If it still hasn't reached the desired temperature, continue roasting for another 5 minutes and check again. Repeat as necessary, but be careful: once the internal temperature is over, it's over. When the desired temperature is reached, remove the roast from the pan and place it on a grooved cutting board to rest.

Let a 2-pound roast rest for 5 minutes; a 4-pounder for 10 minutes. The roast's internal temperature will rise 5 to 8°F while it rests.

TO SERVE: With a carving knife or sharp chef's knife, slice the roast across the grain. The thinner the slice is, the easier it is to chew. A young cow elk's backstrap can be cut 1 inch thick and still melt in your mouth; a bottom round roast from a five-year-old buck should be sliced ¼ inch thick. Fan the slices onto a serving platter, drizzle the meat juices from the cutting board over the slices, sprinkle with salt, and serve immediately.

Serve with the sauces in the serving suggestions and your favorite sides, or try my Cobb Salad (see photo on page 38): Chop 2 small heads romaine lettuce into bite-size pieces and place on a platter. Add the sliced roasted game meat, with any or all of the following: sliced avocado, crumbled blue cheese, crispy bacon pieces, sliced onions, sliced cucumber, chopped tomato, sliced hard-boiled egg. Dress with Basic Vinaigrette (page 315) or Spicy Citrus Dressing (page 315). Top the salad with toasted pepitas or pumpkin seeds.

1 (2- to 4-pound) whole muscle game roast, thawed (see headnote)

2 tablespoons olive oil or vegetable oil

2 tablespoons kosher salt, plus more as needed

1 tablespoon freshly ground black pepper, plus more as needed

SERVING SUGGESTIONS

With Basic Brown Gravy (page 310)

With Balsamic Reduction (page 316)

With red currant, port, and red wine sauce (page 173)

With any one of the compound butters (pages 323) or Green Sauces (pages 320 and 321)

GRILLED VENISON LOIN
WITH CAULIFLOWER PUREE AND BALSAMIC REDUCTION

SERVES 6 (FOR 2 LOINS)

2 venison loins/backstraps, 1 to 2 pounds each, trimmed

Kosher salt

Freshly ground black pepper

Cauliflower Puree (page 333)

1 recipe Balsamic Reduction (page 316)

1 tablespoon chopped fresh chives, for garnish

ALSO WORKS WITH: I've prepared this dish successfully using whitetail deer, mule deer, and elk. Go ahead and use any horned or antlered game.

This is one of several memorable wild game recipes that I cooked alongside my buddy Chef Andrew Radzialowski for a wild game dinner that we did as a fund-raiser for the Theodore Roosevelt Conservation Partnership. (If you like to hunt and fish and care about the future of wildlife in America you should support this group too!) It was the biggest hit of the night, and I begged Andy to let me use it for this book. You'll be glad he said yes. The cauliflower is a perfect accompaniment, especially when a dribble or two of the juices from the meat mixes in with the puree like a drop of blood on snow. It's beautiful.

Remove the loins from the refrigerator about 1 hour before cooking to allow them to come to room temperature. Make sure all the silver skin is carefully trimmed away and the meat is clean and dry.

Prepare a grill (gas or charcoal) for both indirect and direct heat. Smear the loins with oil and sprinkle with a generous amount of salt and pepper, making sure to get all sides. Place the loins on the hot portion of the grill and let a nice sear or crust develop on all sides, 3 to 4 minutes per side. Move to indirect heat and let the meat roast to an internal temperature of 130°F. Pull the loins off the grill and let rest on a cutting board for 10 to 12 minutes to allow the juices to redistribute through the meat. Slice the loins across the grain to your desired thickness.

Place the warm puree down the center of a platter or large plate and place the sliced venison loin fanned out on top. With a spoon, drizzle the balsamic reduction over the meat. Garnish with the chives.

WILD HOG MILANESE
(OR FRIED HOG CUTLET WITH SALAD)

SERVES 5

Every wild game cook should learn the trick of hammering down a cutlet of meat until it's as thin as window glass before coating it in breadcrumbs and frying it in oil. While the dish is most closely associated with Austrian cuisine, where it's known as schnitzel, many cultures have their own version: the French have escalope, and some South American countries have a unique take, Milanese, that was carried to the New World by Italian immigrants. I've eaten it a few times in Argentina and Chile, where it's served in a variety of ways, including on a sandwich. But the best way I've had it, by far, is a stripped-down version where the fried cutlet is plated with a simple salad of spicy greens with a vinaigrette dressing. This is one of those versatile meals that fits just about any occasion. Try it once and you'll be schnitzeling just about anything you can get your hands on.

FOR THE HOG CUTLET: Place the meat between two pieces of parchment paper or plastic wrap. Using a meat mallet, pound the meat really thin (about ³⁄₁₆ inch).

Put the flour, egg wash, and breadcrumbs in three separate trays or shallow bowls. Season the flour with 1 teaspoon salt. Add 2 teaspoons salt and the cheese to the breadcrumbs.

Add oil to a large cast-iron pan or high-sided skillet so it's ¾ to 1 inch deep. Heat over medium-high heat until it reaches 365°F on a deep-fry thermometer. Line a baking sheet with paper towels.

Sprinkle the meat slices with salt and pepper. One at a time, dredge first in the flour, then the egg, and, finally, the breadcrumbs. Carefully slide the breaded cutlet into the hot oil. Fry until golden brown, flipping after 3 minutes to brown the other side. Remove to the prepared baking sheet and sprinkle with salt. Repeat with the remaining cutlets. (If your pan is large enough to cook two at a time, go ahead, but it's important not to crowd them.)

FOR THE SALAD: Combine the greens with the onion, drizzle with the oil, and toss to lightly coat. Sprinkle salt over the greens and toss to coat. Squeeze the juice of half the lemon over the salad. Taste and adjust the seasonings. Cut the other half of the lemon into wedges.

Lay the cutlets on a plate and top with a pile of salad. Serve immediately, with the lemon wedges.

HOG CUTLET

1 pound roast from the rear leg of a wild hog, cut into 5 (3-ounce) slices

1 cup all-purpose flour

3 large eggs, beaten with 2 tablespoons water or milk

2 cups breadcrumbs (panko or coarse Homemade Breadcrumbs, page 324)

Kosher salt

¼ cup grated Parmigiano-Reggiano cheese

About 2 cups olive oil or peanut oil, for frying

Freshly ground black pepper

SALAD

5 cups mixed peppery greens, such as escarole, mizuna, arugula, or watercress

¼ red onion, thinly sliced

3 tablespoons extra virgin olive oil

Kosher salt

1 lemon

ALSO WORKS WITH: I've done this with everything ranging from halibut to wild turkey, so use your imagination.

THREE SPICY BULK GAME SAUSAGE RECIPES

MAKES 10 POUNDS OF SAUSAGE

There are almost as many types of sausages as there are types of people. You've got your gregarious and easygoing varieties that aim to please, such as sweet Italian and bratwurst, and then you've got your blends that are a bit more divisive, like boudin noir and leberwurst. I'll open my door to as wide a variety of these sausages as possible, though the following preparations fall well within the "friendly" category. They're all a bit spicy, but not *too* spicy, and it's easy to turn the heat up or down according to your own tastes. They can be cased in natural hog casings (my preference are casings with diameters between 32 and 35 millimeters) or left uncased as bulk sausage for use in other recipes like soups, stews, tacos, pastas, and patties. Like the big game sausages in my previous book, *The Complete Guide to Hunting, Butchering, and Cooking Wild Game,* Volume 1, these are based on an 80/20 mixture of lean game meat and pork fatback. You can raise the fat level if you prefer, all the way to 70/30, but 80/20 is a flavorful, juicy sausage that's not overly greasy. By the way, a quick tip for any javelina hunters out there: make some chorizo.

ALSO WORKS WITH: You can get away with using any and all big game in these blends. Keep in mind, though, that sausages made from bears, wild pigs, javelinas, and other carnivores or omnivores need to be cooked to a temperature of 160°F to destroy any parasites that might be lurking.

CHORIZO SAUSAGE

BASIC MEAT MIXTURE

8 pounds lean game meat (such as deer, elk, wild hog, etc.), cut into 1-inch cubes

2 pounds pork fatback, cut into 1-inch cubes

20 feet natural hog casings (32 to 35 millimeters in diameter; optional)

CHORIZO SAUSAGE

⅓ cup paprika

3 tablespoons kosher salt

3 tablespoons ground ancho chile powder

2 tablespoon ground árbol chile powder

2 teaspoons dried oregano (preferably Mexican oregano)

1½ teaspoons ground cinnamon

1½ teaspoons freshly ground black pepper

1 teaspoon ground cumin

12 cloves garlic, minced

½ cup white wine vinegar or cider vinegar, chilled

½ cup ice water, as needed

See The Sausage-Making Process (page 47) for basic sausage-making instructions.

SPECIAL EQUIPMENT NEEDED:
meat grinder, sausage stuffer, natural hog casings

MERGUEZ SAUSAGE

BASIC MEAT MIXTURE

8 pounds lean game meat (such as deer, elk, or wild hog), cut into 1-inch cubes

2 pounds pork fatback, cut into 1-inch cubes

20 feet natural hog casings (32 to 35 millimeters in diameter; optional) or

20 feet natural lamb's intestine casings (18 to 22 millimeters in diameter; optional)

MERGUEZ SAUSAGE

1½ tablespoons coriander seeds

1½ tablespoons cumin seeds

1½ tablespoons fennel seeds

⅓ cup kosher salt

¼ cup paprika

1 tablespoon ground cinnamon

2 teaspoons cayenne pepper (or more, as desired)

1 cup harissa sauce, chilled

10 cloves garlic, minced

⅔ cup red wine vinegar or apple cider vinegar, chilled

¼ cup ice water, as needed

For Merguez Sausage: see page 47 for sausage-making instructions, with these notes: To bring out the flavors of the coriander, cumin, and fennel, toast them in a small skillet over medium-high heat until fragrant. Cool, then grind in a spice grinder to a coarse powder. Add the salt, paprika, cinnamon, and cayenne to the spice mixture. Fold the harissa sauce into the sausage along with the minced garlic, vinegar, and ice water after the meat has been ground. Merguez is traditionally cased in lamb casings and left as spirals rather than twisted into links. You can certainly get away with using hog casings, and you can twist them into links, but the traditional methods are a nice touch.

ANDOUILLE SAUSAGE (SMOKED, CREOLE STYLE)

BASIC MEAT MIXTURE

8 pounds lean game meat (such as deer, elk, wild hog, etc.), cut into 1-inch cubes

2 pounds pork fatback, cut into 1-inch cubes

(Alternative mixture: 7 pounds lean game meat and 3 pounds pork belly, cut into 1-inch cubes)

20 feet natural hog casings (32 to 35 millimeters in diameter; optional)

ANDOUILLE SAUSAGE (SMOKED, CREOLE STYLE)

2 onions, finely diced

3 tablespoons vegetable oil

½ cup paprika

12 cloves garlic, minced

3 tablespoons cayenne pepper

3 tablespoons kosher salt

1½ tablespoons garlic powder

1½ tablespoons onion powder

1 tablespoon ancho chile powder

1 tablespoon red chile flakes

2 teaspoons ground allspice

2 teaspoons dry thyme leaves

⅓ cup white wine vinegar or apple cider vinegar, chilled

¼ cup ice water, as needed

See page 47 for sausage-making instructions, with these notes: Cook the diced onions in vegetable oil over medium-high heat until translucent, about 3 minutes. Let cool before mixing into the meat mixture along with the spices. After casing the sausages, heat a smoker to 200°F. Smoke the sausages until the internal temperature of the meat reaches 140°F. If using wild hog, javelina, or bear meat to make this sausage, be sure to test that each sausage has gotten up to 160°F to kill off any parasites. Note: This is not a cured and smoked sausage, so fully hot-smoking is important for safety reasons, and the sausage should be consumed or frozen within a week of smoking.

Here's the basic rundown for making the sausages. Any exceptions to this process will be noted in the particular recipes.

1. TO GET STARTED: Place the cubed fat on a large plate or baking sheet in your freezer until it begins to harden, but don't let it freeze all the way through. Put the cubed meat in your fridge to cool it off. You want everything nice and cold, so that it's on the verge of painful to handle it. Meanwhile, set up your meat grinder according to the manufacturer's instructions and soak the natural hog casings (if using) in lukewarm water. Once the casings are pliable, change the water and give them another soak for 20 to 30 minutes. Then fit one end of each casing over the kitchen faucet and run a cup or two of water into the casing. Push the water all the way through, to rinse the inside of the casing. Set aside in clean water until ready to use.

2. TO GRIND THE SAUSAGE: Combine the chilled cubed meat and pork fat with the dry spices and any herbs or garlic in a large bowl. Mix well so that the meat is evenly coated with spices. Place in the fridge to marinate for 8 to 24 hours. When you're ready to grind the sausage, fill a tub with ice and place the bowl of meat inside the tub to keep it cool. Using a ³⁄₁₆-inch

(4.5-mm) grinder plate, grind the meat mixture into another bowl that's set over ice. (One pass through the grinder will give the meat a nice texture that's appropriate for most sausages. You can get a coarser texture by using a ¼-inch grinder plate; to get a finer texture, pass the meat through the grinder two times. When double grinding, be extra careful about keeping everything cold. Grinders create friction, and friction equals heat.) Using a rubber spatula or large wooden spoon, fold in the liquids and mix well. The mixture should be wet and sticky (like pizza dough), but it should not be sitting in liquid. Cover and refrigerate while you set up your sausage stuffer. Either pack the bulk sausage into 1-pound poly bags or make links using natural hog-middle casings.

3. STUFFING SAUSAGES: Fill the hopper of your sausage stuffer with the sausage mixture and fit the stuffer tube with a cleaned casing. Start pushing meat through the stuffer to clear any air in the stuffer tube. Before meat enters the casing, tie the end with a simple granny knot. Working slowly, stuff the sausage into the casings. Be careful not to overstuff, and expel any large air bubbles inside the casing by pricking it with a sewing needle. When filled, tie off the casing with another granny knot. To create links: make two creases in the casing, one 5 inches from the end and another at 10 inches from the end. Twist the sausage at these two creases about eight times. Now you have two links. Make two more creases at 5-inch intervals and spin these. Continue down the length of the casing. To separate the individual links, gently pull the links apart and snip the middle of the "twist" with a pair of scissors or a knife.

Tip: If possible, freeze your cased sausages in vacuum-sealed bags. Make sure to orient the sausages vertically rather than horizontally in the vacuum bag. Horizontally placed sausages can form a dam in the bag that prevents the sealer from expelling all of the air during the vacuum process. I generally freeze my bulk sausage in poly meat bags, though I like to freeze some bulk sausage in a thin layer inside standard vacuum bags as well. In a hurry, you can toss a vacuum-sealed bag of sausage into a tub of cold water and it'll thaw very quickly.

THE PERFECT VENISON BURGER

SERVES 4

1 pound venison, trimmed

¼ pound fatty bacon ends, pork fat, or beef fat

Kosher salt

Freshly ground black pepper

3 tablespoons olive oil or vegetable oil (to coat the skillet, if needed)

4 slices Cheddar cheese

4 hamburger rolls

Toppings: lettuce, tomato, pickle, mustard, and ketchup

ALSO WORKS WITH: You can use any big game to make burgers. But remember that hamburger made from bears, wild pigs, javelinas, and other carnivores or omnivores needs to be cooked to a temperature of 160°F to destroy any parasites that might be lurking.

SPECIAL EQUIPMENT NEEDED: meat grinder

I might question your judgment if you ground up your venison backstraps to make a cheeseburger. Those tender muscles really are better when they're cooked whole to a medium-rare temperature and then sliced thin. And I might also raise an eyebrow if you ground up all of your venison shanks, as those are pretty damn good after six hours of braising in a 325°F oven. But beyond that, I'm open to the idea of grinding just about any cut of big game as long as it's being prepared with love. Every year, I go through well over one hundred pounds of ground meat. (That might sound like a lot, but keep in mind that I provide protein for a lot of backyard barbecues.) The amount of fat that I use ranges from 10 percent to 20 percent depending on my mood, but if I had to choose a single ratio for the rest of my life, I'd go with around 20 percent. That makes a juicy hamburger that holds together and crisps nicely around the edges. With all the lean meat I eat in the form of roasts and steaks, I don't feel bad at all about having a little grease dripping down my chin when I eat a burger. Beef suet and pork fat can be used interchangeably, depending on personal tastes, and fatty bacon ends can be a nice way to mix things up now and then. Toppings can be what you like: it's about the meat. If you want to get fancy, though, sautéed onions with American cheese is well worth a try.

Slice the venison into 1- to 2-inch cubes. For best grinding, the meat should be extremely cold, almost freezing. Add the bacon ends to the pile and mix together. (This makes a 3:1 meat-to-fat ratio, 25 percent fat). You can spread the pile of meat over a baking sheet and put it in the freezer for 20 to 30 minutes to ensure that it's cold. Run the meat through a meat grinder using a ¼-inch (7-mm) grinder plate. You can stop here, or you can run the meat through the grinder a second time. The twice-ground meat will form a denser patty that holds together better; personally, I prefer a single pass through the grinder.

Prepare a grill (gas or charcoal) for direct high heat. Divide the ground meat into four parts and form patties. Make the patties as loose as you can without risking them falling apart. Be gentle. Salt and pepper the patties; depending on your affinity for salt, you might not need to add any at all, as the bacon ends are plenty salty. Place the patties on the grill (or you can use a cast-iron skillet with the oil) with the grill lid open. Cook for 3 to 4 minutes, flip, cook another 2 to 3 minutes, add a slice of cheese to each patty, close the lid or cover the skillet, and turn off the heat. As the cheese is melting (a minute or two), prep your rolls with the condiments and toppings. Serve immediately.

VENISON STEW
WITH RED WINE AND ROOT VEGETABLES

MAKES 8 1-CUP SERVINGS

I love making stews for my family. For one thing, the kids will eagerly devour them. (Giving them a sliced baguette with some butter on the side always helps.) The other thing is that I cherish the leftovers as a quick, convenient lunch. The fact that it seems to taste better and better over the next few days has me thinking that I should cook it a couple of days ahead of time and let it relax in the fridge before the initial serving. This recipe calls for a few cups of red wine. I'm sure there are some parents who might worry about serving their kids a dish prepared with such a high amount of an adult beverage. But alcohol evaporates out of cooking foods at a temperature of 172°F. Once the stew has simmered for a few minutes, the booze is long gone.

Sprinkle the meat with the salt and pepper. Heat the oil in a large Dutch oven over medium-high heat. Once the oil shimmers, add the meat and brown on all sides, 8 to 10 minutes. (Do this in batches if necessary to avoid crowding.) Remove the meat to a plate.

Add the carrots, celery, and onion to the pot and cook until softened, 5 to 8 minutes, adding more oil as needed. Add the garlic and cook for 30 seconds. Return the meat to the pot along with any juices that may have collected on the plate. Sprinkle the flour evenly over the meat and vegetables and cook, stirring, for 2 to 3 minutes. Pour in the red wine and whisk to get any clumps out. Add the stock, raise the heat, and bring to a boil. Skim and discard any scum that rises to the top. Add the parsley, juniper berries, bay leaf, and rosemary. Cover the pot, reduce the heat, and simmer for 1 hour.

Add the potatoes and turnips and simmer until the meat is very tender and the turnips and potatoes have no resistance when pierced with a fork, 15 to 20 minutes. Discard the bay leaf. Serve immediately.

Note: For potpies, make the recipe as directed and let cool to room temperature. Ladle the stew into a 9 x 13-inch ceramic baking dish or 6 to 8 ramekins (8 to 10 ounces each). Roll out thawed puff pastry dough or Basic Pie Dough (page 324) to 10 x 14 inches. Fit and adhere to either the large baking dish, or cut out circles slightly larger than the diameter of the ramekins, then fit individually to adhere. Make a small slit in the top of the pastry. Chill in the refrigerator for 10 minutes. Preheat the oven to 400°F. Make an egg wash by beating 1 egg with a splash of water. Brush lightly onto the pastry. Bake the potpie(s) until the pastry is golden and the stew is bubbling, about 25 minutes.

3 pounds venison stew meat, shoulder or rump cuts, cut into 1½-inch cubes

2 tablespoons kosher salt

2 teaspoons freshly ground black pepper

¼ cup extra virgin olive oil, plus more as needed

2 large carrots, diced

2 ribs celery, diced

1 large onion, diced

5 cloves garlic, chopped

½ cup all-purpose flour

3 cups red wine

4 cups Brown Game Stock (page 305) or low-sodium, store-bought beef or chicken stock

2 tablespoons chopped fresh flat-leaf parsley

3 juniper berries

1 bay leaf

Leaves from 1 sprig fresh rosemary, chopped

2 russet potatoes, diced

1 small turnip, diced

ALSO WORKS WITH: Make this with pretty much any big game. I find that the texture of bear meat is especially well suited for stews.

VENISON BOLOGNESE

SERVES 6 (SAUCE MAKES ABOUT 8 CUPS)

¼ cup extra virgin olive oil, plus more as needed

1 onion, finely chopped

Kosher salt

3 ribs celery, finely chopped

2 carrots, finely grated

6 cloves garlic, thinly sliced

1½ pounds ground venison (80/20 mix)

1 pound ground pork

8 ounces ground pork fat or pancetta

1 (8-ounce) can tomato paste

Freshly ground black pepper

1½ cups dry white wine

1½ cups milk

3 sprigs fresh thyme

1 bay leaf

1 (6-ounce) bunch kale or other leafy green, thinly sliced (optional)

1½ pounds linguine

½ cup grated Parmigiano-Reggiano cheese, plus more for serving

---

ALSO WORKS WITH: Anything goes, really. It'd be great with bear meat.

Note: If a saucier Bolognese is your preference, cut the tomato paste by half and add 2 cups of canned tomato sauce (or more if you wish) after you add the tomato paste. Omit the milk entirely. Continue to cook for 1 to 2 hours.

This is a pretty traditional Italian-style Bolognese recipe, except that it uses wild game. You'll want to add a good amount of fat for best results. I sometimes grind my wild game as a 90/10 mix of game meat and pork fat or beef suet, though this recipe works well with an 80/20 mix using pork fat. If the ground meat in your freezer is too lean, you can bolster the fat content by mixing in some finely chopped pancetta or bacon. The resulting ground meat mixture will work well for lasagna or any other kind of pasta dish. You'll notice that this recipe uses tomato paste and not tomato sauce. See the Note to learn how to make it saucier if that's your preference. You'll also see that the addition of greens is optional. I like them, because it's a great way to hide some added nutrients into meals that you're serving to kids.

Heat the oil in a heavy-bottomed saucepan over medium heat until it shimmers. Add the onion, season lightly with salt, and cook until softened, translucent, and lightly caramelized, 8 to 10 minutes. Add the celery and carrots, season with salt again, and cook until softened, adding more oil if needed. Add the garlic and cook, stirring, for 30 seconds. Raise the heat to medium-high, add the venison, pork, and pork fat, and brown very well, breaking it up with a wooden spoon, about 15 minutes. When the meat has browned and is audibly frying in its own fat (you should hear a popping sound), push the meat to one side, creating a "hot spot" on the bottom of the pot. Add the tomato paste to the hot spot and caramelize it lightly (being careful not to burn it). Stir to incorporate into the meat and vegetables. Season liberally with salt and pepper. Add the wine and scrape the bottom of the pot with a spoon to release the flavorful browned bits that have accumulated. Add the milk and bring to a bare simmer over medium-low heat. Drop in the thyme and bay leaf and cover. Reduce the heat to low and cook until the flavors come together, 1½ to 2 hours, stirring occasionally to prevent sticking. If using the greens, add after the first hour, along with ½ cup water. After about 2 hours, adjust the seasonings and remove from the heat. Discard the thyme sprigs and bay leaf. Refrigerate if not serving right away. The sauce can be frozen for up to 6 months.

To serve over pasta, reheat 3 cups of the sauce in a large skillet. Bring 6 quarts of water with 3 tablespoons of salt to a rapid boil. Add the linguine and cook until al dente. Add ½ cup of the pasta water to the sauce. Add the pasta to the sauce and stir to incorporate. Remove from the heat, add the grated cheese, and gently mix together. Serve immediately.

VENISON CHILI

SERVES 8

I'd be willing to bet that more pounds of ground venison go into chili than any other type of recipe. I know that I've eaten my fair share. My mom used to make what I think of as a mild "Midwest chili" using whitetail deer and kidney beans on an almost weekly basis in the winter, and I loved every bowl of it. (Thanks, Mom!) This is a more sophisticated version, with poblanos, chipotles, and whole tomatoes. A lot of the magic lies in the toppings, so don't skimp on those. It's fun to let everyone get in there and customize their own bowl.

ALSO WORKS WITH: It's wide open. Use any ground meat.

FOR THE CHILI: Heat a large Dutch oven or other wide, heavy saucepan over medium-high heat. Add 2 tablespoons of the oil. Sprinkle the venison generously with salt and pepper. Working in batches, crumble the venison into the pot in large chunks and sear until browned, 6 to 8 minutes per batch, transferring to a large bowl as each batch is done and adding more oil as needed. Reduce the heat to medium. Add the remaining 2 tablespoons oil, the poblanos, and the onion, scraping up the browned bits at the bottom of the pot. Raise the heat to medium-high heat and cook, stirring often, until softened, 8 to 10 minutes. Stir in the garlic, ancho chile powder, cumin, and oregano and cook, stirring constantly, for 1 minute. Add the tomatoes, crushing them with your hands or mashing them with a potato masher. Add the chipotles, half of the beans, the stock, and the venison with any juices that have accumulated in the bowl. Stir to combine, then bring to a simmer. Cook, partially covered, stirring occasionally, until the venison is tender, about 2 hours.

Add the remaining beans and warm through. Taste and adjust the seasonings.

FOR SERVING: Serve the chili with corn chips or cornbread, cheese, sour cream, onions or scallions, and chiles.

CHILI

¼ cup plus 2 tablespoons vegetable oil

2¼ pounds ground venison

Kosher salt and freshly ground black pepper

3 large poblano chiles, stemmed and diced

1 large onion, chopped

6 cloves garlic, thinly sliced

2 tablespoons ancho chile powder, or to taste

1½ tablespoons ground cumin

1 teaspoon dried oregano

3 (14.5-ounce) cans whole tomatoes, preferably in tomato puree

3 tablespoons minced chipotle chiles in adobo

2 (15-ounce) cans kidney beans or pinto beans, rinsed and drained

3 cups Blonde Game Stock (page 306) or chicken broth

TO SERVE

Corn chips or Cornbread (page 326)

Shredded sharp Cheddar or Pepper Jack cheese

Sour cream

Diced red onions or sliced scallions

Sliced jalapeño or serrano chiles

KIMCHI TACOS
WITH WILD PIG OR JAVELINA

SERVES 4 TO 6

2 pounds bone-in javelina thigh or shoulder, or wild hog shoulder

1 cup soju (Korean rice wine)

⅔ cup gochujang (Korean chile paste)

1 cup soy sauce

1 cup sugar

½ cup grated garlic

½ cup grated ginger

1 to 2 tablespoons toasted sesame oil

1 medium onion, sliced

Corn tortillas

2 cups kimchi

Shredded Oaxaca, Monterey Jack, or other white cheese

4 scallions, thinly sliced on a bias

Some years ago I ended up with about twenty pounds of braised wild hog and a huge jar of homemade kimchi (a spicy pickled cabbage—Korea's national dish) in my refrigerator. It was purely coincidental, but what came out of that situation was a deep respect for a crispy-fried mound of braised pork lying next to a handful of kimchi on a warm tortilla. Since then I've placed everything from javelina thighs to blacktail deer shanks in a similar context, and all of it's great. But there's something about the flavor and texture of white-fleshed hogs and javelina that really lends itself to this preparation.

ALSO WORKS WITH: If you don't have access to wild pigs or javelina but you're dying to try this, do it with a venison shank. Adjust the cooking time so that the meat can be easily pulled away from the bone with your fingers.

Put the meat in a slow cooker and add the soju, gochujang, soy sauce, sugar, garlic, ginger, and just enough water to cover the meat. Cook on low for 5 hours.

Remove the meat, transfer the liquid to a pot, and heat over high heat until reduced by half. Allow the meat to cool to comfortable handling temperature and then pick the meat from the bone. Break the meat up into pieces the size of a ballpoint pen cap and crush them slightly with your fingers. Place the pieces back into the braising liquid.

Heat the oil (enough to coat the bottom) in a medium skillet over medium-high heat. Add the onion and stir until it's translucent and begins to brown, about 10 minutes. Remove the onion from the skillet. Lift the braised meat from the liquid, shaking the pieces off, and then lay them in a single layer in the skillet. Once the meat starts to crisp and the braising liquid begins to caramelize, scrape the bottom of the skillet with a spatula and flip the meat. Don't allow it to burn, but keep frying and scraping until the meat is crispy around the edges. Toss the onions back into the skillet, stir together with the meat, and then remove from the heat.

Warm the tortillas. Arrange rows of meat and kimchi down the center of the tortillas and top with cheese and scallions.

SLOW-COOKED AND GRILLED VENISON RIBS

SERVES 4

I think of this rib recipe, or at least a version of it, as being one of the most important wild game discoveries of my life. Before my brothers and I figured this out, we always deboned the rib meat on our big game animals and used it in hamburger blends. That's because we regarded rib meat on big game as being too tough and stringy for use in standard recipes designed for pork and beef ribs. But then my older brother Matt started experimenting by putting big game ribs in his pressure cooker in order to tenderize them first. Pretty soon that developed into one of my favorite all-time wild game recipes. From then on, I've never looked at a rib cage in the same way—and I've never again deboned rib meat for making hamburgers without feeling at least a little guilty. If you're dealing with an animal that has a lot of fat over the ribs, trim away as much as possible before cooking. It's waxy and not too pleasant to eat. But don't worry if you can't get it all. Most of the remainder will render out during the initial cooking process. There is a lot of guesswork when it comes to pressure cooking ribs, as you can't visually monitor their progress inside the sealed cooker. If you let them go just ten minutes too long, the meat can become so tender that it falls away from the bone. A safer, albeit longer method is using a slow cooker.

ALSO WORKS WITH: Anything goes, as long as there's enough meat to bother with. Smaller whitetails and mule deer, as well as antelope, sometimes have so little meat over and between their ribs that it doesn't warrant the effort of cooking them. In these cases, bone out whatever you can get from the ribs and add it to the trim pile for making burger. In the case of larger animals such as big deer, elk, moose (like the photo shown here), and caribou, it's possible to actually have too much meat. If there's a heavy layer of muscle over the rib cage, fillet it away for the burger pile. On these big critters, there's enough meat between the ribs that you don't need the overlayers to make it worthwhile. See page 16 for how-to on removing the ribs from the animal.

Using a hacksaw or bone saw, cut the ribs perpendicular to the bones to get a 4- to 6-inch strip of connected rib bones. Then cut these strips into pieces containing 3 or 4 ribs apiece. (See the image on page 56.)

Place the ribs, salt, and pepper in a slow cooker and add just enough stock or water to cover them. Cook on high for 2 to 3 hours or on low for 6 to 8 hours. By then the ribs should be fairly tender. The measure of a perfectly cooked venison rib is that the meat clings to the bone but it can be easily pulled away with your teeth, leaving a clean white bone behind. A little resistance when you're chewing is not a bad thing.

1 slab game ribs, cut in half, then cut into 2 or 3 rib bone chunks (see image page 58)

1 teaspoon kosher salt

¼ teaspoon freshly ground fresh black pepper

About 4 cups Blonde Game Stock (page 306) or water (or substitute low-sodium chicken or vegetable broth)

1 recipe BBQ Rub (page 313), or a store-bought rub

1 recipe BBQ Sauce (page 314), or a store-bought sauce

SPECIAL EQUIPMENT:
slow cooker, hacksaw or butcher's saw

Prepare a grill (gas or charcoal) for medium-high direct heat.

Remove the ribs from the slow cooker and then give them a generous rub-down with the rub. Place the ribs on the grill. Since they're already cooked, you're simply reheating the meat and charring the outside a bit. Once the ribs have crisped, about 10 minutes, coat them generously with the BBQ sauce and continue cooking for 1 to 2 minutes to allow the sauce to caramelize and thicken. Serve hot.

WHOLE BRAISED VENISON SHANK ADOBADA

SERVES 6 TO 8

One of my long-standing career goals has been to get hunters excited about cooking and eating shanks. Unaware of the quality of the flesh surrounding the shin bones, too many folks are content to just bone them out for the grind pile or else discard them entirely. My guess is that some folks are intimidated by the cooking process. It can take several hours or more in a 300°F oven to soften the meat. That's a fair bit of pre-planning, but the payoff is heavenly. If you're accustomed to the flavors and textures of traditional wild game roasts, steaks, burgers, etc., you're going to be really surprised by a properly cooked shank. The meat turns rich and silky as the connective tissues and tendons soften during the cooking process. In this case, you're cooking the shanks in a flavorful adobada sauce until they're soft enough to be picked apart with your fingers. It's like magic. Cook this once and you'll never again disrespect a shank. The full-flavored meat can be served with a side of rice and a salad, as suggested here, or with mashed potatoes. Another good option is to make tacos by filling soft corn tortillas (two to four per person) with the meat and garnishing with cilantro leaves, crumbled cheese, and a squeeze of lime.

Pat the shanks dry, then sprinkle with salt and pepper. Heat 2 tablespoons of the oil in a large skillet over medium-high heat. Working in batches, sear the shanks until browned, about 4 minutes per side, adding the remaining 2 tablespoons oil for the second batch. As they are done, transfer to a large container with a lid. Reduce the heat to medium, add the onion, and cook until softened, 6 to 8 minutes. Add to the shanks along with the bay leaves. Pour the adobada over the shanks and turn to coat evenly. Let cool, then cover and refrigerate for 8 hours.

Preheat the oven to 300°F. Transfer the shanks and adobada to a large Dutch oven or small roasting pan. Cover and braise, turning occasionally, until the meat is falling off the bone, 4 to 5 hours. Discard the bay leaves. Transfer the shanks to a platter and set aside until cool enough to handle. Remove the meat from the bones and coarsely shred, discarding any gelatinous chunks. Moisten the meat with some adobada and adjust the seasonings.

Serve hot with warm rice and a simply dressed salad. (For dressing suggestions, see the Basic Vinaigrette on page 315.)

6 pounds whole venison shanks

Kosher salt

Freshly ground black pepper

¼ cup vegetable or canola oil

1 large white onion, chopped

2 bay leaves

1 recipe Adobada (page 314)

Cooked rice, for serving

Green salad, for serving

ALSO WORKS WITH: Anything goes. I haven't yet met a shank that I don't like. When dealing with big shanks from critters like elk and moose, you'll want to saw them down into pieces first. It's easiest if you freeze the whole shank and then saw it like a piece of firewood using a clean hacksaw, butcher's saw, or even a standard carpenter's saw. I've done it quite a few times with an electric reciprocating saw.

OSSO BUCCO
WITH POLENTA AND GREMOLATA

SERVES 4

2 deer shanks, cut into 3 discs measuring 3 inches long (see opposite for more portioning information)

Kosher salt

Freshly ground black pepper

All-purpose flour, for dredging

3 tablespoons extra virgin olive oil

2 carrots, cut into ⅓-inch rounds

2 medium red onions, thinly sliced

1 rib celery, cut into ⅓-inch rounds

4 cloves garlic, thinly sliced

2 tablespoons tomato paste

1 cup dry red or white wine

2 sprigs fresh thyme

1 sprig fresh rosemary

1 bay leaf

1 recipe Polenta (page 330)

1 recipe Classic Gremolata (page 316) (optional)

Freshly grated Parmigiano-Reggiano cheese, for serving

Osso bucco is an Italian dish traditionally prepared with veal shanks. The name translates as "bone with a hole," a reference to the medullary cavity at the center of a bone that is exposed as a round hole when the bone is cut in cross-section. On wild game, the shank is one of the toughest—probably *the* toughest—cuts of meat. It's so packed with sinew and connective tissue that it can clog up an otherwise trusty meat grinder even when cut into small boneless cubes. That's what makes osso bucco such a special recipe. Once the bones are cut into discs, they are braised in a thick broth containing wine and vegetables until the meat becomes so tender and silky that it can be mashed with a fork. The transformation is so stunning that it seems more like magic than science, though the actual explanation has to do with the slow process of collagen being broken down into gelatin through the application of moist heat. The meat is served, nestled around its circle of bone and marrow, over a bed of polenta and under a blanket of rich sauce. Make this once and you'll never again want to jam up your grinder with shank meat. The easiest way to cut the shanks is to saw them with a hacksaw or meat saw while they're still frozen. You can use a reciprocating saw as well.

Tie the shanks around the middle with butcher's twine to hold them in place as they cook. Heat an 8- to 10-quart Dutch oven over medium-high heat. Sprinkle the shank discs well with salt and pepper and lightly dredge them in flour. Add the oil to the pot and swirl to coat. When the oil shimmers, sear the shank discs in batches (avoid overcrowding the pan, as this will steam the meat), 4 to 6 minutes per side. When the meat is well browned on all sides, remove to a plate. Be careful not to let the bits on the bottom of the pan burn, as it will impart a bitter flavor.

Add the carrots, onions, and celery and cook until the onions are browned, 8 to 10 minutes. Add the garlic and cook until fragrant, about 30 seconds. Push the vegetables to one side, creating a "hot spot" on the bottom of the pot. Add the tomato paste to the hot spot and caramelize it lightly, about 1 to 2 minutes, being careful not to let it burn. Stir to incorporate the sauce into the vegetables. Add the wine to the pot and scrape up any browned bits from the bottom of the pan. Allow the wine to reduce slightly.

Return the meat to the pot. Add about 2 quarts water, enough to just cover the meat. Bring to a boil, then reduce the heat to low. Skim off and discard any scum that accumulates on the surface. Add the thyme and rosemary sprigs and bay leaf. Cover the pot and cook at a bare simmer until the meat is very tender but not falling off the bone, 3½ to 4 hours.

Check halfway through to make sure there is still enough liquid covering the meat; add more if needed. Discard the thyme and rosemary sprigs and the bay leaf.

When the shanks are fork tender, remove them from the pot and carefully remove the twine with kitchen shears.

Divide the polenta among dinner plates. Top each puddle of polenta with a shank piece. Spoon the sauce and the vegetables over the meat. Garnish with gremolata, if desired, and some cheese.

ALSO WORKS WITH: Use the shanks of any big game animal, including bears, wild hogs, and mountain lions. A shank from a mature whitetail or mule deer will yield a quantity of three 3-inch discs. Six of these discs should be enough for three or four people, depending on the size of the deer. A single elk shank cut into 3-inch discs will feed four people. With antelope shanks (or a yearling whitetail) you might need a whole shank per person, depending on appetites. Note that the rear shanks of antlered game animals are bigger and meatier than the fronts. On a particular mature female Shiras moose, for instance, the rear shanks weighed 6.5 pounds and the front shanks weighed 5.5 pounds.

SPECIAL EQUIPMENT: hacksaw, butcher's saw, or reciprocating saw; butcher's twine

THE QUEEN MOTHER OF ALL JERKIES

1 (3-pound) roast, frozen for 2 hours

1 cup soy sauce

½ cup pineapple juice

½ cup Worcestershire sauce

¼ cup packed brown sugar

2 tablespoons honey

1 tablespoon red chile flakes

2 tablespoons coarsely ground black pepper

1 tablespoon onion powder

3 cloves garlic, peeled

1 (1-inch) piece fresh ginger, peeled

ALSO WORKS WITH: Any horned or antlered game is suitable for jerky making. I've made jerky with black bear meat as well, but then you've got to cook the finished product to destroy parasites, which diminishes the quality of your end product. It's better to stick with meat that doesn't require the extra hassle. And while it's easier to work with large whole muscles, you can make jerky from just about any little scrap of meat. The end product will lack uniformity of size, and there might be a little more connective tissue to deal with, but that shouldn't dissuade you.

SPECIAL EQUIPMENT: dehydrator, though not necessary

One of the best pieces of jerky I ever ate was from an axis deer I killed on the Hawaiian island of Molokai. My Hawaiian hunting partners marinated thin slices in a peppery homemade teriyaki sauce and then air-dried them out in the sun under a piece of window screen to keep the flies away. This recipe is inspired by that experience, though it takes into account that most of us do not live in a climate that's suitable for air-drying jerky—especially in the fall and winter months. Still, this recipe stays true to the same mixture of salt, sweet, and spice. For the meat, I prefer to work with whole roasts from the ham or shoulder that have been trimmed of fat and silver skin. Before slicing the meat, place it in the freezer for a couple of hours. You want it icy and firm, but not so frozen that a knife can't easily pass through it. This helps you get perfect slices and saves you a lot of aggravation. There are different opinions on whether you should slice with the grain or cross-grain. Slicing with the grain gives you chewier jerky that's hard to bite, but some folks like that. A cross-grain slice gives you more tender jerky that's easy to chew.

Cut the meat into ⅜-inch-thick slices. (See above regarding cross-grain or with-the-grain slices.) Keep the slices as uniform in thickness as possible. If the meat starts to thaw, pop it back into the freezer.

Combine the soy sauce, pineapple juice, Worcestershire sauce, brown sugar, honey, red chile flakes, black pepper, and onion powder. Using a Microplane, finely grate the garlic and ginger into the bowl. Discard the fibrous bits of ginger that don't pass through the Microplane. (If you don't have a Microplane, mince the garlic and ginger with a knife as finely as you possibly can.) Add the meat, mix thoroughly, cover, and marinate in the refrigerator for about 24 hours.

Remove the meat from the marinade and drain. Lay the meat out on the dehydrator trays, leaving space between the slices. Set the dehydrator to 145°F. Depending on the idiosyncrasies of your climate and dehydrator, it probably will take between 2 and 4 hours to finish the job. Start checking the meat at 2 hours and remove pieces as they finish. They should be firm throughout, with no sponginess, and will not break when you bend them. Rather, the fold will reveal a network of thin white lines.

Tip: You can make jerky in a conventional oven by setting it to the lowest possible setting and cracking the door to adjust the temperature. Use an oven thermometer rather than relying on your oven's thermostat, and keep the temperature between 140 and 150°F.

CANNING MEAT

MAKES 1 QUART CANNED MEAT

When I was a kid, a portion of our basement was designated as the "canning room." My dad had installed wooden shelves on either side of a passageway leading to the washer and dryer. My mom kept these shelves stocked with a wide array of home-canned goods. There were a lot of vegetable products from our garden, including tomato sauces and salsa, plus a variety of fruits purchased at a large farmers' market in nearby Muskegon. But the thing that I remember most fondly were the jars of venison all lined up in neat rows. We ate some of it in stews over the winter, but we'd eat the bulk of it the following fall. My dad kept a milk crate of the jars in the back of his truck, and we'd use them for tailgate sandwiches whenever we were out in the woods hunting. There's an image that's burned into my mind of my dad holding back the meat in the jar with his folding knife while he poured off some of the excess stock. Then he'd dig the knife into the jar and pull out a few squares of meat and crush them onto rye bread. A bit of mustard and a slice of onion, and that was it. Then you went back into the woods and started looking for the deer that would make next year's sandwich.

Trim the meat of tallow and heavy tendons or connective tissue, but don't be too persnickety. A little connective tissue or silver skin isn't a problem with this preparation. Cut the meat into approximately 1-inch cubes. Heat the oil in a large saucepan over medium-high heat and brown the cubes on all sides; the meat should still be rare, or undercooked. Remove from the heat. In a medium saucepan, bring the stock to a boil and boil for 5 minutes. Remove from the heat.

Add the salt to a quart jar (or ½ teaspoon per jar if you're using 2 pint jars). Pack the browned meat into the jar, leaving room for stock to cover. Pour the hot stock into the jar, leaving 1 inch of headspace—3 cups (24 ounces) for a quart jar (1½ cups or 12 ounces for a pint jar). Tap the jar gently on the counter and tap the sides with a wooden spoon to release all air bubbles. Follow the recommendations of the manufacturer using 2-piece lids. Process the quart jars at 10 pounds pressure for 90 minutes for a quart jar (10 pounds pressure for 75 minutes for a pint jar). Store the meat in a dark place at room temperature for up to 1 year for optimal quality. This is great for last-minute stews or as a protein source on car or camping trips.

2 pounds game meat

1 tablespoon vegetable oil

3 cups Brown Game Stock (page 305), Blonde Game Stock (page 306), or low-sodium chicken broth

1 teaspoon kosher salt

ALSO WORKS WITH: Use this for virtually any big game, from wild hogs to moose. My brother Matt used to use the same recipe for jackrabbit, and my brother Danny has prepared yet another version with green-winged teal. You're looking for about 2 pound of meat per quart jar, but you can get away with a bit more or less depending on how tightly you pack the meat.

SPECIAL EQUIPMENT: pressure canner and glass canning jars with 2-piece lids (one 1-quart canning jar or two 1-pint canning jars)

Tip: For more information on canning meat or processing at high altitudes, go to the USDA home canning website, http://nchfp.uga.edu/, and search for the guide on preparing and canning meats.

SOUTH TEXAS WILD HOG SHOULDER

SERVES A CROWD

SOP

1 cup white vinegar (I've been using apple cider vinegar with good results)

1 cup water

½ cup (1 stick) unsalted butter

1 cup ketchup

1 cup Worcestershire sauce

2 to 4 lemons, sliced

1 onion, sliced

Kosher salt

Freshly ground black pepper

HOG

1 whole wild hog shoulder, a section of shoulder, whole hindquarter, or section of large hindquarter (also known as barbecue cuts; bone-in is preferred)

Kosher salt

Freshly ground black pepper

ALSO WORKS WITH: Stick with wild pork on this one.

SPECIAL EQUIPMENT: DH smoker, pellet grill, gas grill, charcoal grill, or Dutch oven. Hardwood chips, chunks, or logs. Pecan, cherry, or apple wood work well.

A few years ago I was hanging around with a wild hog trapper outside of Devine, Texas, who does damage control work on the nonnative species. We butchered a few of our hogs on our own and then dropped a few off for processing at Devine Meat Company. We ended up spending the better part of the day there, as the proprietor, Clayton Saunders, slow roasted one of our pork shoulders over his "pit," a large barrel roaster fueled by a live fire of pecan wood. Over the course of four or five hours, he brushed the meat intermittently with a special sop of vinegar, lemon juice, Worcestershire sauce, and other tasty additives. It was the best wild pork I've ever eaten, hands down. Since that day, I've had great luck replicating his recipe on my pellet grill at home. But if you want the full experience of an authentic South Texas barbecue, you should probably stick with the real hardwood fire. That'd make Clayton happy.

FOR THE SOP: Combine the vinegar, water, butter, ketchup, Worcestershire sauce, lemons, onion, and some salt and pepper in a medium saucepan and bring to a simmer. It is now ready to be applied to the cooking meat using a pastry brush or clean kitchen rag.

FOR THE HOG: This is traditionally cooked in a pit barbecue, where the heat source is offset/indirect. The fire, typically made from flavorful hardwoods, is kept up in a firebox and the smoke and heat are funneled to the pit. If you don't own a pit barbecue, you can make do with a pellet grill, a conventional gas or charcoal grill, or even a Dutch oven. Alternate cooking methods are described at the end of this recipe.

If you want to go low and slow, keep the temperature between 200 and 250°F. For a shorter cooking time, start at 300 to 350°F for an hour, and then back it down to 250°F to finish. The internal temperature of the meat must reach 160°F to destroy any parasites.

Start by liberally applying salt and pepper to all sides of the meat. Then place the meat in the preheated pit. It is important to allow a crust, or bark, to form on the meat before starting to sop the meat. The crust should be crisp and firm but not burnt and will take at least 30 minutes to an hour to form. Once the crust is formed, apply the sop every 20 minutes or so. The meat is tenderized by the long low-temperature cooking; it is much more common to undercook it and have a tough product than to overcook it and possibly dry it out. The point here is: give yourself plenty of time. Last, flipping the meat is not necessary. Let the smoke and heat do the work. The meat is ready when you can pull it away from the bone with a fork.

This will usually take between 4 and 6 hours for a medium (100-pound on the hoof) hog's shoulder.

Let the meat rest for 20 to 30 minutes after pulling it from the heat to relax the muscle and allow the juices to flow throughout the meat. The meat can be cut into ⅜-inch-thick slices, or, if it's cooked long enough, picked apart for a pulled pork presentation.

Note: This method could be used to cook a whole hog simply by lengthening the cooking time and having an adequate size pit or grill.

ALTERNATE COOKING METHODS

PELLET GRILL: same as above.

GAS GRILL: If possible, light only a single burner element and place the meat so that it's receiving only indirect heat. You can use wood chips to add some smoke. Soak a handful of hardwood chips in water for twenty minutes, then drain and wrap in heavy duty aluminum foil. Place the foil packet over the heat to create smoke. Refill as necessary.

CHARCOAL GRILL: Soak a handful of hardwood chips in water for 20 minutes, drain, and set aside. You can also use a few chunks of pecan or apple wood (unsoaked) instead. Make coals, set them off to one side of the grill, and then add the meat on the opposite side. Distribute soaked chips among the coals. If using hardwood chunks, add one at a time as needed to maintain a light plume of smoke. Care must be taken to keep the temperature low: even a small pile of charcoal briquettes can raise the temperature beyond what's necessary, overcooking and consequently drying out the meat. Because of the long cooking time, you'll need to replenish the charcoal. It's a good idea to keep another pile of briquettes going in a separate location just for this reason.

DUTCH OVEN: Sear the meat in a Dutch oven. This substitutes for the creation of the bark. Place the lid on the Dutch oven and cook in a 300°F oven for approximately 4 hours, applying sop periodically. This method forfeits the smoking flavor but achieves very tender meat.

Note: The remaining sop makes for a great tangy barbecue sauce. Simply strain the solids from the liquid, bring the remaining liquid to a simmer, and reduce until the desired consistency is reached. More ketchup can be added to thicken the sauce faster. This will also sweeten the sauce. If you like a sweeter barbecue sauce, try adding a few tablespoons of brown sugar.

SMOKED HAM

SERVES A CROWD

1 bone-in venison ham, 7 to 20 pounds, depending on the size of the animal

BRINE

2 gallons water

2½ cups kosher salt

2 cups packed brown sugar

2 teaspoons yellow mustard seeds

20 black peppercorns

8 juniper berries

6 bay leaves

8 cloves garlic

1 tablespoon Prague Powder #1

SPECIAL EQUIPMENT: large stockpot or other container for brining; heavy-duty brine injector; kitchen twine (if using an upright smoker with enough room to hang the ham); smoker; hardwood chips, pecan, apple, or cherry work well

---

Every time I smoke a ham, be it black bear, wild hog, or venison, I'm a little torn about whether or not to remove the femur. With the bone removed, you can truss the ham back together with kitchen twine or food-grade elastic mesh. The advantages of deboning have to do with convenience. A deboned ham brines faster, it's compact, and it's easy to slice. The advantages of leaving the femur in place are more aesthetic, which does not mean less important. A bone-in wild game ham is a bad-ass creation with an undeniably rustic elegance. It's satisfying in a primal way to haul one out of the smoker and plunk it down on a large carving board in front of guests. If you want to see the process for a deboned ham, refer back to *The Complete Guide to Hunting, Butchering, and Cooking Wild Game, Volume 1: Big Game.* If you're willing to move ahead with the bone in place, read on.

It takes a big container and a lot of refrigerator space to brine a whole ham with the shank intact. If you lack the proper container and fridge space, remove the shank at the knee. Don't worry if you have to do this. The bulk of the meat, and the best portions, are all above the knee.

ALSO WORKS WITH: Works best with deer, antelope, black bears, and wild hogs. Anything bigger than a large deer is simply too massive. It would be hard to properly brine and cook, let alone lift up. (A big moose ham will weigh well over 100 pounds; I love smoked hams, but not quite that much.) If you're working with hams from bears or wild pigs, make sure to hit that safe internal temperature of 160°F to destroy any parasites.

PREPARE THE HAM FOR BRINING: Clean the ham, trimming away as much fat as possible. Pierce and perforate the ham all over with a fillet knife. This will allow the brine to penetrate throughout the muscles faster.

FOR THE BRINE: In a large stockpot, combine the water, salt, brown sugar, mustard seeds, peppercorns, juniper berries, bay leaves, garlic, and Prague Powder #1 and bring to a boil. Remove from the heat and let cool to room temperature, then let it chill in the refrigerator.

Remove 1 quart of the liquid and inject it into the meat all over, deep in the muscles—as deep as the bone. It is sufficiently saturated when liquid begins to seep from the injection and perforation holes.

Submerge the ham in the brine. If necessary, use a plate to weight it down so that it stays submerged. Brine for 4 or 5 days in the refrigerator. Inject the meat daily (this helps shorten the overall brining time).

Prepare your smoker according to the manufacturer's instructions using a mild wood such as apple, cherry, or pecan. Adjust the temperature to 180°F, or as close as possible without falling under 180°F. Remove the meat from the brine. Discard the brining liquid. Rinse the meat well and pat dry. If you're working with an upright smoker, use kitchen twine to create a strong loop tied to the bone. Hang the ham in the smoker. If using an offset smoker, or a stack smoker, lay the ham down on the rack as you would a brisket, pork butt, or other large roast.

Smoke consistently for 8 to 10 hours, until the internal temperature reaches 150°F when checked with an instant-read thermometer. (If curing a hog or a bear ham, the internal temperature of the meat has to reach 160°F. To reach this higher temperature, you may need to raise the heat of the smoker to 200°F after 8 hours.)

Serve warm, or let cool to room temperature and wrap well. The ham will keep for up to 2 weeks in the refrigerator. The ham can be sliced and frozen in vacuum-sealed bags at this point as well.

SANDWICHES WITH CHEDDAR CHIVE BISCUITS

For this you'll need leftover smoked ham slices and a batch of Cheddar Chive Biscuits (page 325). Use freshly baked biscuits, or warm them if they're premade. Slather the cut side of the biscuits with your condiment of choice: spicy mayo or grainy mustard work, or you could even try Herbed Tartar Sauce (page 318). Top the bottom biscuit half with sliced ham and pickles, if you like, cover with the top half of the biscuit, and serve.

02 SMALL GAME

INTRODUCTION

The term *small game* is a surprisingly slippery classification. Some hunters use it as a catch-all to describe everything with feathers or fur ranging from a one-pound gray squirrel to a twenty-five-pound wild turkey. That's a little too broad for my tastes. While I tend to think of turkeys as turkeys, I'm willing to lump them in with upland birds for the sake of organizational convenience. But my willingness to lump things together finds its limits when it comes to upland birds and waterfowl, which I view as entirely distinct categories of wild game. So that narrows "small game" down to squirrels, rabbits, and hares—at least if we're speaking of conventional game species that are commonly hunted around the country. This includes gray squirrels, fox squirrels, cottontail rabbits, snowshoe hares, and a couple of jackrabbit species. Nonconventional small game species—unadventurous folks might classify them as oddball, weird, or worse—include muskrat, beaver, nutria, raccoon, porcupine, and opossum, all of which are legal to harvest according to specific regulations set forth by the state where you happen to do your hunting. While we do give a nod or two to these rogue outliers of the small game world, a full treatment on these species falls outside the scope of this book.

Once upon a time, small game was a universal gateway drug into hunting. Most hunters got their start on squirrels and rabbits and then graduated, years later, into the big leagues of deer and turkey hunting. That has changed over the past couple of decades, partly because of ecology, partly because of shifting trends, and partly because of regulatory changes. From the ecology end of things, there are simply a lot more deer and turkeys in a lot more places than there were thirty years ago. For deer and turkey hunters, right now is the good ol' days. Seasons are long, bag limits are high. The widespread availability of deer and turkeys has, in turn, affected what hunters are interested in. People want to pursue these bigger and more glamorous species, and interest in small game has waned proportionately. What's more, the legal age at which a person can begin hunting has generally gone down. For instance, you had to be fourteen to hunt deer with a firearm in Michigan when I was a kid. Now there is no minimum age requirement as long as the kid is accompanied by an adult mentor. Gone are the days when you had to hunt squirrels while dreaming of chasing deer.

Regardless, I still feel that small game hunting is the best place to begin for someone who's eager to start hunting. First off, small game seasons are generally very liberal. While big game seasons for deer or elk might run for just a few weeks or even a few days, in many states you can hunt squirrels and rabbits more days out of the year than you can't. In New York, squirrel season runs from September 1 to February 28. In Kentucky, you can hunt squirrels from the third Saturday in August through to the end of February, and again for a monthlong spring season. In California, the season for rabbits and snowshoe hares runs from July 1 to January 29, and it never closes for jackrabbits. In Montana, where squirrels and rabbits are administered as nongame species, you can hunt year-round. And the cost of a small game license is hardly a hindrance. In most states, a resident hunter can get permitted for around twenty dollars.

It's also helpful that small game weapons restrictions are not very restrictive. No matter what you're hunting, your "method of take" is going to be limited to some extent. Many states have separate big game seasons for firearms and archery equipment, and each of these methods can be further regulated with regard to calibers, broadhead types, technological enhancements, ammo types, shot sizes, and so on. Small game restrictions are relatively lax. In most states you can hunt squirrels and rabbits with air rifles, archery equipment, small-caliber rifles such as the .22 LR and .17 HMR, and even crossbows and slingshots in some states.

Finally, squirrel and rabbit populations are generally abundant and readily accessible. Of course, this depends somewhat on natural population cycles that are dictated by weather, predation, and availability of food resources. But still, it's a rare year when you can't find good numbers of small game if you're looking in the right places. And "right places" abound. Small game populations can thrive on small, isolated parcels of land that are often overlooked by other hunters. Getting permission to hunt private land is far easier when

the ask involves squirrels and rabbits rather than the more coveted deer and turkey. Furthermore, the high fecundity of small game species translates to high bag limits. In most states, you'll find that you're allowed around five squirrels and five rabbits every day. When you imagine those liberal daily bag limits spread out over a six-month-long season, with a hunting license that costs half as much as a tank of gas, you'll begin to see the seductiveness of small game hunting.

And let's not forget the meat, which is tasty, versatile, and relatively easy to deal with. From barbecue to tacos to stews to buffalo-style squirrel "wings," small game will get you cooking wild. In the big game section of this book, I voiced my belief that successful big game cooking requires you to consider the particular cut of meat that you're dealing with. A great recipe for venison shanks is certainly not a great recipe for a venison sirloin, and vice versa. I would never say the same thing about small game. When it comes to squirrels, rabbits, and hares (and raccoons, for that matter), I use the

whole animal in my recipes with little or no regard to what particular "cut" it is.

There are a couple of different reasons for this. First, the cooking methods that are necessary to tenderize small game are usually aggressive enough to limit or altogether negate the very subtle distinctions that differentiate the front shoulders from, say, the loins. Second, you need to consider the small size of the animals. In all my years of hunting, I've never been in a position to eat half a squirrel and then freeze the other half for later. The small size of the animals pretty much dictates that you're going to be using several of the whole animals all at once in order to have serving-size portions for your family or a group of friends.

Almost all small game animals benefit from long and slow braises, be they recipes from this chapter or those in Big Game, Waterfowl, or Upland Birds. You'll see that most of these recipes can be used interchangeably with squirrels and rabbits, with some adjustments. In fact, I'll often mix squirrels and rabbits together in a single recipe. When I'm hunting rabbits,

I'll usually get a squirrel or two, and when I'm hunting squirrels, I'll sometimes get a rabbit. Besides the similarities in the quality of flesh, it makes sense to lump them together sometimes just for the sake of having enough meat to feed your family. But don't despair about quantities if an outing to the woods yields only a single squirrel or rabbit. With a little thinking, you can reduce these recipes by half or a quarter in order to produce appetizers.

Or, better yet, save up your small game in a freezer. Take an empty gallon-size milk jug or a two-liter soda bottle, cut off the top, and wash it out. When you get a squirrel or rabbit, place the meat in the bottom and add just enough water to cover it up. Pop it into the freezer. Next week or next month, when you get another critter or two, place the meat atop the layer of ice and add just enough water to cover that. Refreeze and repeat, until some midwinter afternoon when you decide to make a giant batch of Kevin Murphy's Kentucky-Style Squirrel Gravy with Cathead Biscuits (page 92). Then you can revel in the glory of a being a small game hunter.

THE NATURE OF THE BEAST

Squirrels

When most people talk about squirrel hunting, they're talking about hunting for **gray squirrels** and **fox squirrels**. There are two species of gray squirrel, eastern and western, which are indistinguishable from the perspective of someone eating a prepared dish of squirrel meat. Black squirrels are common in many areas, though those are just a melanistic color phase of the eastern gray squirrel and there's no difference in the quality of meat. For that matter, the meat of a fox squirrel is basically the same as a gray squirrel's, just in bigger portions. The meat is similar in color to a dark chicken thigh, though more packed with flavor. You can grill squirrel legs if you tenderize them with a strong marinade, and they can be fried and baked. They work especially well in slow-cooked dishes.

Most squirrel hunters who live in the vicinity of gray and fox squirrels will pay no attention to pine squirrels, of which there are a handful of species. The most widely distributed is the **American red squirrel,** which is very common in the northern United States and the boreal forests of Canada. Squirrel hunters ignore them because of their diminutive size and their bad reputation as table fare. The size issue is warranted, as they weigh only about a fourth of what a fox squirrel does. The quality of flesh issue isn't quite so fair. While they do feed heavily on conifer cones, which makes people think they taste "piney," the meat is actually quite comparable to gray and fox squirrel.

Rabbits

The true rabbits of North America that attract hunter interest are variants of the cottontail rabbit. There are many, and they all look quite similar to the common **eastern cottontail**. However, they do range in size wildly. The **swamp rabbit** runs up to 6 pounds, while the **mountain cottontail** is only around 2½ pounds. All are excellent. The color is much like chicken breast, and it is mild. As with other small game, you can use everything on a cottontail all in the same recipe. The differences between "cuts" aren't enough to warrant separating the pieces out for different uses. Cottontail can be baked, grilled, fried, slow-cooked—you can do just about anything with it that you'd do with chicken.

Hares

The **snowshoe hare** of the northern United States is the most commonly hunted hare of North America. The flesh is leaner and darker than cottontail and can be a bit tougher. It's particularly suitable for any kind of slow-cooking, which allows the meat to tenderize. The addition of fat is a good idea, as snowshoe hares are very lean. Don't let this frighten you away from snowshoe hares. With the proper methods and recipes, it's a worthwhile quarry to pursue.

Despite the name, **jackrabbits** are actually hares. While not as popular as snowshoe hares, jackrabbits are certainly edible and can be quite delicious. Their meat is darker still than snowshoe hare, and also tougher. The loins can be fried, or else marinated and grilled, but you'll want to remove the silver skin on the outside of the loin first. The legs should be cooked for a long time at a low heat, which is the secret of success with jackrabbits.

Aquatic Rodents

Part of the reason that hunters don't pursue **musk-rats** and **beavers** as sources of meat is because these animals have valuable pelts that are sought after by the garment industry. They are generally regulated as fur-bearers rather than as game animals, meaning that you need a special fur harvester license to pursue them. (These licenses are not hard to get.) Always check your state's regulations before pursuing muskrat or beaver. In many states, it's illegal to shoot them; they must be trapped. Beavers and muskrats both have excellent meat. Beaver is dark, almost like beef, and muskrat is red with a purplish tint. There are areas in the country where they are regarded as delicacies. For each, slow-cooking methods are the way to go. That includes slow-roasting in a barbecue.

Some Rogue Outliers

Just about every animal is edible, but this quick listing of alternative small game animals will focus on those species that are widely available and generally open to hunting no matter where you live. **Raccoon** is a tad greasy, though not necessarily in a bad way; people often soak them in vinegar-based marinades before cooking them. **Porcupines** are good to eat, and surprisingly mild in flavor, though you have got to be careful when skinning them; the quills can give you nasty infections. **Opossums** are stronger flavored and a tad musky; in the old days, folks would catch opossums and put them in a cage in order to fatten them on a diet of grain before butchering them. I'm told they're quite good that way.

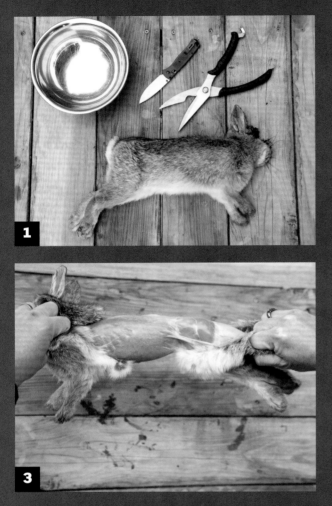

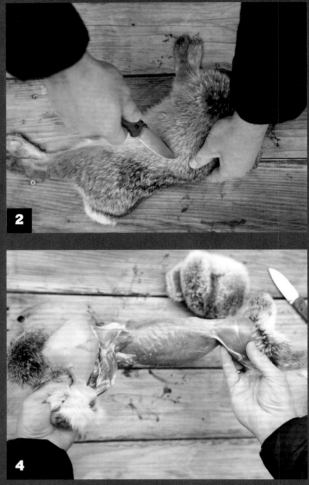

1. Cottontail rabbits used to be one of America's most popular game animals. It's a shame more people don't get after them, since they are widely available, easy to hunt, and a crowd pleaser on the dinner table. The shirt and pants method of skinning works well for rabbits and squirrels.

2. Make an incision through the skin at the top of the back. Now cut completely around the middle of the rabbit. Be sure to cut just the hide and not into the flesh or gut cavity.

3. At the cut, grab the hide along the back with each hand. Pull the hide toward the front and back legs at the same time. Rabbits peel easily, but squirrels will take a little more effort.

4. Pull the hide free on the pants half of the rabbit until you reach the bony shins on the back legs. On the shirt half of the rabbit, peel the hide free from the legs to the ankle, and off the shoulders to the neck.

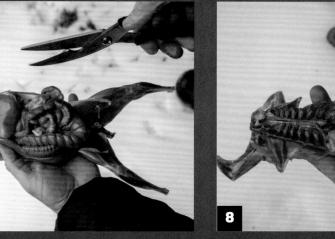

5. Next, use game shears to remove the head and feet.

6. At the anus, cut through the pelvis bone with game shears.

7. Continue cutting through the upper paunch and rib cage, just below the back. With one side of the belly and ribs removed, the guts can be easily discarded. Save the heart and liver, as they can be used in many recipes.

8. Cut the paunch and ribs free from the opposite side of the rabbit. Wash the carcass and remove any bloodshot meat or shotgun pellets.

SQUIRREL TAIL SKINNING

Squirrels are among the tastiest small game animals available to hunters, and they are an underutilized resource throughout America. Once you get the hang of it, the tail skinning method is a fast, simple way to cleanly remove a squirrel's tough pelt.

Tail Skinning

1. You'll need a sharp knife, a pair of game shears, and a cinder block or tree stump.

2. Start by making a cut through the underside of the tail, through the tailbone just above the anus. Stop short of completely removing the tail, leaving the hide attached to the carcass.

3. Next, lay the squirrel on its back and step firmly on the tail where you made the first cut. Get a good grip on the rear legs and slowly lift.

4. The hide will separate cleanly from the carcass as you lift.

5. When you reach the front legs, insert a finger into the gap between the hide and legs and continue to lift and pull the hide free of the forelegs.

6. The squirrel will still have some remaining hide on the lower belly and rear legs. Hold the squirrel firmly behind the front legs, and with the other hand pull the hide from the belly and rear legs down to the feet.

7. Pull the hide past all four ankles, and then use a game shear to remove the feet by cutting at the ankle joints. Remove the head and innards and, if needed, remove any hair or dirt and wash the carcass.

DISASSEMBLING RABBIT OR SQUIRREL

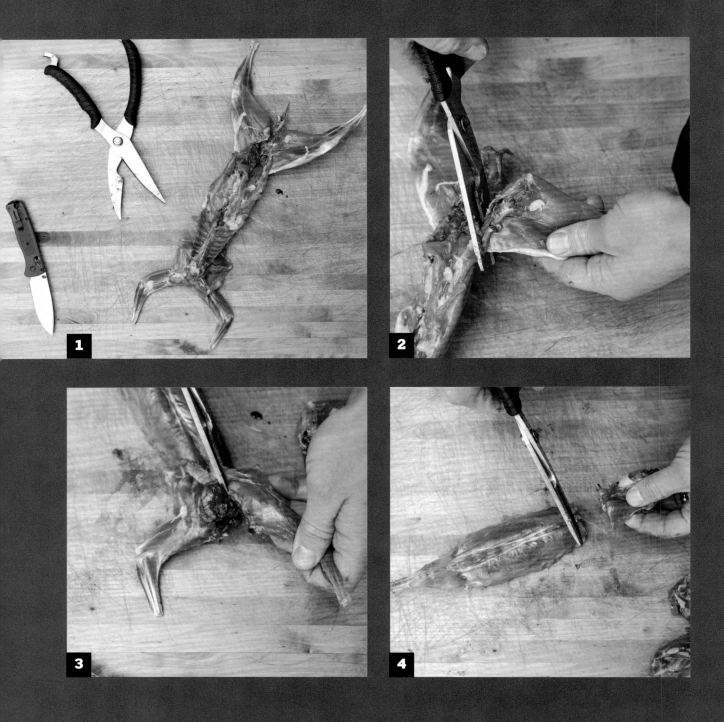

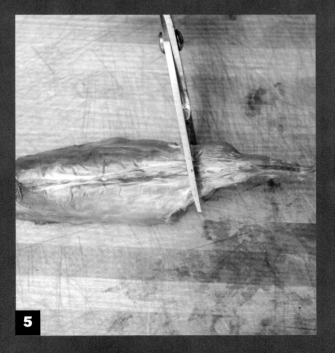

Rabbits and squirrels can be left whole after skinning and gutting or they can be broken down into pieces. It all depends on how you'll be cooking them. You can braise whole rabbits or squirrels, but if you're going to fry them, they will need to be disassembled.

1. You can do the job with a game shear or small knife.

2. Remove each back leg by cutting along the pelvis and through the hip's ball and socket joint.

3. Next, cut the front legs free.

4. Cut through the spine just forward of the loins to remove the shoulder area from the carcass.

5. Now separate the hips and tail from the back end of the carcass with a cut through the spine just behind the loins.

6. The four leg quarters and the back loins, or saddle, are ready to be cooked. Use the bony shoulder and hip pieces to make a small batch of stock for gravy.

BUFFALO HOT LEGS

SERVES 4

One of my older brothers did a semester or two of college at Ferris State University in Mecosta County, Michigan. I would visit him often, and we'd always do a lot of squirrel and cottontail rabbit hunting in the surrounding country. We'd find cottontails around the beaver ponds and squirrels up in the hardwoods. At night, after hunting, we would head to a bar that offered a happy hour deal of ten-cent draft beers and five-cent Buffalo chicken wings. Ever since then I've associated small game hunting with Buffalo wings. This recipe formally unites those two things in the perfect appetizer to be served with cold beer. Squirrels and cottontail rabbits can be used interchangeably here, though I do have a subtle preference for squirrel meat. It's darker and more flavorful, though rabbit does have a coloration and texture more in line with the traditional barroom buffalo chicken wings that many of us have spent our whole lives eating.

Cut the squirrels into 4 leg pieces and 2 back pieces. Cut the rear legs of cottontails into 2 pieces and the back into 3 or 4 pieces.

Sprinkle all the pieces with 1½ teaspoons of the salt and the pepper. Heat the oil in a medium pot or Dutch oven until it registers 300°F on a deep-fry thermometer. Group the pieces of meat by size—front legs together, rear legs together, back pieces together. Carefully lower 6 to 8 small pieces into the hot oil and cook until light golden brown in color, moving the pieces around occasionally to ensure they don't stick to the bottom, about 6 minutes. Drain on paper towels and repeat with the remaining smaller pieces. Fry the larger pieces for a total of 8 minutes.

While you're frying, prepare the buffalo sauce by warming the hot sauce, maple syrup, vinegar, and the remaining ¾ teaspoon salt in a small saucepan over low heat. Slowly stir in the butter until it has fully melted, then remove from the heat.

Raise the heat of the oil to 375°F and fry the squirrel or rabbit pieces for a second time to finish crisping the exterior, about 3 minutes per batch. Transfer the pieces to a large draining rack.

Toss half of the piping hot pieces in a bowl with half of the buffalo sauce, coating them thoroughly. Repeat with the remaining meat and sauce. Serve immediately—so you maintain that double fried crunch—as you would traditional Buffalo wings, with celery, carrots, and blue cheese dressing.

2 to 3 squirrels and/or cottontail rabbits

2¼ teaspoons kosher salt

¾ teaspoon freshly ground black pepper

2 quarts peanut oil

1½ cups Frank's Red Hot Original Cayenne Pepper Sauce

5 tablespoons maple syrup

3 tablespoons distilled white vinegar

¾ cup (1½ sticks) unsalted butter

Celery and carrot sticks, for serving

Blue cheese dressing, for serving

ALSO WORKS WITH: See above comments. Works with both squirrels and cottontail rabbits.

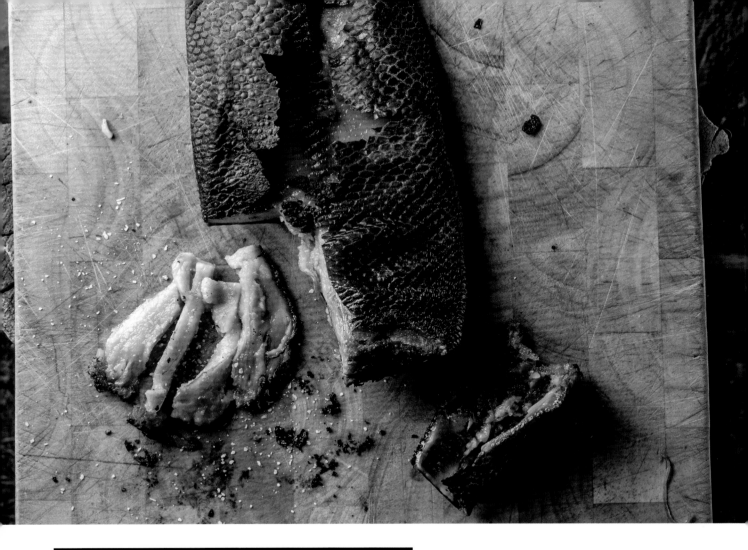

FIRE-ROASTED BEAVER TAIL

SERVES UP TO 10 PEOPLE AS A NOVELTY APPETIZER

ALSO WORKS WITH: Nothing else comes even close; a beaver tail is its own special thing.

Food is capable of doing a lot more than just tasting good. In this case, it can bring you back in time to the heyday of the mountain man era, when bad-asses such as Jed Smith, Jim Bridger, and Hugh Glass were working the wild Rockies for beaver pelts while dodging perils such as grizzly bears, frozen rivers, and scalping knives belonging to the rival indigenous hunters upon whose land they trespassed. Even the most casual history buff who reads about the mountain men will find references to beaver tail, which is usually described as the official favorite food of these bygone trappers. You'd never guess it from looking at one, but the interior of a beaver tail is almost pure fat and gristle, making it an essential food item for men who were living on a diet comprised almost exclusively of lean red meat. My brothers and I had several failed attempts at cooking beaver tail, which led us to believe that the history books were lying to us. But then, through trial and error, I finally figured out how mountain men were probably preparing this dish. Once I got it right, I was blown away by the visual qualities and pleasantly surprised by the taste. If possible, use a beaver killed in the fall for this preparation. A beaver's tail serves as the animal's fat reserve. After a hard winter, the tail can be too thin to bother messing with it.

1 beaver tail

Kosher salt

Build a small cooking fire. Try to use dry wood from deciduous trees. Due to the nature of a beaver's habitat, it's safe to assume that more beaver tails have been roasted over fires made of aspen, willow, and cottonwood than any other fuel source. You're looking for more than just a bed of coals, as a few flames are necessary to complete the cooking process.

As the fire builds up a hot bed of coals, pierce the base of the beaver tail with a knife and insert the sharpened end of the skewer into the slit. Now, position the beaver tail so that it's close to the fire but not too close—look for a place where you can hold your hand for about 2 seconds before you have to pull it away. The tail can get licked by a flame or two but should not be engulfed. Imagine that you're trying to roast a marshmallow without letting it burn. You can use rocks and a forked stick to support the skewer, but don't wander off.

Within 5 or 6 minutes, the scaly skin of the beaver tail will begin to bubble and lift away from the fatty interior. Adjust the tail's position so that the blistering occurs evenly across the side of the tail that's facing the fire. Use the blade of a knife to test whether or not you can lift or scrape the skin away from the fat. Once that's done, rotate the tail on the skewer and repeat the process on the opposite side. Keep in mind that you're trying to cook the inside of the tail at the same time that you're bubbling the skin away, so don't rush it. If the entire process takes 15 minutes, you're in good shape.

Lay the cooked tail on a stump, rock, or platter and let it cool enough so that you can begin peeling the skin away. What remains should look like fatty gristle from a beef steak with a tailbone running down the middle. That's mountain man's gold. Slice as thin as possible, either lengthwise or crosswise, and sprinkle each slice with a bit of salt. Enjoy the taste of history.

SPECIAL EQUIPMENT: a stout skewer, as thick as your thumb, cut from a green tree or shrub, sharpened on one end

KENTUCKY-STYLE SQUIRREL GRAVY
WITH CATHEAD BISCUITS, STRAIGHT FROM KEVIN MURPHY

SERVES 6

2 fox squirrels or 4 gray squirrels

Kosher salt

Freshly ground black pepper

All-purpose or self-rising flour

Vegetable or peanut oil, for frying

Dollop or two of melted lard

2 to 3 cups milk, or a little more if needed

Cathead Biscuits (page 95)

Curly leafed parsley (optional garnish)

ALSO WORKS WITH: This might annoy Kevin, but I'd feel comfortable using cottontail rabbits or snowshoe hares to make this recipe.

My buddies and I have dubbed our friend Kevin Murphy "the world's greatest small game hunter" without a lick of irony. While most hunters cut their teeth on small game and then move along to larger quarry, Kevin has stayed true to his foundational pursuits. He hunts the same patches of public land in Kentucky that he hunted with his dad when he was just a kid, and his primary passion is chasing squirrels with his small pack of squirrel hounds. If he's not doing that, he prefers to be chasing marsh rabbits and eastern cottontails with his small pack of rabbit hounds. If not that, he likes chasing grouse and quail with his bird dogs. You get the point. Kevin is also faithful to his culinary roots. He still likes to prepare the same dishes that his mother made for him as a kid when he brought home squirrels and rabbits for the family dinner table. He's prepared his squirrel gravy and cathead biscuits a number of times for me, and I like them so much that I asked him to give me the recipes exactly in his own words so that nothing is lost in translation. (If you're wondering, it's called a cathead biscuit because that's how big they ought to be.)

Cut the squirrels into 4 leg pieces and 2 back pieces; if you have larger squirrels, cut the rear legs into 2 pieces and then cut the back into 3 or 4 pieces.

Season and flour your squirrel pieces. Heat the oil in a seasoned cast-iron skillet over medium heat, then add the lard, cover, and steam for at least 20 minutes, until cooked through. Squirrels for the most part have very little fat reserves, unless you catch them in the fall of the year, just before winter. With a limited food source, they will consume just about everything available in the woods, from black gum berries to pine cones; in my opinion, squirrels feeding on pine cones do not taste like pine trees. (I have not seen them actually eat locusts, but in the years they emerge from the ground, which is about every seven years for a major hatch, the squirrels are mud-ball fat, and I have always assumed this was from eating locusts.) In times of food shortages, squirrels try to put on and retain weight so they can make it through the winter until the trees start budding in late winter or early spring. Water maple is the first to bud, followed by elm. Once this occurs, squirrels will become more active and spend more time out of their den or nest!

OK, back to our gravy. After the squirrel has been cooked, remove it from the skillet.

You should have a couple of tablespoons of rendered squirrel drippings and flavored fried squirrel-seasoned crispies. Scrape the bottom of the skillet clean and mix with the drippings. If you don't have 2 tablespoons, add enough lard to make up the difference. Add about 2 tablespoons flour. Adjust the heat level to medium to medium-high. Work the flour into the drippings until the flour browns and add ¼ teaspoon salt and ¼ teaspoon pepper. You can season again after the gravy is made.

Next is the tricky part of the process. Have on hand 2 to 3 cups of whole milk, maybe a little more just in case your gravy is too thick. (It's much easier to make thick gravy thin than to make thin gravy thick!) Raise the heat to high and, with a whisk in one hand, start incorporating the milk while working the edge of the browned flour. It will start to rise, bubble, and expand immediately. Keep whisking away and adding milk until all the lumps are dissolved and you have a velvety thin gravy. Now is a good time to season with salt and pepper again. Reduce the heat to medium and cook, constantly stirring, for 3 to 5 minutes, maybe a little longer. You don't want the gravy to stick to the bottom of the skillet. Remove it at a thinner stage than you like to eat it because it will thicken as it cools. Gravy making is a skill that will develop with time just like any outdoor skill. Serve over cathead biscuits.

CATHEAD BISCUITS

MAKES 5 BISCUITS

Preheat the oven to 425°F.

Mix the flour, salt, and sugar in a large mixing bowl. Rub the lard or shortening (or cut the butter) into the flour. When you're done it should look like coarse cornmeal.

Pour in the buttermilk and gently mix it into the flour with your hands to where it feels and looks like brick mortar (firm, but wet enough that it can still flow). Sprinkle in more flour as needed; the dough will be wet and sticky, but not so wet and sticky that it clings to your fingers or won't scrape off the counter. Place on a hard floured surface. Pat out into a rectangle about 7 by 9 inches. Fold into thirds like a letter. Pat the dough out again into a rectangle about 1 inch high. Lightly flour the top, then cut 3 biscuits with the mason jar. Then re-form to cut out 1 more, and re-form one more time for the last biscuit. Grease up a 10-inch cast-iron skillet with lard, shortening, or butter. Arrange the biscuits around each other, leaving about a ½-inch gap between them. Brush a little melted butter on top of the biscuits, if desired (it will help with the browning).

Bake until puffed and lightly golden brown on top, 13 to 15 minutes. Turn the oven light on to check the biscuits (don't open the door or you'll lose your heat). If you think the bottoms of the biscuits are done, you can turn your broiler on for 30 seconds or more to brown the tops of your biscuits.

2 cups self-rising flour, plus more for sprinkling

¼ teaspoon kosher salt

½ to 1 tablespoon sugar (depending on how sweet you like them)

2 tablespoons lard, shortening, or unsalted butter (cut into small pieces), chilled, plus more for the pan

1 cup buttermilk

1 tablespoon unsalted butter, melted (optional)

SPECIAL EQUIPMENT: 1 mason jar (diameter of a cat head, 3 inches)

RABBIT CURRY

SERVES 4 TO 6

I get a kick out of cooking regional foods with meats that would be totally out of place in the dish's place of origin. Such is the case with this curry recipe, so long as you're using any of the rabbits or hares available to American hunters. Making this dish with native wild game is its own strange form of fusion cuisine, a global melding of tastes and ideas.

ALSO WORKS WITH: You could get away with using 3 squirrels instead of 2 cottontails, but you'd want to increase the cooking time in order to tenderize the squirrels. It would also work with snowshoe hares or even jackrabbits.

Remove the ribs and lower spine from the rabbits. Cut into 6 pieces each (2 sets of legs and two back pieces, with the loins still attached to the backbone).

Mix the yogurt, curry powder, salt, chili powder, turmeric, cardamom, cayenne, garlic, and ginger in a large bowl. Add the rabbit, stir to coat, cover, and refrigerate for at least 2 hours or up to overnight.

Pour enough oil into a heavy soup pot to cover the bottom and heat over medium-high heat. Add the onion and cook, stirring occasionally, until golden brown, about 15 minutes. Push the onion to the side and add the tomato paste to the middle. Cook, stirring, until it browns, about 3 minutes. Add the rabbit, reserving the yogurt marinade. Working in batches if necessary and adding more oil if needed, cook the rabbit on each side until the meat browns a bit, about 3 minutes per side. Return all the rabbit to the pot. Stir in the reserved yogurt marinade, the tamarind, butternut squash, and enough water to cover. Bring to a boil, then reduce the heat to low, cover, and simmer until the rabbit is very tender and nearly falling off the bone, 1 to 1½ hours. By this time, the butternut squash should be beginning to fall apart. (Use your spoon to mash it against the side of the pot if it isn't.) The butternut squash acts as a thickener here. If the liquid appears curdled or broken, whisk vigorously to emulsify. Raise the heat to medium, add the bell pepper and yellow squash, and cook, uncovered, until the vegetables are softened and the curry has thickened into a stew, about 10 minutes. Season with salt and pepper.

Serve over steamed white rice and garnish with cilantro leaves. Each person gets a leg or two plus a piece of the back.

2 cottontail rabbits

1 cup plain yogurt

2 teaspoons curry powder

1½ teaspoons kosher salt, plus more as needed

1 teaspoon chili powder

½ teaspoon ground turmeric

¼ teaspoon ground cardamom

¼ teaspoon cayenne pepper

3 cloves garlic, grated

¾-inch knob ginger, peeled and grated

2 tablespoons canola oil, plus more as needed

1 large onion, cut into ¼-inch slices

1 tablespoon tomato paste

1 teaspoon tamarind concentrate or fresh lime juice

½ butternut squash, peeled, seeded, and diced

1 large red bell pepper, cut into ¼-inch slices

1 large yellow squash, cut into ¼-inch half-rounds

Freshly ground black pepper

Steamed white rice, for serving

Fresh cilantro leaves, for garnish

SMALL GAME AND SAUSAGE GUMBO

SERVES 10 TO 12 (MAKES 15 CUPS)

About 3 pounds squirrel and/or rabbit

1½ cups plus 2 tablespoons vegetable oil

3 tablespoons Creole Seasoning (page 312), or use store-bought

1½ cups all-purpose flour

12 to 16 ounces Andouille Sausage (page 45) or other smoked sausage, cut into ½-inch-thick half moons

1 medium onion, diced

1 large green bell pepper, diced

1¼ cups diced celery

1 tablespoon chopped garlic

2 bay leaves

2½ to 3 quarts Blonde Game Stock (page 306), Brown Game Stock (page 305), or low-sodium chicken broth

ACCOMPANIMENTS

Hot cooked white rice

Thinly sliced scallions and/or chopped fresh parsley

Gumbo filé (aka filé powder)

Hot sauce

ALSO WORKS WITH: Just about any combination of small game, upland birds, and waterfowl.

Gumbo is the hunter's best friend, especially if the hunter is a generalist who likes to do it all. What other dish can accommodate such a disparate array of ingredients? The last batch I made—and I'm not kidding here—had two species of ducks, three species of upland bird, a goose breast, some marsh rabbit, and one gray squirrel. It was a little bit of Noah's Ark in every bowl. This version calls for rabbit and/or squirrel, along with sausage, but no one's going to complain if you dig through your freezer and add in a few surprises. The trickiest part is making the roux. The old-fashioned way of doing this is to whisk the fat and flour over low heat until your arm's ready to fall off. If you're attentive, you can do as some Southern chefs do and make a speedier version over medium-high heat. Just be sure not to get distracted and walk away. If you do, you could quickly end up with a burned and bitter mess.

If you made your own andouille (see page 45) back in the fall, break it out for this recipe. If not, a store-bought version will do.

Cut the squirrels or rabbits into 4 leg pieces and 2 back pieces. On larger rabbits, cut the back legs into two pieces.

Heat 2 tablespoons of the oil in a large skillet over medium-high heat. Sprinkle the rabbit with 1 tablespoon of the Creole Seasoning. Working in batches if necessary, sear the rabbit until golden brown, about 2 minutes per side. Transfer the rabbit to a platter.

Heat the remaining 1½ cups oil in a Dutch oven over medium-high heat. Gradually add the flour, whisking until smooth. Cook, whisking constantly, until the roux thickens and turns dark, like coffee with a splash of cream, 8 to 10 minutes. Reduce the heat to medium. Carefully add the sausage, onion, bell pepper, celery, and garlic (it may splash and splutter) and cook, stirring constantly, until the vegetables soften, about 5 minutes. Add the remaining 2 tablespoons Creole Seasoning and the bay leaves. Slowly whisk in the stock to desired thickness. Add the rabbit and bring to a boil. Reduce the heat to maintain a simmer and cook, uncovered, until the rabbit is tender, 1 to 1½ hours. Skim off and discard any oil or scum that rises to the surface.

Transfer the rabbit to a shallow pan or platter and set aside until cool enough to handle. Remove the meat from the bones, discarding the bones, and shred into large pieces. Discard the bay leaves. If necessary, whisk the gumbo to emulsify. Return the rabbit meat to the gumbo and adjust the seasonings. Serve over rice and garnish with scallions and/or parsley, filé, and hot sauce.

RABBIT OR SQUIRREL IN CREAMY MUSTARD SAUCE

SERVES 4

2 cottontail rabbits

Kosher salt

Freshly ground black pepper

2 tablespoons vegetable oil

3 tablespoons unsalted butter

¼ cup finely chopped shallots

1 large clove garlic, minced

1 cup dry vermouth or white wine

1 cup Blonde Game Stock (page 306) or low-sodium chicken broth

3 tablespoons grainy Dijon or country-style mustard

1 large sprig fresh tarragon

¼ cup heavy cream

1 tablespoon chopped fresh tarragon or thyme

3 tablespoons chopped fresh flat-leaf parsley

1 pound hot freshly cooked egg noodles

This recipe is well suited for folks who enjoy sophisticated food but might not be totally comfortable with the idea of wild game. It's a dish with deep traditions in Europe, where rabbit is a much more common menu item than it is in the United States, so it's got a nice cosmopolitan pedigree. And there's enough going on with the creamy mustard sauce and buttered noodles to distract people away from the idea that you shotgunned the thing out of some nearby woodlot. However, any guise of true refinement will be lost when someone finds a bit of shattered bone and a shotgun pellet. That's why I always like to introduce a fun game to my guests before I serve small game: whoever finds the first shotgun pellet gets to kiss the cook.

ALSO WORKS WITH: Squirrels and snowshoe hares are a good idea, though remember that you might need an extra 20 or 30 minutes of cooking to fully tenderize the meat.

Cut the cottontails into 4 leg pieces and 2 back pieces. Sprinkle the pieces generously with salt and pepper. Heat the oil in a large, heavy skillet over medium-high heat. Working in batches if necessary, sear the rabbit until nicely browned on both sides, 3 to 4 minutes per side. Transfer to a plate when done.

Remove the skillet from the burner for a couple of minutes to let it cool a little. Reduce the heat to medium and melt in 1 tablespoon of the butter. Add the shallots and cook, scraping up the browned bits at the bottom of the skillet, until softened, 3 to 5 minutes. Add the garlic and cook for about 30 seconds. Add the vermouth and bring to a boil. Let it reduce by half, about 5 minutes. Add the stock, mustard, tarragon sprig, all of the browned rabbit, and any accumulated juices to the skillet. Bring to a boil, then reduce the heat to maintain a simmer. Cook, covered, until the meat is tender, about 1 hour. Transfer to a platter and discard the tarragon sprig.

Bring the sauce to a boil and cook until reduced by half, about 5 minutes. Stir in the cream, tarragon, and parsley. Taste and adjust the seasonings. Simmer for 3 to 5 minutes, then add the rabbit and turn each piece to coat. Toss the hot noodles with the remaining 2 tablespoons butter and serve with the rabbit.

BBQ SMOKED BEAVER SANDWICHES

SERVES 6

When you serve someone a good dish that features beaver meat, you're probably going to have to argue with them about whether or not it's really beaver. For some reason, people have a hard time believing that the flesh from an aquatic rodent with a scaly tail can taste so similar to beef pot roast. When cleaning a beaver, it's important to work carefully around the castor glands. Remove the glands quickly, and then wash your hands and knife to make sure you're not spreading the oils to the meat with your fingers or knife.

FOR THE BEAVER: Rinse the thighs under cold running water and vigorously scrub them with your hand. This helps ensure that there's no castor oil on the meat. Pat dry with paper towels and completely cover the meat with 6 tablespoons of the rub, working it into all areas of the thigh.

Prepare your smoker according to the manufacturer's instructions at 225°F and smoke the beaver with your favorite hardwood chips (I love the smell of hickory and mesquite) for 2½ hours. Remove the thighs and place them in a roasting pan or Dutch oven.

Preheat the oven to 300°F.

Add the stock to the pan, cover tightly with aluminum foil, place in the oven, and braise for 1½ hours, or until the meat is very tender and easily pulls away from the bone with a fork. Put the meat aside until it's cool enough to work with. Meanwhile, strain the braising liquid into a shallow pan and refrigerate to allow the fat layer to solidify on top. Once you can handle the meat, shred it into small pieces. This can be done up to a day ahead of time.

FOR THE SLAW: Whisk the mayonnaise, vinegar, sugar, mustard, granulated garlic, salt, onion powder, and pepper in a medium bowl until smooth. Combine the cabbage, scallions, and carrots in a large bowl. Add the dressing to the cabbage and toss until it is completely coated.

TO SERVE: Preheat the oven to 375°F. Skim the fat off of the braising liquid. Whisk ½ cup of the liquid with ½ cup of the BBQ sauce in a small bowl. Place the shredded meat in a large bowl and pour the BBQ sauce over the meat, tossing well. This will make the meat moist but not very saucy. Spread the meat out on a baking sheet and sprinkle with the remaining rub. Place the meat in the oven and heat until hot, 8 to 10 minutes. Serve on buns with coleslaw, the remaining BBQ sauce, and pickles.

BEAVER

2 bone-in beaver thighs

½ cup BBQ Rub (page 313)

2 cups Blonde Game Stock (page 306) or low-sodium chicken broth

1½ cups BBQ Sauce (page 314)

SLAW

½ cup mayonnaise

¼ cup apple cider vinegar

3 tablespoons sugar

1 tablespoon Dijon mustard

1 tablespoon granulated garlic

1 tablespoon kosher salt

1 teaspoon onion powder

1 teaspoon freshly ground black pepper

½ head green cabbage, cored and thinly sliced

4 scallions, thinly sliced

1 carrot, grated

6 burger buns

Sweet bread-and-butter pickles

ALSO WORKS WITH: I'd like to try this with a javelina thigh, but haven't done it yet.

RABBIT CACCIATORE

SERVES 4 TO 6

One of the things that makes this dish so good is that it's served over a bed of Italian-style polenta with grated Parmigiano-Reggiano cheese. There are a number of small game dishes in my personal repertoire that involve sauces and polenta. It's a brilliant combination, in my opinion, and almost guaranteed to please (but it's equally tasty over pasta or a hunk of crusty bread). What's especially cool about cacciatore is that it's an Italian word that translates as "hunter." In Italy, when a dish is described as *alla cacciatore,* or "hunter's style," it means braised with traditional ingredients of tomatoes, herbs, onion, and wine. You'll see that this dish calls for a bit of game stock. You can always substitute low-sodium chicken broth, but making game stock is a lot of fun and it puts to good use the bones and trimmings from your kill.

FOR THE RABBIT: Cut the rabbits (or squirrels) into 4 leg pieces and 2 back pieces. On larger rabbits, cut each back leg into 2 pieces and the backs into 3 pieces. Sprinkle the meat liberally on all sides with salt and pepper. Heat the oil in a heavy-bottomed saucepan over medium-high heat until it shimmers. Brown the meat on all sides, about 10 minutes. Remove to a plate. Add the onion and cook until translucent, about 8 minutes. Add the celery and mushrooms and cook until softened, about 8 minutes. Add the garlic and red chile flakes and cook, stirring, for 30 seconds, or until fragrant. Add the wine, scraping any browned bits from the bottom of the pot. Put the tomatoes in a bowl, crush them with your hands, and add them to the pot. Pour in the stock and season with a pinch of salt. Add the meat back to the pot and bring to a simmer. Add the rosemary sprigs and bay leaf. Reduce the heat and cook at a low simmer until the meat is tender and just beginning to release from the bone, up to 1½ hours or more for a wild rabbit, depending on its size. Discard the rosemary sprigs and bay leaf.

Spoon the rabbit onto a platter. Top with the sauce and garnish with the parsley and cheese. Serve over polenta, freshly cooked pasta, or with a hunk of crusty bread.

2 rabbits

Kosher salt

Freshly ground black pepper

Extra virgin olive oil, as needed to cover the bottom of the pan

1 onion, finely chopped

2 ribs celery, thinly sliced

10 ounces cremini mushrooms, sliced

5 cloves garlic, sliced

Pinch of red chile flakes

1¼ cups dry white wine

1 (28-ounce) can whole peeled tomatoes, drained

1 cup Blonde Game Stock (page 306) or low-sodium chicken broth

2 sprigs fresh rosemary

1 bay leaf

Leaves from 1 bunch fresh flat-leaf parsley, chopped

Freshly grated Parmigiano-Reggiano cheese

1 recipe Polenta (page 330)

ALSO WORKS WITH: Squirrel and snowshoe hare, even a younger jackrabbit.

03 **WATERFOWL**

INTRODUCTION

When I was a teenager, we hunted a local marsh that offered dynamite action on wood ducks in mid-October. It was hardly bigger than a basketball court and full of dead trees. The local woodies used it as a roosting pond. They'd come bombing into the marsh just five or ten minutes before the end of legal shooting light. Because of all the timber and the waning light, you could never actually see the ducks coming until they were right on top of you. They'd all of a sudden materialize, already in range, flying low and fast and then cupping their wings as they whizzed past your face. A few nights a year, for just a few minutes per night, that pond provided an exhilarating place to miss a bunch of ducks and maybe, if you were lucky, hit a few.

What amazed me about those ducks, beyond their speed and agility as they maneuvered through the trees, was how well fed they were. They'd spend their days down in the deep ravines of the aptly named Mosquito Creek, gorging themselves on beechnuts. Their crops would be so packed full of the nuts that their necks would feel like marble bags when you picked them up. After we cleaned the ducks, my mom would stuff them with chopped apples and raisins and roast them under a sheet of aluminum foil in a hot oven. Just before removing the birds, she'd pull off the foil and let them brown under the broiler. They tasted magical, moist and almost steak-like. Served alongside acorn squash from our garden, it was the perfect fall meal.

With those birds as my foundational experience, as I grew up it would surprise me when I'd meet other hunters who didn't really like eating waterfowl. I'd hear hunters tell me that ducks and geese were "pasty" or "livery" or "dry" or whatever, and it honestly was hard for me to relate to what they were saying. At least, that is, until I had the opportunity to eat a few birds that were poorly handled in the field and then grossly overcooked on a grill or pan. The fact that many of these low-grade meals were prepared by otherwise proficient wild game cooks eventually led me to the realization that ducks and geese present the most vexing challenges of all wild game categories.

To understand those challenges, it's helpful to understand just how many types of waterfowl are out there. An American waterfowl hunter who's not afraid to travel around the country might in his or her lifetime encounter around forty species. These birds are organized in a confusing fashion that will puzzle just about anyone. While some folks are familiar with the straightforward method of grouping that places waterfowl into two categories—ducks and geese—avid waterfowl hunters go a bit deeper and categorize their waterfowl into dabbling ducks, diving ducks, sea ducks, dark-colored geese, and light-colored geese.

Dabbling ducks, often called puddle ducks, primarily reside in shallow freshwater ponds, lakes, and rivers. There are about a dozen species. The classification includes some of our most popular and easily recognizable ducks, including the ubiquitous mallard, the beautifully colored wood duck, and the diminutive green wing and blue wing teals. They generally feed by tipping forward in the water, submerging their heads while leaving their tails up in the air. They are surefooted and can walk on land. If you see a duck walking in a crop field, that's a puddle duck. Another indicator is a bright, iridescent speculum, or wing patch. Puddle ducks are largely herbivorous. Most people who eat a

lot of ducks will tell you that puddle ducks taste better than diver ducks, which tend to feed below the water's surface and eat a lot more animal matter.

Diving ducks reside primarily on deep lakes, big rivers, and coastal bays and inlets. They do most of their feeding underwater. When taking flight, they can't jump off the water's surface and get airborne as quickly as a dabbling duck. Instead, they have to "run" along the water's surface before taking flight. Another reliable distinguisher is that they lack the iridescent speculum, or colored wing patch, that typifies dabbling ducks. In addition to aquatic vegetation (more or less, or none, depending on the species), they feed on fish and a wide variety of invertebrates such as mollusks, aquatic insects, marine worms, and freshwater shrimp.

There are about twenty species of diving ducks in North America, and many hunters are content to use that single classification for all of them. But guys who really geek out on waterfowl will readily draw a distinction between diving ducks and sea ducks. They'll tell you that the "diving duck" classification should be limited to a tribe of birds known as the pochards. These include the most popular of the diving ducks: canvasbacks, redheads, ringnecks, and scaups (both greater and lesser). The sea duck category contains a lot of birds that most hunters will never encounter, such as king eiders, harlequins, and long-tailed ducks. Some other sea ducks such as buffleheads and goldeneyes are quite common on interior freshwater waterways.

And then there are the geese. For convenience's sake, these are broken into classifications of light-colored and dark-colored. Dark-colored geese include brants, white-fronted geese, and the lookalike Canada geese and cackling geese. (If you really want to get confused, you might investigate the process by which taxonomists condensed dozens of species of "white-cheeked geese" down into a handful of Canada and cackling subspecies.) The light-colored geese include greater snow geese, lesser snow geese, and Ross's geese. These vary in size, but it takes a trained eye to tell them apart.

Finally, you've got a handful of birds that are considered to be waterfowl species, which aren't actually ducks or geese. These range from the sandhill crane, which has the most highly esteemed meat of all waterfowl, down to the American coot, which has perhaps the lowest.

In addition to the huge variety of waterfowl species out there, there's a lot of variability within species. The quality of a duck has a lot to do with where it's from and what it's been up to. A mallard that's been fattening itself in the grain fields of southern Illinois for two months is going to be one of the very best ducks you'll ever eat. A mallard that was born and raised on the tidal flats of southeast Alaska, where it eats crustaceans and salmon eggs, will seem like an entirely different creature. Anyone who takes up the challenge of hunting and cooking waterfowl in its many forms will encounter tastes and textures known only to a very small fraction of the world's citizens. There is no commercially available product that comes anywhere close to, say, a bufflehead or a sandhill crane, so a wild game cook who wants to get serious about cooking such birds is headed into unfamiliar territory.

Thankfully, you don't need to head into this strange land without a map. There are countless little secrets when it comes to handling waterfowl—how to remove tendons from the legs, how to burn off pin feathers, how to get a nice crispy skin on roasted ducks, what to do with the hearts and livers, how to perfectly butcher a puddle duck—that can add up to make the difference between merely acceptable dishes and dishes you'd serve to impress your future in-laws. Get out on the water with your shotgun and have a good day. Then come back inside and open this book.

THE NATURE OF THE BEAST

Dabbling Ducks

In general, this is the best category of ducks with regard to tablefare. Dabbling ducks are mild and tender. The fat and skin on dabbling ducks is usually very good. Exceptions occur when they are feeding heavily on animal matter, such as when mallards feed on salmon eggs or aquatic invertebrates, but cases like that occur only in isolated situations.

Teal (green wing, blue wing, and cinnamon teal) are small birds, but some of the best. They have delicate, relatively light-colored flesh and are suitable for many applications.

Wood ducks sometimes eat a diet similar to deer and squirrels, as they like to walk from the water into hardwood forests to feed on acorns, beechnuts, and other mast crops. They'll even eat berries. These ducks are superb.

Mallards, pintails, and **black ducks** are large and excellent, especially when fat. If you don't like these, you don't like ducks. They are good for anything that can be done with ducks.

American wigeons and **gadwalls** are not as highly esteemed as mallards and pintails, though most people would be hard-pressed to distinguish a nice fat wigeon from a nice fat mallard. They are mild, flavorful, with good fat.

Northern shovelers are the least tasty of the dabbling ducks. They eat a higher proportion of animal matter (mollusks, insects, crustaceans) than other dabblers. Their flesh suffers because of it. This is the one puddle duck whose skin you'll probably want to discard before cooking.

Diving Ducks

A common complaint about some species of diving ducks is that they have a powerful, sometimes "fishy" taste. When present, these off-putting flavors are concentrated largely in the skin and fat. A good rule of thumb when preparing diving ducks is to discard the skin and fat and use only the meat. The pochards (canvasbacks, redheads, ring-necked ducks, and scaup) are usually an exception to this rule. Their fat can be delicious.

Canvasbacks, redheads, ring-necked ducks, and **scaup** (both greater and lesser) are the best-tasting of the diving ducks. These are sizable birds with mild flesh that can be used for many applications, though you still might want to discard the skin and fat. Taxonomically, these species are classified as pochards. You'll notice that the skin of pochards peels away much more easily than it does with other diving ducks, though it's not always necessary to skin them. Try one with the skin first; if it's fishy, discard the skin on the rest of your haul.

Scoters (black, surf, and white-winged) stand out as another exception among the diving ducks, though not as remarkable an exception as the pochards. My friend Brandt has eaten more diving ducks than most people have seen, and he's insistent that their flesh is milder and more tender than most divers. Discard the skin and fat.

Buffleheads and **goldeneyes** (both common and Barrow's) are representative of diving ducks as a whole. You're not going to throw a breast on the grill and serve it rare with a pinch of salt, as you would with a fattened mallard, but there are still plenty of things that you can do with them: curries, stir-fries, jerky, slow-cooked recipes. Just make sure that you're adding some flavor and avoiding the use of the skin and fat.

Mergansers, both common and hooded, are hotly debated birds. Hunters like to argue about whether or not they're actually edible. If you peel away the skin and use them for a heavily seasoned dish like gumbo, you probably won't be able to tell them apart from many species of diving ducks.

Geese

Goose meat has as much in common with red meat as it does with duck. It's beefy, deep red, and very good if properly handled. Geese are best when they're well fed and fatty. A goose that's been migrating long distances in harsh conditions, with little food, might be poor in quality with lean breasts.

Canada geese are by far the most widely hunted species of geese. Fattened on green grass and agricultural crops, a Canada goose breast is on par with a quality steak. Geese that are feeding in saltwater estuaries sometimes consume enough animal matter (aquatic invertebrates, fish eggs, and so on) to give their meat a strong, sometimes fishy flavor. Discarding the skin and fat on these geese is helpful.

White-fronted geese, or specklebelly geese, are regarded by many as the finest-tasting of all geese.

Snow geese are not as highly esteemed as Canada geese and white-fronted geese. Many are killed along migration routes when the birds have exhausted their fat reserves and their flesh is a bit lean and tough. However, a fat snow goose is as good as a fat Canada goose, only smaller, so don't let the negative hype fool you. Any snow goose is worth your effort and deserves to be handled properly.

Cranes

Sandhill cranes are the best of the best. A crane breast is like some kind of magical fork-tender steak; if you get your hands on one, cherish it.

NO GUTS, NO GLORY: PUTTING BIRD ORGANS TO USE

You're depriving yourself if you're not retaining giblets from your waterfowl and upland birds. You can make a number of tasty concoctions from these gems, including rich pâtés, aesthetically pleasing heart skewers, and crowd-pleasing jars of what my brother and I lovingly refer to as "gib pickles." By giblets, or course, we're referring to three internal organs that you'll find when you gut your birds: the liver, heart, and gizzard. (See photograph on this page of cleaned wild turkey liver, heart, and gizzard.) These occupy the extremes on a spectrum of hardiness. The liver is so fragile that a hasty gutting job can mash it to smithereens, while the gizzard, or gastric mill, is tough enough that it would seem appropriate for industrial applications. A gizzard's toughness makes sense when you consider the job that it performs. It's part of the bird's digestive tract. The bird swallows gravel, or "grit," and this goes into the gizzard. When food passes into the gizzard, the muscle churns it together with the grit and pulverizes it into a digestible mush. Think of it as what happens when you chew, except that the gizzard acts as your jaw muscle and the grit acts as your teeth.

Because of the anatomy of a bird, the gutting incision is made down near the vent, while the organs are hidden behind the breastbone—you never actually see the organs *in situ*. Everything must be done by feel. After making your cut, which runs from the vent up to the point of the breastbone, slip your fingers inside and feel around for the smooth and silky liver. Draw this out first, or else you'll end up with a mashed and segmented mess. (You might end up pulverizing it later for a pâté or mousse, but it's easier to handle and it's much prettier in its pristine state.)

Once you get the liver free, you can reach all way up into the cavity and pull out the heart and gizzard. All you need to do is give the heart a light rinse to wash away any coagulated blood. Any bird from a dove up to a mallard has a small enough heart that you can prepare it as one bite-size piece. Bigger than a mallard and you'll probably want to halve it. Bigger than a goose and you'll want to quarter it.

Gizzards take a bit more work. Start out by using a sharp knife to slice about halfway through the organ. Then pry it open by hand like you're opening up a clam. Inside, you'll find a bunch of gravel and some pulverized food. Rinse this stuff away. The internal pouch containing the gravel and food has a tough, slightly abrasive liner. Depending on the bird species, you can either peel this liner away by hand or else you'll have to slice it away. On smaller birds, that's all that needs to happen. The gizzard is now recipe-ready. On larger birds, say anything from a Canada goose up to a turkey, you'll want to slice away the outer wall that the abrasive liner is connected to. You'll end up with four matching quarters that are rubbery, beautiful, and rich with promise.

I generally eat my bird livers fresh, either sautéed in butter and splashed with a bit of brandy, tossed into stuffing, or whipped into a mousse. Hearts and gizzards are more resilient and can be stored away for later use. I freeze mine in water. At the beginning of hunting season, when I kill my first birds, I'll take a two-liter soda bottle and cut away the upper, tapered portion. I toss whatever giblets I've got into the bottle, cover them with water, and place it in the freezer. Then, as the season progresses, I'll keep adding layers of giblets and water until the bottle is filled up. When that happens, it's time to whip up a batch of gib pickles. See *The Complete Guide to Hunting, Butchering, and Cooking Wild Game: Volume 2*, for details.

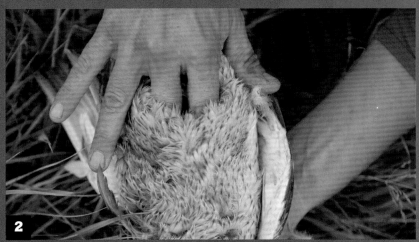

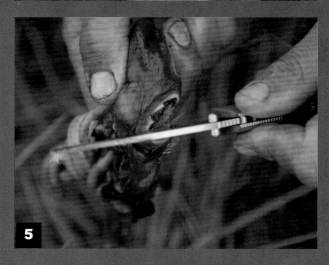

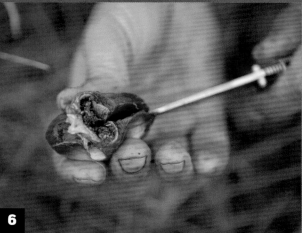

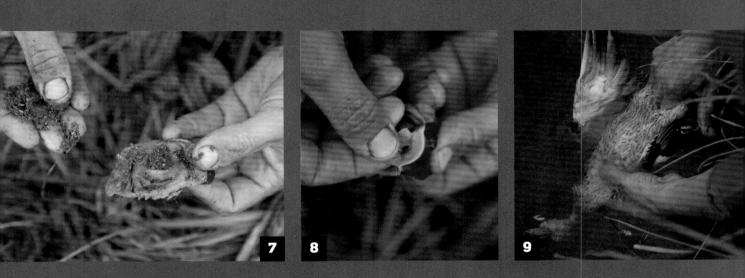

It is always a good idea to gut upland game birds and waterfowl in the field, soon after they've been killed. This allows the carcass to begin cooling and the hunter to properly clean out the gut cavity. The gutting process is the same whether you're dealing with a small quail or a large goose.

1. Start by making a small incision below the lower end of the breastbone—you can pluck the feathers here to make this area more visible. Continue making a shallow cut through the skin of the gut cavity down to the cloaca (anus).

2. Use your finger to open up this cut to expose the innards. Reach into the gut cavity with your fingers. You want to reach past the digestive organs until you feel the top of the chest cavity.

3. Now begin scooping downward and outward. You will feel the organs in the chest cavity pull free. Continue pulling. All of the guts should come out in one package.

4. Separate the heart, liver, and gizzard from the rest of the guts. The gizzard is a large, purplish, oval-shaped, muscular organ that pulverizes a game bird's food.

5. You'll need to cut the gizzard from the digestive system.

6. Slice down the middle of the gizzard lengthwise.

7. Now open up the gizzard and remove any bits of food and grit. You'll see a thin, light-colored layer of tissue that lines the interior of the gizzard.

8. Peel away the interior lining of the gizzard.

9. Take the time to wash the gut cavity and edible organs.

PLUCKING A DUCK

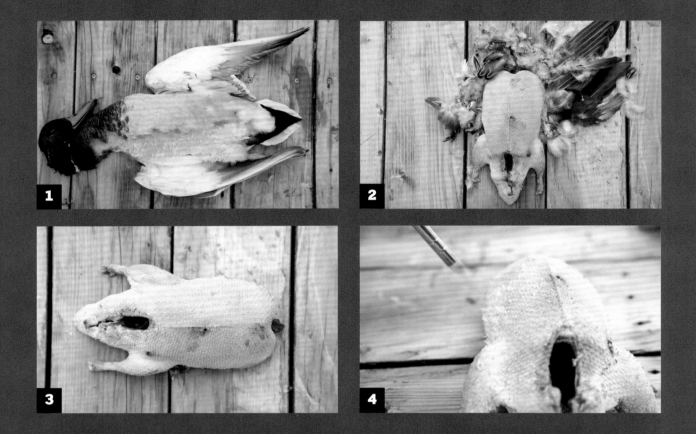

Too many hunters don't take the time to pluck waterfowl and upland game birds. This is a huge mistake and a mortal sin according to author Jim Harrison. Plucking is a somewhat tedious job, but eating a whole, plucked bird with crispy skin and moist, tender meat makes it worth the time and effort involved.

1. Start by plucking the larger breast feathers just below the neck. Work with grain methodically downward and be careful to avoid tearing the skin. Once you have the larger feathers plucked, go back and pluck the smaller, downy feathers that remain attached to the skin. Also pluck any small replacement feathers that are still embedded in the skin.

2. After you've plucked the breast, move on to the wings, legs, and back. These feathers are well-anchored and easier to pluck against the grain. Use a pair of game shears to cut the lower legs and wings from the carcass.

3. Now you have a plucked bird with only small, hair-like pin feathers remaining attached to the skin.

4. The easiest way to quickly remove these tiny feathers is with a handheld propane torch. Pass the flame lightly over the skin without burning it. This will quickly singe the remaining feathers away. You may need to use a toothpick to remove any shot or feathers stuck under the skin. The end result should be able to pass for a store-bought chicken, albeit one sporting a few pellet holes.

HOW TO PULL TENDONS OUT OF A DUCK LEG

1. Removing the leg tendons from ducks and other game birds makes an otherwise tough piece of meat more tender. Start by making a shallow cut around the circumference of the lower leg joint.

2. Now bend the leg joint backward in the opposite direction it would normally move until it pops.

3. Slowly twist and pull the lower leg away from the upper leg. With a little effort, the tendons will slide out of the muscle. With the stringy tendons removed, you won't wear out your jaw muscles chewing on tough game bird legs.

REMOVING BREAST WITH LEG ATTACHED (SKIN-ON)

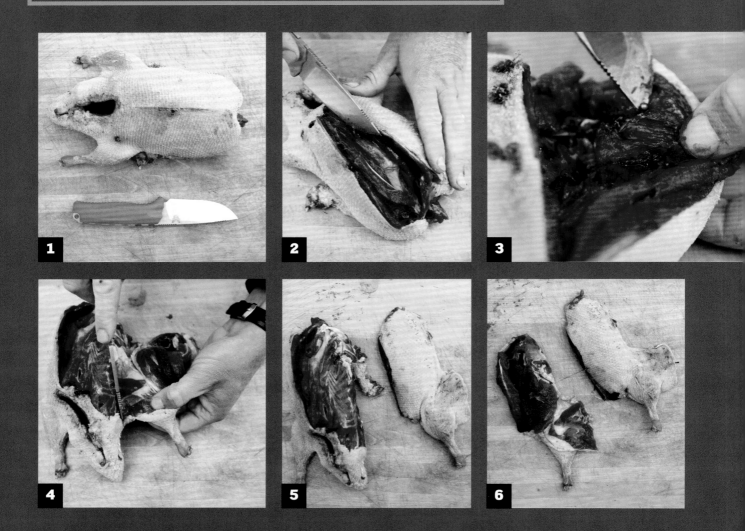

1. Leaving skin-on breasts and legs attached to each other makes for a great presentation, and the fatty skin keeps the meat moist during cooking. Start with a clean gutted and plucked duck.

2. Make your first cut through the skin and muscle parallel to the breastbone.

3. As you cut, watch for pellets or feathers embedded in the meat and remove them along with any bloodshot meat.

4. Continue to separate the breast from the chest cavity, stopping short of removing it completely from the carcass. Where the thigh muscle joins the body, find the hip's ball joint. Cut through this and the upper thigh muscle to separate the leg from the carcass.

5. Now cut through the skin along the rear and back to remove the breast and leg in one piece.

6. Next, repeat the process on the other side of the duck. This cut is ideal for grilling or searing and then finishing in the oven.

REMOVING SKINLESS BREAST FILLETS

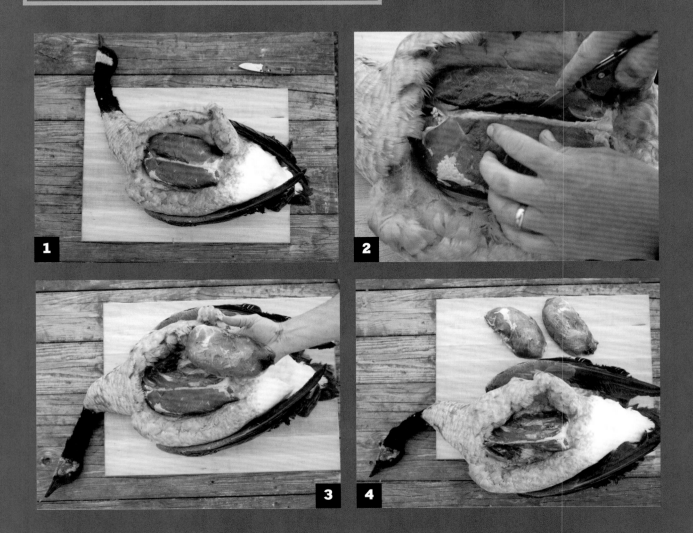

Removing skinless, boneless breasts from most geese, puddle ducks, and upland game birds is quick and easy.

1. Start by making a shallow cut through the skin on top of the breast. Now use your hands to peel the skin completely back from both sides of the breast. Birds that have been allowed to freeze are much harder to skin once they've been thawed out. The skin from some diver and sea duck species can be difficult to peel away, but since the skin can have a strong, fishy taste, it should be removed before cooking.

2. Cut along the bone that runs down the center of the breast to begin removing one side.

3. Now fillet the entire boneless breast off the underlying bones of the breast plate.

4. Repeat the process on the other side, and don't forget to save the legs.

WATERFOWL
LIVER PÂTÉ
PAGE 123

WILD GOOSE PASTRAMI
PAGE 128

BRANDIED CHERRIES
PAGE 318

GAME BIRD TERRINE
PAGE 159

VENISON
LIVER MOUSSE
PAGE 30

TEA-SMOKED
DUCK BREASTS
PAGE 134

SPICY PICKLED
RED ONIONS
PAGE 318

SEARED TONGUE
PAGE 36

WATERFOWL LIVER PÂTÉ

SERVES 6 TO 8 AS AN APPETIZER (MAKES 2 CUPS)

While I do freeze waterfowl livers, I'll admit that it comes at a cost. They are delicate organs, and freezing them changes the texture and consistency in a noticeable way. However, freezing livers is often necessary if you're trying to save up enough to do something major with them. By major, I'm talking about preparation like this waterfowl pâté, which requires a pound of livers. You and your buddies might get enough livers in a single day of hunting if everything falls into place, but it's more likely that you'll have to accumulate the livers over the course of a few outings. This recipe is similar to the Venison Liver Mousse (page 30) in that it uses the classic French technique of hard-boiled eggs as an emulsifier. But the flavor profile here is decidedly different. The orange, anchovies, and thyme make it lively and zesty.

ALSO WORKS WITH: Try this with livers from any upland birds or waterfowl. If you don't have a full pint in your freezer, substitute the remainder with chicken livers.

Remove 3 strips of zest from the orange with a peeler. Save the partially zested orange for another use.

Heat the butter in a large sauté pan over medium heat. Add the shallot and cook until translucent, 3 to 5 minutes. Add the livers, orange zest, thyme, anchovies, garlic, bay leaf, red chile flakes, and the whole hard-boiled egg. Sprinkle with a generous pinch of salt and pepper and cook until the livers are just cooked through (you will notice that blood will begin to appear on the surface of the liver), about 4 minutes. It's OK if they are a little pink in the middle. Remove the pan from the heat and pour in the brandy. Return the pan to the heat, step back, and carefully tip it away from you slightly so the brandy ignites. Let the alcohol cook off for about 1 minute, gently shaking the pan every few seconds. Toss to coat well. Remove from the heat. Discard the orange zest, garlic, bay leaf, and thyme. Cut the hard-boiled egg into quarters.

Transfer the livers, egg, and shallot to a food processor and process until smooth. Taste and season with salt and pepper as needed.

Serve on baguette slices or saltines with capers as an accompaniment.

See the photograph of pâté on charcuterie spread on page 122.

1 orange

¼ cup (½ stick) unsalted butter

1 large shallot, thinly sliced (about ⅓ cup)

1 pound goose livers (about 1 pint)

2 fresh thyme sprigs

2 anchovy fillets

2 cloves garlic, smashed

1 bay leaf

Pinch of red chile flakes (optional)

1 large hard-boiled egg, peeled

Kosher salt

Freshly ground black pepper

¼ cup brandy or bourbon

Baguette slices or saltines, for serving

Capers, for serving

SPECIAL EQUIPMENT NEEDED:

food processor

SKEWERED AND GRILLED DUCK HEARTS
AND GRAPES AND WALNUT PESTO

MAKES 6 HEARTS

2 tablespoons balsamic vinegar

2 tablespoons extra virgin olive oil

Leaves from 2 small sprigs fresh rosemary

Leaves from 2 sprigs fresh thyme

2 bay leaves

1 clove garlic, smashed

½ pound duck hearts, cleaned (about 6 hearts)

Small bunch of grapes (on stem)

Kosher salt

Freshly ground black pepper

Lightly grilled baguette slices

Walnut and Mint Pesto (page 320)

SPECIAL EQUIPMENT:

wooden skewers (optional)

First off, this dish is visually stunning. The grilled hearts and grapes come together like a work of art. There are interesting flavors and textures here as well. The hearts are little firecrackers of meaty flavor, and the experience of having a warm, smoke-flavored grape burst inside your mouth will forever change your impressions of this fruit. You can make this dish on a gas or charcoal grill, but I highly recommend an open fire. Start the blaze an hour or so ahead of time. When you're ready to cook, use a small shovel to build an off-to-the-side bed of embers and position your grilling rack above it. Keep the fire burning and add additional embers as needed. Plan on at least two or three hearts per person.

ALSO WORKS WITH: Try this with hearts from any upland game birds or waterfowl. If you're using Canada geese hearts, cut them in half lengthwise. For a wild turkey's heart, you'll want to quarter it. This recipe also works well with hearts from big game animals, though you'll have to treat them like kabobs, cubing a larger heart into 1-inch pieces then skewering as directed in the recipe.

If using wooden skewers, soak them in water to cover for at least 30 minutes to prevent them from burning.

Combine the vinegar, oil, rosemary, thyme, bay leaves, and garlic in a wide shallow bowl. Transfer half of the marinade to a resealable plastic bag, add the duck hearts, toss around to coat, then marinate in the refrigerator for 2 to 3 hours.

Heat a grill over high heat. Gently toss the bunch of grapes in the bowl of reserved marinade to coat. Sprinkle the grapes with salt and pepper, then grill, covered, turning occasionally, until slightly charred in spots, about 5 minutes. Return to the bowl of marinade until ready to serve.

Remove the duck hearts from the marinade, place them on skewers, if using, then sprinkle generously with salt and pepper. Grill the hearts, covered, until desired doneness, 4 to 5 minutes for medium-rare, turning halfway through. Serve with the grapes, baguette, and walnut pesto.

Note: You can skewer the grapes as well, as in this image. If they are clinging tightly to their bunch, try to grill them whole; it makes for a dramatic presentation.

GRILLED DUCK NACHOS

MAKES ONE 9 X 13-INCH PAN (SERVES A CROWD AS APPETIZERS)

Like most Americans, I spent the better part of my life making nachos with ground meat. I did it that way because . . . well, it's just the way that people always did it. This preparation gets away from that by using grilled, thinly sliced duck breast for the protein. I almost hate to mention this, because I don't want to dissuade you from making this recipe, but you might end up liking the grilled duck so much that you skip the tortilla chips on your next go-around and just use the duck as a main course with some grilled veggies on the side. When cooking with duck breasts, make sure not to forget about the rest of the bird. Use the legs and the wing bones to make a stock, or you can braise them down and shred the meat for all manner of uses (see the Red Curry Duck recipe on page 132). You can even take the shredded meat and toss it in some oil, then fry it until it's crispy and add it to your nachos.

Prepare a gas grill over medium heat.

FOR THE DUCK: Score the skin of the breasts in a crosshatch pattern without cutting into the meat. Combine the coffee, salt, brown sugar, garlic powder, onion powder, cayenne, and cinnamon in a small bowl. Rub the coffee mixture all over the duck. Grill the duck skin-side down, covered, until the skin has rendered its fat and is charred in spots. (The more fat your duck has, the longer this will take, but a thin-skinned duck should only take about 4 minutes.) Flip the breasts over and grill until desired doneness (127°F on an instant-read thermometer for medium-rare, 130 to 135°F for medium). Transfer to a cutting board skin-side up and let rest for 5 to 10 minutes. Cut in half lengthwise, then thinly slice crosswise into short strips.

FOR THE NACHOS: Mix the lime zest into the sour cream in a small bowl. Spread half of the chips on the bottom of double layered 9½ x 13½-inch disposable foil lasagna tray, or a metal cake pan of similar dimensions. Top with half of the duck, beans, cheese, and jalapeños. Repeat the layering with the remaining chips, duck, beans, and cheese, holding back the remaining jalapeños. Grill, covered, until the cheese is melted, 10 to 15 minutes. Remove from the grill and top with the remaining jalapeños, scallions, and cilantro. Serve with the lime sour cream and salsa.

DUCK

2 pounds duck breasts

1 tablespoon finely ground coffee beans

2 teaspoons kosher salt

2 teaspoons packed brown sugar

½ teaspoon garlic powder

½ teaspoon onion powder

¼ teaspoon cayenne pepper

¼ teaspoon ground cinnamon

NACHOS

Zest and juice of 1 large lime

16 ounces sour cream

6 ounces restaurant-style tortilla chips

1 (15-ounce) can black beans, rinsed well and drained

1 pound shredded Monterey Jack or Mexican-style blend cheese

2 large jalapeños or red Fresno chiles, thinly sliced

Thinly sliced scallions, for garnish

Fresh cilantro leaves, for garnish

Salsa, for serving (pico de gallo shown in photograph)

ALSO WORKS WITH: As is, this recipe is intended for dabbler duck species such as mallards, wood ducks, pintails, and teal, which are largely vegetarian. If you intend to use a diver duck species, which eats a lot more fish and invertebrates, make sure to discard the skin.

WILD GOOSE PASTRAMI

SERVES 4 TO 6

CURE

¼ cup Morton's Tender Quick

¼ cup freshly ground black pepper

¼ cup packed dark brown sugar

2 tablespoons granulated garlic

2 teaspoons ground coriander

2 teaspoons onion powder

2 teaspoons dried thyme

RUB

3 tablespoons freshly ground black pepper

1 teaspoon ground coriander

1 teaspoon granulated garlic

½ teaspoon onion powder

½ teaspoon smoked paprika

½ teaspoon dried thyme

GOOSE

2 goose breasts (about 1 pound each)

Mustard and pickles, for serving

SPECIAL EQUIPMENT NEEDED:

smoker or grill outfitted for smoking

With populations of snow geese and Canada geese at near record-high levels, pastrami is a goose hunter's best friend. This is a great way to get through a big haul of birds and turn them into something that your friends and family will be begging you to share. We've done as many as ten geese like this in a single batch. They're best served fresh out of the smoker alongside some good seedy mustard, bread-and-butter pickles, and maybe a handful of mixed greens tossed with a vinaigrette. After that initial serving, you can start piling leftovers into sandwiches. Keep in mind, too, that you can freeze your finished product. Just slip a breast or two into a vacuum-sealed bag and freeze it for up to a few months. The frozen pastramis are a good option for overnight hunting and fishing trips when you need a simple meal plan. Even if you don't have the time or gear needed to warm them up, you can just thaw them out and eat 'em at room temperature. If "room temperature" is below freezing, tuck one into the pocket of your down jacket for a few hours. For a photograph of the finished goose pastrami, see the charcuterie spread on page 122.

ALSO WORKS WITH: This recipe is tailored for wild geese, though sandhill cranes are going to taste even better if you have access to them. You can also make pastrami out of your big game animals. Elk and moose briskets work great, or you can use whole muscle roasts from deer or bear. Start with a 1- to 2-pound roast and go from there. See the note opposite for alternate curing/smoking times for big game.

FOR THE CURE: Mix the Morton's Tender Quick, pepper, brown sugar, granulated garlic, coriander, onion powder, and thyme in a small bowl.

FOR THE RUB: Mix the pepper, coriander, granulated garlic, onion powder, paprika, and thyme in a small bowl.

FOR THE GOOSE: Rub the goose breasts heavily with the cure, making sure to cover the whole piece of meat. Place in a resealable bag and add the remaining cure on top of the meat. Remove as much air as possible from the bag and refrigerate for 3 days. Flip the bag once each day. After 3 days, remove the meat from the bag and rinse it thoroughly. Soak the goose breasts in cold water for 30 to 45 minutes to remove all the cure. Remove the goose from the water and pat dry with paper towels.

Rub the goose breasts with the spice rub on all sides. Prepare a smoker with fruit wood to 225°F and place the breasts skin-side down on the smoker racks. Smoke until the internal temperature reaches 150°F, 1½ to 3 hours. Rest for 10 minutes. Slice the meat against the grain. Serve with your favorite mustard and pickles.

The pastrami will keep in the refrigerator for up to 2 weeks, or freeze in vacuum-sealed bags for up to 6 months. To reheat after refrigerating, slice very thinly across the grain and put the meat into a very hot sauté pan. Toss a few times to start to release the fat, about 1 minute, and then add ¼ cup water and cover for another minute to minute and a half, tossing a few times. This steam method keeps the meat moist and allows the flavors of the crust to coat the entire slice of meat.

Note: To make the pastrami with a venison roast or large brisket, rub the meat heavily with the cure, making sure to cover the entire brisket. Place the brisket in a resealable bag and add the remaining rub on top of the meat. Refrigerate for 4 days. Flip the bag once every day. After 4 days, remove the meat from the bag and rinse it thoroughly. Soak the brisket in cold water for 30 to 45 minutes to remove all the cure. Remove the brisket from the water and pat dry with paper towels. Rub the entire brisket with the spice rub. Prepare a smoker to 225°F and smoke the meat until fork tender, or to an internal temperature of 170°F, about 5 hours. Let the meat rest for 10 minutes. Slice the meat against the grain. Serve with your favorite mustard and pickles.

SOY SAUCE DUCK

SERVES 2

I love the look of a wild duck that's been cooked whole. It has a primal beauty, and every time I see one I want to rush for my carving knife. The problem is that they aren't always as good as they look. There are big differences between the breast meat and the leg meat on a wild duck. While the breasts are tender, moist, and best served rare, the legs can be rubbery and require a lot of cooking in order to tenderize them. Because of this discrepancy, you often end up with perfect legs and a breast that's dry and overdone or else a perfect breast and legs that are nearly impossible to eat. This recipe helps address that conundrum because the bird is submerged in liquid and simmered at a relatively low temperature. This prevents the breast from getting dried out too quickly while still allowing the legs plenty of time to get the heat that they deserve. The finished product is sweet and salty. Try this on folks who say they don't like wild ducks. This will change them for the better.

Remove the duck from the refrigerator about 1 hour before cooking.

Heat the oil in a tall 10-quart stockpot over medium heat. Add the ginger slices and cook, stirring, for 30 seconds. Add the garlic and scallions and cook, stirring, for another 30 seconds. Carefully add the wine, then the star anise and cinnamon. Bring to a simmer and cook for about 1 minute. Add both soy sauces, the brown sugar, orange zest, and water. Bring to a boil, then reduce the heat and simmer for about 30 minutes.

Add the duck to the pot breast-side down. Maneuver the duck so that the soy sauce mixture enters the cavity of the duck. Bring to a simmer and cook for 25 minutes, basting the top of the duck that is not submerged. (It can help to weight down the bird with a plate or small pot lid.) Immediately remove from the heat, cover, and steep the duck in the soy sauce basting liquid for 1 hour.

Remove the duck and transfer to a cutting board. When cool to the touch, proceed to carve. Serve with the ginger-scallion oil, additional sauce from the pot, and a side of rice.

1 whole mallard, pintail, or other large wild duck

1 tablespoon vegetable oil

7 thin slices ginger

2 cloves garlic, smashed

2 scallions, cut into 2-inch pieces

1½ cups Shaoxing wine

5 star anise pods

2 cinnamon sticks

1½ cups dark soy sauce

1½ cups light soy sauce

1 cup packed dark brown sugar

5 strips orange zest

10 cups water

Ginger-Scallion Oil (recipe follows)

Cooked rice, for serving

ALSO WORKS WITH: Stick with dabbler ducks on this one. Diver ducks usually need to be skinned before cooking them, and you want the skin intact for this. See page 112 for more information. Getting your portions right with wild ducks can be tricky. A large dabbler such as a mallard is plenty of meat for two people. Wood ducks, which run a bit smaller, fall in the middle; bigger appetites will eat the whole bird, smaller appetites will want to share. With teal, a single person might want one or two birds for themselves. This recipe is intended for ducks on the larger end of the spectrum, such as mallards, though it should be little problem for you to make adjustments to accommodate smaller birds.

Tip: The soy sauce basting liquid can be stored in the freezer and used over again; it's considered a master sauce that turns richer with each use. When the liquid has cooled, strain and transfer to airtight containers and store in the freezer. Add a fresh batch of ingredients when using again, plus more water if necessary.

GINGER-SCALLION OIL

MAKES ⅓ CUP

Heat the oil in a small saucepan or skillet over low heat. Add the ginger, scallion, and salt and cook for 5 minutes. Transfer to a heatproof dish and allow to cool before serving. The oil can be made a day ahead and stored in the refrigerator.

½ cup vegetable oil

1-inch piece ginger, finely chopped (about 1 tablespoon)

1 large scallion, finely chopped (about ¼ cup)

1 teaspoon kosher salt

RED CURRY DUCK

SERVES 4 TO 6

BRAISED LEGS

1½ pounds duck and/or goose legs (roughly 18 to 22 legs), skin removed

1 onion, halved

4 cloves garlic

1-inch piece ginger, peeled, sliced into coins, and smashed

5 fresh cilantro stems

1 quart Blonde Game Stock (page 306) or low-sodium chicken broth

RED CURRY

2 tablespoons vegetable oil

2 cups fresh pineapple chunks

1 cup grape or cherry tomatoes

2 (14-ounce) cans unstirred full-fat coconut milk, chilled

4 to 6 tablespoons red curry paste

2 tablespoons fish sauce, plus more for serving

1 tablespoon brown sugar

1 medium eggplant, cut into 1-inch pieces

1 cup fresh Thai basil leaves, plus more for garnish

Hot steamed white rice, for serving

Lime wedges, for serving

Sliced Thai or serrano chiles, for garnish (optional)

Fresh cilantro leaves, for garnish

ALSO WORKS WITH: Use the skinless legs from any waterfowl, including geese. After cooking, finely mince the skin and add it back into the shredded meat. When using diver ducks, discard the skin before cooking. Use already cooked, leftover duck.

Admittedly, wild duck legs are a lot harder to deal with than the breasts. There's a lot of tendon and bone inside a leg, so the ratio of edible to non-edible meat is pretty low. And the meat that is there, at least on a roasted bird, can be tough enough to resist your best efforts at chewing. That's why many of my favorite recipes for duck legs begin with slow-cooking them until the meat is tender enough to be picked off the bone. Once that's taken care of, you have something magical on your hands. There are a hundred things that you can do with it, though this red curry recipe belongs at the top of the list.

FOR THE BRAISED LEGS: Combine the duck and/or goose legs, onion, garlic, ginger, and cilantro stems in 6-quart saucepan. Add enough stock to just barely cover the meat. Bring to a boil over high heat, skimming and discarding any foam that may rise to the top. Reduce the heat to low, cover, and simmer until the leg meat is very tender but not yet falling off the bone, about 2 hours and 40 minutes.

Remove the meat to a plate. Strain the cooking liquid and discard the solids. Measure out 1½ cups of the liquid and discard the rest or reserve for another use.

FOR THE RED CURRY: Place an empty pot over medium-high heat and add the oil. Add the pineapple. Cook, stirring once or twice, until browned in some spots, about 3 minutes. Transfer the pineapple to a separate plate. Add the tomatoes and cook, stirring occasionally, until the skins start to split, about 2 minutes. Add the tomatoes to the pineapple.

Skim the thick coconut cream from the tops of the coconut milk and add to the pot along with the curry paste. Bring to a simmer, stirring often and scraping the browned bits from the bottom, about 2 minutes. Add the remaining coconut milk, the reserved braising liquid, the fish sauce, and the brown sugar. If the curry broth is too thin, reduce at a simmer to thicken it slightly. Add the eggplant and continue to simmer until the eggplant is tender, 10 to 15 minutes.

Shred the duck into bite-size pieces. Stir in the duck, pineapple, tomatoes, and basil and cook until warmed through, 3 to 5 minutes. Adjust the seasonings by adding a little extra fish sauce or salt as needed.

Serve over rice, with lime wedges and a garnish of chiles, if using, cilantro, and torn basil leaves.

ROAST DUCK
WITH POMEGRANATE GLAZE

SERVES 2

I mention in the introduction to this chapter that my love affair with eating wild ducks began with the oven-roasted woodies that my mom prepared when I was a kid. She stuffed the birds with raisins and chopped apples and cooked them hot and fast. They were simple and nearly perfect. The one drawback was that the fruit stuffing was locked up inside the chest cavity and the flavors never fully integrated with the meat. This recipe helps correct that, because here the fruit is paired more aggressively with the meat as a glaze of pomegranate molasses. The carved meat is then garnished with pomegranate seeds as a fun and surprising accompaniment. The key here, as with all roasted ducks, is not to overcook the bird. You want to hit that sweet spot where the legs are cooked through and the breast is still moist. Have a meat thermometer on hand in order to hit your preferred temperature without going over.

Rinse the duck inside and out with cold water, then pat dry with paper towels. Place the duck on a wire rack and refrigerate, uncovered, for 8 to 24 hours (this air-drying helps to crisp the skin but can be skipped).

Preheat the oven to 425°F. Line a roasting pan with foil. Bring the duck to room temperature.

If your duck strikes you as being a fatty specimen, do not bother brushing it with oil. But if the layer of fat looks thin (I know, this requires some guesswork, but do your best), then you'll want to rub it with a thin layer of oil. Sprinkle the duck generously with salt and pepper, including the cavity. Stuff the cavity with the onion and bay leaf. Put the duck on a wire rack and place over the prepared roasting pan.

Roast until an instant-read thermometer inserted lengthwise along the breastbone (the thickest part of the breast) registers 127°F for medium-rare or 130 to 135°F for medium.

Raise the oven temperature to 450°F. If fat has accumulated on the bottom of your pan, carefully pour it off and reserve it for another use, if you like. Baste the duck with oil. Return to the oven and roast until the skin is crisp and golden, 5 to 10 minutes. Brush the pomegranate molasses all over the duck several times while the duck rests, about 10 minutes. Discard the onion and bay leaf. Carve the duck and transfer to a platter. Sprinkle pomegranate seeds over the top.

1 whole duck

½ cup extra virgin olive oil, if needed

Kosher salt

Freshly ground black pepper

1 small onion, quartered

1 bay leaf

¼ cup pomegranate molasses (see Tip below on making your own corn syrup)

Pomegranate seeds, for garnish

ALSO WORKS WITH: Whole roasted geese (Canada, speckled, brants, etc.) are great. You'll have to adjust your cooking time (longer, obviously) and you'll likely have to pour off some rendered oil mid-process if it's a fatty goose. As for ducks, stick with dabblers or the pochard species. See page 112 for more information. Getting your portions right with wild ducks can be tricky. A large dabbler such as a mallard is plenty of meat for two people. Wood ducks, which run a bit smaller, fall in the middle; bigger appetites will eat the whole bird, smaller appetites will want to share. With teal, a single person might want one or two birds for themselves. This recipe is intended for ducks on the larger end of the spectrum, such as mallards, though you should be able to make adjustments to easily accommodate smaller birds.

Tip: You can make your own pomegranate glaze by reducing (simmering) pomegranate juice down to a syrup, adding sugar if necessary.

TEA-SMOKED DUCK BREASTS
WITH BLUEBERRY PORT COMPOTE

SERVES 3 TO 4

The genius of this recipe is that it brings together three things that combine into something magical: duck breasts, smoke, and chutney. Instead of traditional smoking fuels of fruitwood or hardwood, the breasts are treated to a gentler and more aromatic smoke from tea, cinnamon, and star anise. Don't worry, you do not need an outdoor smoker or smokehouse to pull this recipe off. You can do it on a conventional stovetop burner right in your kitchen, or else on a simple outdoor barbecue grill. The compote here captures some of the same flavors as the smoke, along with a bit of zip from crushed red pepper. I recommended making a double batch or more. Keep the remainder in your fridge for up to a couple of weeks or up to six months in your freezer. It's an excellent accompaniment to pretty much any roast meat, from wild hog to venison to pheasant. The Shaoxing wine and Sichuan peppercorns are available in Asian grocers or online if you can't find them at your local stores.

If you can't get everything on the list, riffing on the smoking spices and marinade ingredients is totally acceptable. As long as you use a black tea and soy sauce, you'll be onto something good. See page 122 for a photograph of my finished charcuterie platter.

Toast the salt and peppercorns in a small, dry, heavy skillet over medium-low heat, shaking the pan occasionally until the salt begins to color slightly, about 5 minutes. Set aside to cool, then grind in a mortar and pestle.

Score the duck skin in a crosshatch pattern. Rub the duck all over with the salt mixture.

Combine the soy sauce, wine, ginger, star anise, cinnamon, and scallions in a resealable plastic bag. Add the duck breasts, close securely, and refrigerate for at least 8 hours or overnight.

Bring the duck to room temperature, about 30 minutes. Remove the duck from the marinade, reserving the star anise and cinnamon. Line a wok (with a lid) with 2 long sheets of wide heavy-duty foil, crossing them in the center like a "t." They should drape over the edges of the wok by a couple of inches (see photo).

Combine the brown sugar, tea leaves, rice, and reserved star anise and cinnamon and spread out over the foil. Place a round cake rack about an inch above the smoking mixture. If necessary, use balls of aluminum foil to raise the rack (see photo). Turn the exhaust fan on. Heat the wok, uncovered, over high heat until the smoking ingredients start to let off smoke, 3 to 4 minutes. Place the duck, skin-side up, in a single layer on the rack. Cover the wok and crimp up the foil around the lid so it's tightly sealed. Reduce the heat to medium and let smoke for 8 minutes. Remove the wok from the heat, but leave covered and undisturbed for another 10 minutes, or until the internal temperature is 125 to 130°F.

Cut a slice to check for desired doneness; it should be rarer than you really want to eat it.

Uncrimp the foil and carefully uncover the wok—it will be smoky. Pat the skin dry, then place it skin-side down in a large heavy skillet over medium heat. Sear until the skin is golden and crisp, 2 to 3 minutes, or to desired doneness (135°F for medium-rare/medium). Let rest for 5 to 10 minutes before slicing on the bias. Serve as part of a charcuterie plate (see photo on page 122) with the blueberry port compote.

1½ tablespoons kosher salt

2 teaspoons Sichuan peppercorns

2 pounds duck breasts (4 breasts)

3 tablespoons soy sauce

3 tablespoons Shaoxing wine

3 (⅓-inch) slices unpeeled ginger, smashed

3 star anise pods

2 cinnamon sticks

2 scallions, cut into 2-inch pieces

½ cup packed brown sugar

½ cup loose black tea leaves (such as pu-erh or Lapsang souchong)

½ cup uncooked rice

Blueberry Port Compote (page 317)

ALSO WORKS WITH: Any waterfowl. With cranes and geese, cooking times will need to be adjusted. If you're using diver ducks, make sure to remove the skin.

SPECIAL EQUIPMENT NEEDED:
mortar and pestle; wok with lid, or, alternatively, a gas or electric grill outfitted with an aluminum tray directly over the heat to hold the aromatics

SEARED GOOSE BREAST
WITH APPLE, CHERRY, AND SAGE CHUTNEY

SERVES 4 AS AN ENTRÉE, 8 AS AN APPETIZER

CHUTNEY

1½ pounds Granny Smith apples or other tart apples, skin on, cored and cut into medium dice

½ cup apple juice

⅓ cup packed brown sugar

¼ cup apple cider vinegar

½ cup dried cherries

¼ cup golden raisins

2 tablespoons honey

2 tablespoons finely chopped fresh sage

1 tablespoon finely chopped fresh rosemary

1 tablespoon minced garlic

Juice of 1 lemon

Kosher salt

Freshly ground black pepper

GOOSE

4 boneless goose breasts, skin on

Kosher salt

Freshly ground black pepper

Olive oil, to coat the pan

1 tablespoon unsalted butter

ALSO WORKS WITH: Cranes, or any large dabbler ducks with a good layer of fat. A crane breast or a large Canada goose breast will easily feed two. Smaller goose breasts are good for one to two people, depending on appetites. With larger dabbler ducks, plan on a breast for each person.

I've cooked countless ducks and geese (and a handful of sandhill cranes) using this method. It's perhaps my favorite waterfowl recipe because it showcases the main ingredient in its pure form; the bird really gets to speak for itself. It's best when you're working with a bird that has a nice layer of fat beneath the skin. That way, the breasts do a bit of self-basting as the fat renders out, and the skin turns a beautiful golden brown. When you slice the finished breasts, you've got a piece of medium-rare meat crowned with a halo of crispy fat and skin. Put a dollop of the chutney on there and your trigger finger will start getting itchy in anticipation of your next goose hunt.

FOR THE CHUTNEY: Combine the apples, apple juice, brown sugar, vinegar, dried cherries, raisins, honey, sage, rosemary, garlic, lemon juice, and salt and pepper to taste in a medium saucepan and cook over medium heat until the mixture starts to bubble. Reduce the heat to low and simmer, stirring occasionally to prevent sticking, until the fruit is soft and pulpy, the liquid is mostly absorbed, and the chutney is fairly thick, 25 to 35 minutes. Remove the chutney from the pot and let cool.

FOR THE GOOSE BREASTS: Remove the breasts from the refrigerator about an hour before you're ready to cook and let them come up to room temperature. Preheat the oven to 400°F.

Sprinkle a liberal amount of salt and pepper on the breasts. Place a cast-iron pan big enough to hold both breasts over high heat and add enough oil to just coat the bottom of the pan. Once the oil begins to shimmer, carefully place the breasts in the pan skin-side down. Let the meat develop a nice brown sear, but be careful not to let it burn. Once the skin side is golden, flip the breasts over in the pan and place the entire pan in the oven. Cook for 4 minutes, then open the oven and put the pat of butter in the pan. After another 3 minutes, quickly remove the pan from the oven, tilt the pan to one side so all the juices and butter pool on the edge of the pan, and use a spoon to baste the breasts several times. Place the pan back in the oven and finish cooking until it achieves an internal temperature of 125°F for rare (or cook to desired doneness); this may take 5 to 7 more minutes depending on the size of the breasts. Remove the pan from the oven, baste the breasts a few more times, then let rest on a cutting board for 10 minutes. Place the chutney in the hot pan and let the residual heat gently warm it up. Thinly slice the breasts and serve with the chutney.

RED WINE-BRAISED WATERFOWL

SERVES 4 TO 6

Here's a recipe that's good for virtually any specimen of waterfowl, regardless of size or condition. I recommend using this with legs and thighs, though there's no reason you can't add some breasts as well in order to get the right amount of meat. This recipe works as a stand-alone dish, with the braised meat served atop rice, polenta, or pasta, or with mashed or roasted potatoes and vegetables. The boneless meat can also double as a base or additive for other dishes such as soups or pasta sauces. In the recipe on page 138, it's used to build the filling for the Duck Ravioli with Port and Red Wine Sauce. In following this recipe, you're going to be cooking the bone-in legs until the meat can easily be picked free of the bones. But be careful not to overdo it. You want to stop the cooking once the meat can be picked, not after it falls away from the bones on its own.

ALSO WORKS WITH: As mentioned above, it's good for any and all waterfowl.

Preheat the oven to 325°F.

Sprinkle the legs with salt and pepper. Heat the oil in a large Dutch oven over medium-high heat. Working in batches, sear the waterfowl until golden all over, about 8 minutes per batch. Transfer to a platter as done.

Pour off all but 2 tablespoons of the rendered fat from the pot and reserve. Add the garlic, carrots, celery, onion, thyme, and bay leaves to the pot and cook until the vegetables begin to brown, 3 to 4 minutes. Add the wine, bring to a simmer, and simmer, scraping the bottom of the pot, until the wine reduces by half. Pour in the stock. Return the waterfowl and any accumulated juices to the pot. Cover and braise in the oven until the meat is very tender, 1½ to 2 hours.

Transfer the waterfowl to a platter and let cool. Strain the braising liquid, discarding the solids and any fat that rises to the top.

If making the Duck Ravioli with Port and Red Wine Sauce on page 138: reserve the liquid for Duck Ravioli and shred the duck meat, discarding the skin and bones. Or serve over pasta, polenta, or rice or with mashed or roasted potatoes and vegetables.

2 pounds skinless, bone-in waterfowl legs

Kosher salt

Freshly ground black pepper

1 tablespoon vegetable oil

4 cloves garlic, smashed

2 carrots, cut into 2-inch pieces

2 ribs celery, cut into 2-inch pieces

1 onion, cut into wedges

4 sprigs fresh thyme

2 bay leaves

2 cups red wine (such as cabernet, pinot noir, or malbec)

3 cups Brown Game Stock (page 305) or low-sodium chicken broth

SPECIAL EQUIPMENT:
large Dutch oven

DUCK RAVIOLI
WITH PORT AND RED WINE SAUCE

SERVES 6 (MAKES ABOUT 48 RAVIOLI)

If I were in urgent need of help, you can bet your ass that I'd call a hunting buddy way before I'd call a drinking buddy. There's a bond that forms among hunting partners that is hard to replicate among any other group of friends. If you're wondering why I'm mentioning this in an introduction to a ravioli recipe, it's because making ravioli is the kind of thing that's best accomplished while working hand-in-hand with your most trusted buddies. A little bit of camaraderie goes a long way when you're doing the arduous work of assembling dozens of tasty little pasta packets. But don't fret if you can't get your hunting buddies together to make this dish. Your spouse will work just as well; better still if you can get a couple of kids involved. The group effort will add a fresh and welcome dimension to mealtime.

ALSO WORKS WITH: We're using the Red Wine–Braised Waterfowl from page 137 as a filling for this recipe, but any wild game-based ravioli filling will work as a substitution.

SPECIAL EQUIPMENT NEEDED: food processor

FOR THE FILLING: Melt 1 tablespoon of duck fat in a large heavy skillet over medium heat. Add the onions, season with salt, add the sugar, and toss to coat. Cut a round of parchment paper just slightly smaller than the diameter of the pan, then cut a ½-inch hole in the center. Place the parchment paper on top of the onions. Cook, lifting the parchment paper occasionally to stir, about 20 minutes. Remove the parchment paper and discard it. Continue to cook, stirring often, until the onions are jammy, sweet, and browned, 45 to 55 minutes. Transfer to a food processor.

Raise the heat to medium-high. Add remaining tablespoon of duck fat or butter if the pan is dry. Sprinkle the livers with salt and pepper, then sear quickly, about 2 minutes per side. Transfer the livers to the food processor. Add the thyme and parsley and process until smooth. Let cool.

Add the shredded waterfowl and pulse (4 or 5 short pulses) until a chunky paste forms. Transfer to a wide, shallow bowl, fold in the chestnuts, and season with salt and pepper.

FOR ASSEMBLY: Sprinkle 2 baking sheets with flour. Keep the dumpling wrappers loosely covered with plastic wrap while you're working to prevent them from drying out. Set a small bowl of water next to the work surface. Spoon 2 teaspoons of filling onto a wrapper. With your finger, swipe the perimeter of the wrapper with water. Fold the wrapper in half. Starting at the mound of filling, press outward to push air out of the ravioli and seal. Repeat forming raviolis with the remaining filling and wrappers, laying them on the prepared baking sheets in a single layer as they are done. If not cooking immediately, refrigerate until ready to use or freeze the ravioli until hard, then transfer to freezer bags or a container with a tight-fitting lid and freeze for up to 3 months.

FOR THE PORT AND RED WINE SAUCE: Melt the duck fat in a wide, heavy pan over medium-high heat, add the garlic and mushrooms, and toss to coat. Cook undisturbed until the mushrooms release their moisture and the liquid mostly evaporates, 5 to 6 minutes. Stir, then continue to cook, stirring occasionally, until golden, 3 to 5 minutes. Season with salt and pepper and transfer to a plate.

Deglaze the pan with the red wine and port, then simmer, scraping up the browned bits on the bottom of the pan, until reduced by half. Add the reserved braising liquid and stock and cook until reduced and it coats the back of a spoon, about 25 minutes.

Meanwhile, add 2 tablespoons salt to a large saucepan of water and bring to a boil. Working in batches if necessary, cook the ravioli in the boiling water until they float to the top of the pot. Drain, reserving 1½ cups of the cooking water.

Add the butter and ¾ cup of the cooking water to the mushroom mixture and simmer until the butter is melted. Stir in 1 tablespoon of the chives. Gently add the ravioli to the pot and toss gingerly to coat well, adding more cooking water as necessary to create a silky sauce.

Divide the ravioli and mushrooms among 6 pasta bowls. Garnish with the remaining 1 tablespoon chives and grated cheese. Serve immediately.

FILLING

2 tablespoons duck fat or unsalted butter

1½ pounds yellow onions, thinly sliced

Kosher salt

Pinch of sugar

4 ounces duck livers, trimmed and patted dry

Freshly ground black pepper

1 tablespoon fresh thyme leaves

3 tablespoons chopped fresh flat-leaf parsley

3 cups shredded, cooked duck meat, from Red Wine–Braised Waterfowl (page 137)

1 (4¼-ounce) package peeled roasted chestnuts, coarsely chopped

ASSEMBLY

All-purpose or semolina flour, for sprinkling

48 round dumpling wrappers, plus some extra as backup

PORT AND RED WINE SAUCE

1 to 2 tablespoons duck fat or unsalted butter

1 clove garlic, smashed

10 ounces cremini mushrooms, stems trimmed, sliced

Kosher salt

Freshly ground black pepper

¾ cup red wine (such as cabernet, pinot noir, or malbec)

¾ cup tawny port

Reserved strained braising liquid from Red Wine–Braised Waterfowl (page 137), plus enough Brown Game Stock (page 305) or low-sodium chicken broth to yield 3 cups total

5 tablespoons unsalted butter

2 tablespoons chopped fresh chives

Freshly grated Parmigiano-Reggiano cheese, for serving

04 **UPLAND BIRDS**

INTRODUCTION

My early exposure to upland birds was pretty limited. We had almost zero pheasants in the area of Michigan where I grew up and there was no dove season. I never ran into any quail, sharptail grouse, or chukar. The few turkeys in the state at that time were managed through a lottery-draw system, and even those were located well north of my home. (The place is now crawling with turkeys, one of the great conservation success stories of our time.)

What we did have available were ruffed grouse and woodcock, the woodcock being more sporadically available than the ruffed grouse. They'd migrate through in October, usually in small numbers but now and then in impressive groupings. I remember one time when I was running my trapline for fox and flushed a dozen or so woodcocks out of a single stand of poplars. I ran back to my truck and grabbed my Savage Model 24C, a break-open combination gun with a .22 rifle barrel mounted over a 20-gauge shotgun barrel. I went back into the poplar grove and kicked up another half-dozen birds. I downed two of them, making that my single best year for woodcocks. As for the ruffed grouse, I can't remember my brothers and I ever killing more than five or six in any given season. The ones we did get were shot incidentally while chasing more favored quarry such as cottontail rabbits, squirrels, and waterfowl. Those few upland birds that did come into our kitchen were treated as casually as store-bought chickens. They ended up in stir-fries, or else cut into leg and breast pieces that were browned in a skillet and then tossed into an oven. That I never developed any strong, well-informed opinions about cooking and eating upland birds should go without saying.

Then Montana happened. I moved out there in the mid-nineties to attend graduate school. Suddenly I was hunting for upland birds that I barely knew existed a year or two earlier. In the mountains I had access to not only the familiar ruffed grouse, but also spruce grouse and dusky grouse. Turkeys were available to the east and northwest of where I lived. Pheasants were scattered throughout the larger valley bottoms. Out on the Great Plains, less than a day's drive away, I could find sharptail grouse, sage grouse, and Hungarian partridge. In a normal hunting season I'd be dealing with five or six species of birds; I encountered even more in my out-of-state travels, which were increasing in frequency. Several species of ptarmigan in Alaska; bobwhite quail in southern Illinois; chukar in Wyoming. At some point thereabouts, I went from being naive to experienced in the ways of upland birds.

The most important thing that I learned about cooking them is that they can't be treated like domestic chickens and turkeys. This might seem perfectly obvious to many folks, but it's something that begs to be pointed out in any discussion around cooking upland birds. Many home cooks treat store-bought chicken as a blank slate upon which to add additional layers of flavor in the form of sauces and accompaniments with little consideration for the actual meat. The flesh is regarded as bland and relatively fail-safe—it's almost hard to mess it up. That's because store-bought birds are usually just a few months old, they are grossly overfed, and they've never flown or walked more than a handful of steps in any one direction. They are fatty blobs of nothingness. Upland birds, on the other hand, have qualities that are far more nuanced. They are lean and vigorous creatures that are powerful fliers. Some of them grow to be several years old, or even older.

They are far more flavorful and richly textured than domestic fowl, and also far less forgiving. Instead of using these birds as a characterless base upon which you build your dish, you need to use a gentler approach that highlights their idiosyncratic flesh and wild beauty. Half-assed attempts at cooking them can result in meat that is tough and dry. Believe me, I have eaten my way through enough mess-ups to know how true that is. It's my hope that by following the procedures and recipes laid out in this chapter, you'll avoid similar mistakes and produce meal upon memorable meal with your hard-earned birds. Anyone who has been startled and then thrilled by the explosion of a pheasant rising up suddenly from the brush beneath your boots, or by the silence-shattering gobble of a wild turkey in the spring woods, will agree that these birds deserve every bit of love that a cook can muster.

THE NATURE OF THE BEAST

Dove

Mourning doves are the most prolific and heavily harvested game animal in the United States. Hunters typically harvest well over ten million a year. The meat is dark, almost a deep purple, and excellent. Most of the meat is in the breast fillets, which are bite-size, but the legs can and should be cooked as well. Care must be taken to keep them from drying out. Add a fat, such as bacon, butter, or oil, and don't overcook. **White-winged doves** are a bit bigger, though the flesh is hard to distinguish from mourning doves.

Grouse

Ruffed grouse and **sharptail grouse** are the two grouse species that are most likely to be compared to chicken. The meat is white and mild relative to other grouse, and very approachable.

Blue grouse (often known as dusky and sooty grouse, depending on location) have a slightly worse reputation than ruffed grouse. This is totally undeserved. They are excellent, one of the best game birds.

Spruce grouse have a reputation for being "piney" or "gamey," which isn't entirely unwarranted. It's better to use them as an additive to dishes than the main show. They are great for dishes such as stir-fries, pâtés, and gumbo.

Sage grouse are the meatiest of the grouse species, both in terms of size and the color of the flesh. They have dark breasts; the legs are lighter colored. Some might think of the meat as strong-flavored, but it is good when properly handled.

Pheasant

Light colored and mild, the **ring-necked pheasant** is very approachable. Young birds, hatched in the spring of the year, are especially good. Birds over a year old can be tough; generally, it's a good idea to slow-cook or braise them.

Pigeon

The **common street pigeon,** a nonnative species in North America, is edible as an adult, though not really that great; the flesh can be dryish and gray. The young, when killed before they begin to fly, are called squabs. Their meat is pinkish, tender, and superb. The **band-tailed pigeon,** a pigeon that's native to the United States, is similar in taste and texture to doves.

Ptarmigan

Hunters either love or hate **willow ptarmigan, rock ptarmigan,** and **white-tailed ptarmigan**. The three species are nearly identical in taste and texture—tender, but with hints of liver. Some ptarmigan enthusiasts say they taste better in the late summer, when feeding on berries, than they do in the winter when their diet switches to willow buds and alder catkins. Put your ptarmigan into pâtés or a Chinese hot pot and you'll hopefully become a lover rather than a hater.

Wild Turkey

Wild turkeys are truly excellent when properly prepared. You can do just about anything with a wild turkey that can be done with domestic varieties. If handled carelessly, they can be tough and dry. The birds benefit from the addition of fat when cooking. Mild brines are helpful.

Partridge

The **chukar,** a nonnative bird introduced to the United States and Canada, is one of our best game birds. Light colored and with flavorful flesh, they are comparable to sharptail grouse and are highly versatile. **Hungarian partridge,** another nonnative, are a bit darker and also excellent.

Woodcock

Woodcock are a connoisseur's item. They are renowned as a delicacy, but those who expect all birds to taste like chicken will be disappointed. These birds have a wild flavor and fairly dark meat. They are best when roasted simply with some basting or a piece of bacon laid over the breasts.

Quail

All six species of quail—**bobwhite, Gambel's, valley, Mearn's, scaled,** and **mountain**—are exceptional. The meat is tender and well-flavored. The less you do to a quail, the better. They are best when plucked, brushed with seasoned butter, and grilled over a hot flame.

PLUCKING AND GUTTING A TURKEY

1

2

3

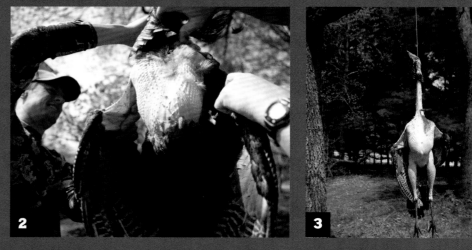

4

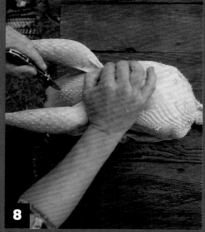

5

6

7

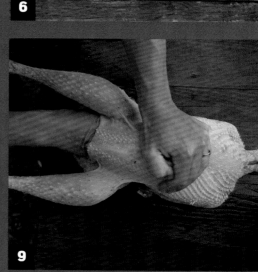

8

9

Just like plucking waterfowl and smaller upland game birds, it's worth taking the time to pluck wild turkeys. You'll appreciate the culinary rewards that result from this job, which goes a lot faster with help from your hunting buddies.

1. Start by suspending your bird by the neck at a comfortable height for plucking.

2. Pluck the breast first, then work on the legs, neck, and back.

3. Now pluck the wings out to the first joint. Beyond that point, there is very little meat, and the wing feathers are extremely hard to remove.

4. Next, cut each wing free at the elbow joint.

5. Now cut the lower legs free at the joint below the drumstick.

6. Remove the head. You can save the neck for making stock if it is not too shot up.

7. Remove the tail fan by cutting below the base of the feathers just above the vent.

8. Make a gutting incision from the end of the breastbone down to the vent. See page 116 on gutting birds.

9. Remove the innards, reserving the heart, liver, and gizzard. See "No Guts, No Glory" on page 114.

10. In the pocket where the two sides of the breast split on the upper chest, you'll find the bird's crop. The crop is a pouch where game birds store food before it is ground up by the gizzard and digested. Cut the skin around the crop to expose it.

11. Pull the crop free by hand. Around and underneath the crop, you'll find a layer of fatty material called the sponge. The sponge is foul-tasting and should be cut away from the breast. Next, wash the gut cavity, inspect the bird, and remove any pellets, embedded feathers, or bloodshot areas. See page 118 for information on singeing pin feathers.

HALVING A TURKEY

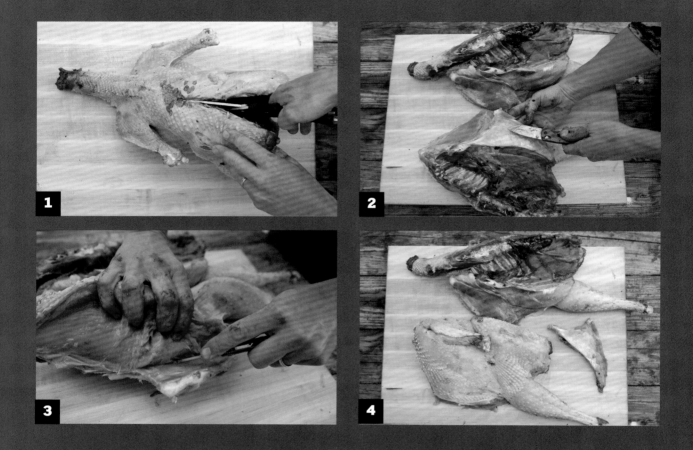

Halving large game birds like wild turkeys or geese makes packaging and transporting them home easier, especially for traveling hunters. One half of a turkey is more than enough to feed several people. By splitting your birds, you can spread out the meals and try more than one preparation.

1. You'll be cutting bone, so you'll need a sharp, sturdy pair of game shears. Start at the rear and begin cutting through the back alongside the spine toward the neck. At the base of the neck, change the angle of your cut so it runs above the shoulder and wing.

2. Now flip the bird over so the breast side is facing up. Make a cut with a knife through the breast meat along one side of the breastbone. Now, use game shears to split the bony part of the chest cavity un-derneath the breast meat. You may need to make a couple more small cuts to completely separate the bird into two halves. One side of the bird will still have the plate-like breastbone attached to the breast meat.

3. This bone is easily removed by filleting it away from the breast muscle.

4. Now you have two bone-in, skin-on halves ready for the oven, grill, or smoker.

SEPARATING TURKEY PIECES

Breaking a turkey (or any sizable game bird) down into individual cuts gives a wild game chef the ability to prepare many different types of meals. With just a single turkey, it's possible to make everything from fried turkey nuggets to brined and smoked thighs to breakfast sausage.

1. Starting with a whole plucked and gutted bird, remove the two breasts (1) first. A small "tender" (2) is connected to each breast by a membrane. You can separate the tender by pulling it away with your fingers. See page 120 for instructions on removing breasts.

2. Next, remove the legs by cutting through the upper thigh and separating the ball joint at the hip.

3. Now separate the thigh (3) and drumsticks (4) by cutting through the knee joint.

4. Remove the wings (5) by cutting through the shoulder joint.

5. The carcass will have remaining pockets of meat that can be trimmed away or left on for making soup or stock.

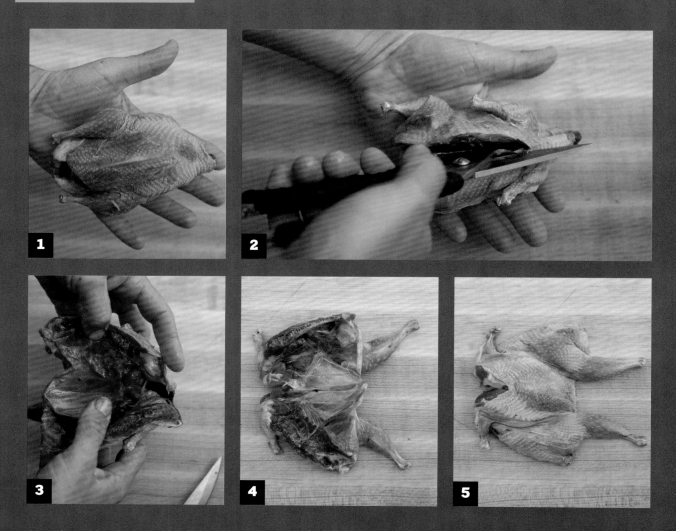

Spatchcocking is a butchering process used on game birds to butterfly, or split them open, in preparation for grilling. Spatchcocking allows the meat to cook faster and more evenly. Small birds like doves and quail lend themselves well to spatchcocking, as do medium-size birds like grouse and ducks.

1. Start with a whole gutted and plucked game bird.

2. Use a pair of game shears to split the back of the bird open from the rump to the neck.

3. Gently pull the bird apart so it can be laid out flat.

4. Wash the interior of the bird and remove any pellets, bone fragments, or damaged meat.

5. Now the bird is ready for the grill, skillet, or oven.

DOVE (OR QUAIL) JALAPEÑO POPPERS
WITH BACON-SCALLION CREAM CHEESE

SERVES 4 AS AN APPETIZER

Quail and dove hunting tend to be social affairs, and this is a social kind of recipe. Ideally, you'll pull this off with your hunting buddies within a few hours of the hunt, while you're still pumped up and excited with the thrill of being alive and well in the great outdoors. Make the bacon-scallion cream cheese ahead of time and you'll have this dish ready in a flash. If you get skunked, you can always throw it in your fridge overnight and spread it on some bagels in the morning.

Prepare a charcoal grill for direct heat.

Mix the cream cheese, mustard, garlic powder, bacon, and half of the scallions in a small bowl. Evenly stuff the jalapeños with the cream cheese. Place a strip of dove or quail on top. Sprinkle with a little salt. Place on the grill meat-side up, cover, and roast until the meat is cooked through, the peppers are lightly charred, and the cream cheese is soft, about 10 minutes. Garnish with the remaining scallions.

4 ounces cream cheese, softened

1 tablespoon yellow mustard

¼ teaspoon garlic powder

3 slices cooked bacon, chopped

2 scallions, chopped

12 to 16 jalapeño chiles, stemmed, halved lengthwise, seeds removed

12 to 16 dove breast fillets, or 6 to 8 quail breast fillets (if using quail, slice the breasts lengthwise in half as if opening a burger bun)

Kosher salt

ALSO WORKS WITH: You could use the breast meat from any upland game bird, though I'd avoid wild turkeys. Slice the breasts into sushi-size pieces and go from there.

GRILLED QUAIL LEGS WITH RANCH DRESSING

If you're wondering what to do with the quail or dove legs left from making jalapeño poppers, try this on the same grill. Take 12 to 16 dove legs (or 6 to 8 quail legs), ½ cup ranch dressing (I suggest Hidden Valley Ranch), plus more for dipping, and some vegetable oil to rub on the grates of the grill to keep the meat from sticking. Prepare a grill for direct heat. Combine the quail and ranch dressing while the grill heats. When ready, oil the grates, place the quail on the grill, and cover. Grill until lightly charred, about 2 minutes. Flip, then grill until charred and cooked through on the other side, about another 2 minutes. Serve garnished with sliced chives or scallions with additional ranch dressing for dipping.

FRIED WHOLE MOURNING DOVES

SERVES 4 AS AN APPETIZER

Peanut or vegetable oil for deep frying

1 cup fine- or medium-grind cornmeal

½ cup all-purpose flour

3 tablespoons Creole Seasoning (see page 312, or use a prepared blend such as Tony Chachere's)

8 whole mourning doves

Kosher or fine salt

1 bunch fresh curly parsley

ALSO WORKS WITH: quail

SPECIAL EQUIPMENT NEEDED:
electric deep-fryer or Dutch oven

This is the kind of recipe that prompts everyone to bust out their phones and start taking pictures. They can't help but comment on how the birds look like miniature Thanksgiving turkeys. The word *cute* gets thrown around a bunch, too. What I like about this preparation, beyond the mini-turkeyness and the cuteness, is that it utilizes the whole plucked dove so that there's no waste or leftovers. When you pull the birds out of the fryer, just give them a few minutes to cool and then you can break them apart with your fingers and devour the meat. All that remains are a few picked-clean bones.

Pour oil into an electric deep-fryer or a Dutch oven to a depth of about 3 inches, enough to submerge the doves.

Combine the cornmeal, flour, and 2 tablespoons of the Creole seasoning in a large bowl. Sprinkle each dove with a small pinch of the remaining Creole seasoning and rub it into the breast and legs. Working with one or two at a time, toss the doves into the cornmeal mixture and coat thoroughly on all surfaces. Working in two batches, fry the doves in the oil for about 4 minutes, rolling them around a few times as they cook, until all sides are browned and crispy. Remove from the oil and place them on a platter lined with paper towels to cool and immediately sprinkle with salt.

After the last batch of doves is cooked, divide the bunch of parsley into several bundles containing a few sprigs each. Drop the bundles into the hot oil and fry for 1 minute. Garnish the platter with the crispy bundles of parsley and serve as soon as the doves are cool enough to handle.

GAME BIRD TERRINE

MAKES 1 TERRINE (SERVES 18 TO 20 AS AN APPETIZER)

You could spend a week studying the distinctions between terrines and pâtés and still not fully understand it all, but here's a good primer: a terrine is a type of pâté that's cooked in a particular type of loaf-shaped pan, commonly called a terrine mold. Making a terrine is a lot of work, but it's well worth the effort when you want to make a lasting impression on your guests. See a photograph of the terrine with my charcuterie spread on page 122.

Cut the 8 ounces of breast meat into ½-inch cubes and place them in a small container that has a tight-fitting lid. Place the 1 pound of mixed boneless breast, leg, and organ meat in a separate container. Sprinkle the mixed meat with salt and pepper. Divide the juniper berries, garlic, thyme, bay leaf, brandy, and oil between the two containers and toss everything to coat. Cover and refrigerate for at least 8 hours and up to 48 hours.

Preheat the oven to 350°F. Grind the mixed meat and pork belly through a ³⁄₁₆-inch grinder plate into a large bowl. Add the ground pork, 1 tablespoon salt, a generous amount of pepper, the parsley, tarragon, and thyme and mix well again. Add the cubed breast meat, cream, and pistachios and mix well.

Line the bottom and sides of a 5-cup ceramic terrine mold or loaf pan with overlapping pancetta slices, allowing the pancetta to hang over the sides of the mold. Reserve 2 slices of the pancetta. Pack the mold with the pâté mixture. Arrange the remaining pancetta slices on top of the mixture, then fold the hanging ends of the pancetta over the pâté. Cover the mold with a sheet of heavy-duty foil and crimp tightly to seal.

Place the mold in a roasting pan and fill with boiling water to come halfway up the sides of the mold. Bake until an instant-read thermometer inserted into the center of the pâté reads 160°F, 1 to 1½ hours.

Remove the terrine from the water bath and remove the foil. Cover the top with plastic wrap, then place a terrine board or another board with 2 or 3 heavy cans on top to weight the pâté down. Let the terrine cool on a wire rack, then chill in the refrigerator overnight to let the flavors meld.

To serve, put the mold in a roasting pan of hot water for several minutes to melt the fat surrounding the pâté. Invert the pâté onto a plate and bring to room temperature. Transfer to a clean platter, then slice and serve with crusty bread and Brandied Cherries (page 318) or Spicy Pickled Red Onions (page 318).

8 ounces whole boneless upland bird breast

1 pound boneless upland bird meat (which can include a mix of legs and breasts and, if available, the hearts and livers)

Kosher salt

Freshly ground black pepper

6 juniper berries, lightly crushed

4 cloves garlic, crushed

4 sprigs fresh thyme

1 small bay leaf, torn in half

½ cup brandy or cognac

1 tablespoon extra virgin olive oil

6 ounces skinless pork belly, cut into chunks, chilled

8 ounces ground pork

¼ cup chopped fresh flat-leaf parsley

1 tablespoon chopped fresh tarragon

1 teaspoon fresh thyme leaves

½ cup heavy cream

¼ cup shelled pistachios

12 (4-inch round) slices pancetta

ALSO WORKS WITH: Virtually any combination of small game or upland birds, including hare, ptarmigan, or dove. When cooking with hare or rabbit, substitute loins for the cubed bird breast.

SPECIAL EQUIPMENT NEEDED: meat grinder with a ³⁄₁₆-inch grinder plate; 5-cup ceramic terrine mold or loaf pan; a small board or a terrine board (¾-inch board that is the precise area of the inside dimensions of your terrine), plus 2 or 3 cans of food to use as weights

WILD BIRD HOT POT

SERVES 4

MEAT

Around 4 ounces of raw meat per person (see headnote). Could be a single ingredient, such as ptarmigan or venison loin, or a combination of fish, birds, and various red meats.

SOUP STOCK

1 tablespoon vegetable oil

6 thin slices ginger

2 scallions, cut into 2-inch sections

2 to 3 dried árbol chiles (omit if you prefer less heat)

3 whole cloves

2 star anise pods

1 cinnamon stick

8 cups Blonde Game Stock (page 306) or low-sodium chicken broth

Kosher salt

DIPPING SAUCE

½ cup reduced-sodium soy sauce

2 tablespoons toasted sesame oil

4 scallions, finely chopped

Chile oil or hot sauce (optional)

SOUP INGREDIENTS

2 small carrots, cut into thin rounds

1 potato, peeled and cut into cubes

4 ounces shiitake mushrooms, stems removed

3 ounces enoki mushrooms (optional)

4 cups spinach leaves

5 to 6 napa cabbage leaves, cut into pieces

1½ pounds fresh udon noodles

The premise of hot pot, a dish said to have originated in Mongolia or Northern China during the Yuan dynasty, is simple and fun. Place a simmering pot of heavily seasoned soup broth in the center of your table and let everyone dunk in all manner of raw ingredients, from seafood and sliced red meat to leafy vegetables. It's a dream for the generalist hunter and angler who has a lot of good things in her freezer to bring to the table. Karl Malcolm, a wildlife biologist with the U.S. Forest Service, once had me over for a hot pot that featured about a dozen vegetables and fungi along with raw slices of walleye, elk, mule deer, turkey heart, turkey gizzard, and pronghorn heart arranged around a double-burner Coleman camp stove that supported twin pots of broth—one spicy with Sichuan peppers and the other kid-friendly. You can do this recipe with endless variations of wild game, though I implore you to include a sampling of upland birds in the mix if at all possible. Trust me, it's a radical departure from anything you've made before. You'll be struggling to rethink your vocabulary around the taste of game birds.

ALSO WORKS WITH: Just about anything (see headnote). To date, a thinly sliced ptarmigan breast was the best thing that I've ever added to a hot pot. The scalded yet still rare meat seemed to dissolve in my mouth like some sort of culinary magic trick. If you live in ptarmigan country, or know someone who does, I highly recommend that you try it.

FOR THE MEAT: Place pieces of meat in the freezer for 15 or 20 minutes until firm but not frozen. Slice as thin as possible and arrange on a plate. When using game birds, the skinless legs can be left whole.

FOR THE SOUP STOCK: Use a large open pot that can also be used to cook at the table. Heat it over medium heat, and then add the oil, ginger, scallions, chiles, cloves, star anise, and cinnamon and cook until fragrant, 1 to 2 minutes. Add the broth and the ptarmigan legs and wings. Bring to a boil, then reduce the heat to maintain a simmer and cook for 30 minutes, lightly skimming the surface if necessary. Season with salt, if needed; it shouldn't be too salty.

FOR THE DIPPING SAUCE: Whisk together the soy sauce, sesame oil, and scallions in a small bowl.

FOR THE SOUP INGREDIENTS: Arrange the raw ingredients on platters, keeping the vegetables, meats, and noodles separate. Have a portable stove on the dining table along with small ladles, small slotted spoons, or sieves. Divide the dipping sauce into individual bowls and have plates for each person. Allow guests to adjust the heat of their personal dipping sauce with chile oil, to their liking.

Transfer the soup stock onto the portable stove, keeping it at a simmer. Cook the bird legs, carrots, and potato first, 15 to 20 minutes, until tender. Mushrooms take about 3 minutes. Spinach and cabbage cook in 1 to 2 minutes. Thin breast meat cooks in about 1 minute. Thin slices of red meat, such as venison, can be cooked for less than a minute. The noodles take 3 to 4 minutes. Remove the cooked ingredients with a ladle or sieve and place on individual plates. Dip in the sauce and eat.

The broth at the end can be enjoyed as a soup, flavored with any remaining dipping sauce, if needed.

SPECIAL EQUIPMENT NEEDED: a large open pot that can also be used to cook at the table; portable tabletop stove

SLOW COOKER TURKEY POSOLE

SERVES 8 TO 10 (MAKES ABOUT 18 CUPS)

2 tablespoons vegetable oil

About 4 pounds turkey legs and wings, with the legs broken down into thighs and drumsticks

Kosher salt

Freshly ground black pepper

1 large white onion, finely chopped

5 cloves garlic, thinly sliced

1 to 2 quarts Blonde Game Stock (page 306) or low-sodium chicken broth

2 (16-ounce) jars salsa verde

2 (15-ounce) cans hominy, rinsed and drained

2 (4-ounce) cans diced green chiles

2 tablespoons ground cumin

1 tablespoon dried oregano

2 bay leaves

ACCOMPANIMENTS (OPTIONAL)

Chopped avocado

Thinly sliced radishes

Fresh cilantro leaves

Lime wedges

Sour cream

Tortilla chips

SPECIAL EQUIPMENT NEEDED:

slow cooker

Most turkey hunters would agree that wild turkey breasts are one of the best things to ever come from a bird. They are flavorful, versatile, easy to handle, and plenty big enough to feed a gathering of friends and family. The legs and wings of wild turkey are not as universally appreciated. The complaint is that they are prohibitively chewy. There's some merit to this, but the problem is easily remedied with the application of low and steady heat. If you're skeptical, this recipe will make you a believer. As for the accompaniments, don't worry about getting everything on the list, but do make sure to get more than a few of them. And have extra broth on hand, because the shredded turkey soaks it up like a sponge.

ALSO WORKS WITH: You could absolutely do this with pheasant legs, but it'd take several birds to get enough meat. This recipe can be halved to cook smaller meat quantities.

Heat the oil in a large skillet over medium-high heat. Sprinkle the turkey generously with salt and pepper. Working in batches, brown the turkey on all sides, 6 to 8 minutes per batch. Transfer to a platter as done. Add the onion to the skillet and cook, scraping up the browned bits from the bottom of the skillet and stirring occasionally, until the onion is softened, about 6 minutes. Add the garlic and cook for another minute. Transfer the onion and garlic to a slow cooker.

Stir in 1 quart of the stock, the salsa, hominy, chiles, cumin, oregano, bay leaves,1 teaspoon salt, and pepper to taste. Add the turkey and any accumulated juices to the slow cooker. Cover and cook on low until the turkey is very tender, about 6 hours.

Transfer the turkey to a platter and set aside until cool enough to handle. Shred the meat and discard the skin and bones. Discard the bay leaves. Return the turkey to the slow cooker and stir to combine. Taste and adjust the seasonings. If you like your posole brothier, add more hot stock and adjust the seasonings. Serve with your choice of accompaniments.

TURKEY APPLE SAUSAGE

MAKES 14 (4-OUNCE, 3-INCH-WIDE) SAUSAGES

A batch of wild turkey sausage is the best way to stretch out a bird for the maximum amount of enjoyment over the maximum amount of time. Frozen in half-pound quantities, you can get more than twenty meals out of a single bird. Turkey sausage is also a nice break for anyone who generally just makes their sausage from big game animals. The white-colored meat and radically different flavor of a turkey will get you excited about sausage making all over again. With apple, nutmeg, cinnamon, and bacon, this is a perfect blend for breakfast patties.

ALSO WORKS WITH: Bone out the carcasses of any white-fleshed upland birds to make this sausage.

Place the turkey meat and bacon on a baking sheet and place in the freezer for 30 to 45 minutes so that it becomes firm but not frozen.

Meanwhile, heat the oil in a large nonstick skillet over medium heat. Add the onion and cook, stirring, until softened, about 8 minutes. Stir in the apples and continue to cook until softened, 6 to 8 minutes. Transfer to a large plate, spread in a thin layer, and let cool in the refrigerator.

Grind the turkey and bacon into a large bowl set over a large bowl of ice. Add the cooled onions and apples, the brown sugar, thyme, salt, pepper, cinnamon, nutmeg, and lemon zest. Mix well with your hands. Pinch off a small bit of the sausage mixture and cook in a little oil in a skillet to test for seasoning. Adjust the seasonings and sweetness as necessary. Cover and refrigerate until ready to use.

Form patties with a slightly wet hand. I like to make them 3 inches in diameter because they're easy to throw on the grill or in a pan, but you can make them any size you want.

Preheat a cast-iron pan over medium heat and put a little oil in the pan. Working in batches, sear the sausage patties until browned on both sides and cooked throughout, 4 to 5 minutes per side.

2 pounds skinless, boneless turkey legs (or a mix of legs and breast), cut into 1½-inch cubes

14 ounces thick-sliced bacon, cut into large pieces

2 tablespoons olive oil, plus more as needed

1 large onion, diced

2 medium sweet-tart apples, such as Honeycrisp, peeled, cored, and cut into ¼-inch cubes

2 to 2½ tablespoons packed brown sugar

2 tablespoons fresh thyme leaves

2 tablespoons kosher salt

1½ tablespoons freshly ground black pepper

¼ teaspoon ground cinnamon

¼ teaspoon ground nutmeg

Zest of 1 lemon

SPECIAL EQUIPMENT NEEDED:

meat grinder

Note: To freeze, stuff the bulk sausage meat into poly meat bags in ½-pound or 1-pound quantities, depending on how many people you typically serve.

GRILLED GROUSE
WITH CAYENNE BUTTER

SERVES 2 TO 4

CAYENNE BUTTER

2 small cloves garlic

1 cup (2 sticks) unsalted butter, softened

1½ teaspoons cayenne pepper

¼ teaspoon kosher salt

Zest of 1 small lemon (about 2 teaspoons)

Juice of ½ small lemon (about 1 tablespoon)

GROUSE

2 spatchcocked grouse (ruffed or sharptail)

Kosher salt

Vegetable oil

ALSO WORKS WITH: Any white-fleshed game bird up to the size of a pheasant, and also squab. (In case you're wondering, a squab is a baby street pigeon. Check out my book *The Scavenger's Guide to Haute Cuisine* if you want to get the full scoop on that subject.) If you're using quail for this recipe, plan on 2 to 4 birds per person. A ruffed or sharptail grouse can feed 1 to 2 people; a mature pheasant is plenty for 2 people.

SPECIAL EQUIPMENT NEEDED:

food processor

This is a flexible preparation that can be used on a wide variety of game birds. It's mind-blowingly good for ruffed and sharptail grouse (also sooty and dusky grouse), and I've used it with great success on everything ranging from squab to quail to pheasant. You'll want your birds to be plucked and spatch-cocked. The skin on a grouse is thin and delicate, so do the plucking as gently as possible so you don't tear it. As for spatchcocking, I recognize that it might seem like a complicated process. But it's really very easy, I promise, and you'll get the hang of it quickly. (See page 154 for spatchcocking instructions.) The cayenne butter that's described here is meant to be friendly and approachable in terms of heat. Feel free to crank it up to your liking.

FOR THE CAYENNE BUTTER: Put the garlic in a mini food processor and process until chopped. Break the butter up into chunks and add to the bowl of the processor. Add the cayenne, salt, lemon zest, and lemon juice and process until smooth. Scrape onto 2 pieces of parchment paper, roll into logs, and refrigerate until firm.

FOR THE GROUSE: Rinse the birds in cold water and pat them thoroughly dry with paper towels. Give the birds a sprinkling of salt on both sides and then brush them with a light coating of oil. Place them breast-side down on a medium flame grill and close the lid. Cook for 6 to 7 minutes, periodically checking the birds. A light bit of charring on the underside is good, but adjust the flame if you see any burning or blackening. Flip the birds over, baste the charred underside with the cayenne butter, and cook breast-side down for an additional 3 or 4 minutes. Flip the birds again, so that they're breast-side up, and baste the breasts with cayenne butter. Go sparingly so that you're not creating oil fires from the dripping butter. Let them cook for another 2 to 3 minutes, basting every minute or so. Be careful not to overcook. When you can prick the thickest part of the breast and the juices bubble up as a clear oily liquid, it's time to pull them. Another indicator that they're done is that the breast feels firm, like a cooked chicken breast. Baste them one last time while they're still piping hot. Serve with a simple side salad dressed with Basic Vinaigrette on page 315.

SPLIT AND SMOKED TURKEY
WITH BBQ SAUCE

SERVES A CROWD

Over the past few years I've been splitting most of my wild turkeys in half by cutting them down the spine. (See page 152 for instructions.) This particular recipe is well suited for a bird butchered in such a way, as it fits handily inside a pellet grill or on the rack of a smoker. The brine makes the bird juicy with a bit of salty sweetness, and the smoke adds a rustic woodsiness. When you're making this, you could cover the bird in strips of bacon if you're a bacon kind of person. A pound should be plenty. Yet another option is to make one of the compound butters on page 323. Chill the butter and slice it thin, then place a liberal scattering between the breast meat and the skin.

FOR THE BRINE: Combine the water, salt, brown sugar, peppercorns, and bay leaves in a large pot and bring to a boil. Remove from the heat and let cool to room temperature, then place the brine in the fridge to cool. Add the split turkey to the brine and brine for 12 to 24 hours.

Remove the split bird from the brine and rinse under cold water. Set on baking sheets and pat dry. Discard the brining liquid. Rub the outside of the bird well with oil and sprinkle generously with salt and pepper. Rub the BBQ rub, if using, evenly all over the bird.

Prepare a smoker to 275°F following the manufacturer's instructions. Use any mild flavored wood (such as cherry, apple, or pecan). It's smart to fill a foil roasting pan with an inch of water to act as a drip pan beneath the bird.

Set the turkey halves cut-side down on the smoker rack(s). After about 1 hour of smoking, begin basting with the melted butter (or substitute Clayton Saunders's BBQ Sop; page 313). Smoke the turkey to an internal temperature of 150 to 155°F (about 30 minutes per pound). The turkey can be carved and served right away, finished with BBQ sauce, or stored as described below.

To finish with BBQ sauce: If using a combination grill/smoker, raise the heat to high and baste the turkey halves with the BBQ sauce, flipping occasionally to caramelize the sauce and acquire a little char. If you just have a straight-up smoker, begin basting the turkey when the internal temperature reaches 150 to 155°F.

Serve warm with your favorite sides. Store cooled leftovers in vacuum-sealed bags in the refrigerator for up to 10 days or in the freezer for up to 6 months.

BRINE

1 gallon water

1 cup kosher salt

1 cup packed brown sugar

10 black peppercorns

3 bay leaves

8 pounds ice (1 gallon water)

TURKEY

1 turkey, split in half down the spine with breast plates removed

Olive oil

Kosher salt

Freshly ground black pepper

¼ cup BBQ Rub (optional; page 313)

1 cup (2 sticks) salted butter, melted

1 recipe BBQ Sauce (page 314)

1 recipe Cornbread (optional; page 326)

1 recipe Coleslaw (optional; page 333)

ALSO WORKS WITH: Try the same preparation with pheasants and grouse, though it's better to spatchcock those smaller birds rather than split them in half so that you're cooking the whole thing all at once.

SPECIAL EQUIPMENT NEEDED:
smoker

ROASTED WILD TURKEY

SERVES 6 TO 8

1 whole wild turkey

2 heads garlic

4 sticks (1 pound) unsalted butter, at room temperature

1½ tablespoons dried thyme

Zest and juice of 2 lemons (reserve the rinds)

Kosher salt

Freshly ground black pepper

2 carrots, cut into large chunks

1 Vidalia onion, quartered

4 sprigs fresh rosemary

4 sprigs fresh sage

6 thick-cut slices smoked bacon (optional)

ALSO WORKS WITH: Use this same method for roasting whole upland birds such as pheasants and grouse. Cooking times will need to be adjusted accordingly.

I like to point out to people that there's no solid evidence suggesting that the pilgrims actually ate wild turkeys for the first Thanksgiving meal. They used the word *turkey* as a catchall for large edible birds, and some historians suggest that it's more likely they were eating waterfowl. Either way, the tradition of roasting a whole turkey for Thanksgiving is here to stay. The trouble for turkey hunters is that roasting whole wild birds can be tricky. If you don't take the necessary precautions, you can end up with a dry, leathery mess. My brother Matt has long recognized this problem, and he began searching for a solution by providing wild turkeys to his friend Shannon Harper, a private chef at a Montana dude ranch. With a little trial and error, Shannon hit upon the ultimate roasted wild turkey recipe. This is your best path to the perfect Thanksgiving.

Bring the bird to room temperature 1 hour before roasting. Rinse the bird with cold water, inside and out. Then dry it well—inside and out—with a clean kitchen towel. (Ideally, let the bird sit in your fridge uncovered overnight to fully dry. This helps to get crispier, caramelized, and more flavorful skin.)

Preheat the oven to 350°F.

Peel and mince 2 cloves garlic, then mash into the butter along with the thyme, lemon zest, and lemon juice. Sprinkle the bird inside and out with salt and pepper. Cut the remaining garlic heads in half horizontally and stuff them into the turkey's cavity along with the lemon rinds, carrots, onion, rosemary, and sage. Smear about half of the herbed butter all over the exterior of the bird. Leave no part uncovered—even the pope's nose. Put the remaining butter in a saucepan or bowl on top of the stove to melt so you can baste the turkey while it roasts. If you choose to use the bacon, drape it over the turkey's breast with each slice slightly overlapping the next. Put the turkey in the oven. After 45 minutes, baste with the melted herb butter. After 30 more minutes, crank the oven to 375°F and baste again. Baste with the butter every 20 minutes until the butter is used up or the internal temperature of the turkey reaches 160°F. To test the internal temperature of the bird, insert the thermometer into the fattest part of the thigh. For accurate measurement, be sure that the probe is not touching the bone.

After the turkey is fully cooked, place it on a cutting board or platter, cover loosely with foil, and let it rest for 20 minutes before carving.

ROAST PHEASANT
WITH ROOT VEGETABLES AND RED CURRANT, PORT, AND RED WINE SAUCE

SERVES 4

ALSO WORKS WITH: Try this with grouse or chukars. These smaller birds will require shorter cooking times to hit a temperature of 160°F.

When roasting whole pheasants, it's best if you're working with young birds that were born in the spring of the same year that you killed them. These are more tender than older birds and easier to cook to perfection. (They are also more abundant; typically, young birds will far outnumber older birds.) Thankfully, it's easy to age a pheasant by looking at its wing feathers. Stretch the bird's wing away from the body and look at the primary feathers. If the three outermost primaries are shorter than the rest, it's a bird-of-the-year. If the outer primaries are fully grown, it's probably gonna take some time in a slow cooker in order for that bird to reach its full potential as tablefare. You'll see that this recipe calls for some brining, which, in my opinion, is generally a good idea when it comes to roasting upland birds. The challenge is to fight dryness, and brines help you win that battle.

FOR THE PHEASANTS: Add the pheasants to the brine and brine for 4 to 8 hours. Remove the pheasants from the brine and pat dry. Bring the birds to room temperature for 30 minutes. Preheat the oven to 450°F.

Stuff each pheasant with a lemon wedge, onion wedge, and 2 thyme sprigs. Rub oil or butter all over the birds, then sprinkle with salt and pepper. Place the pheasants in a large, heavy oven-safe skillet.

FOR THE VEGETABLES: Arrange the mushrooms, potatoes, parsnips, and onion on a baking sheet and drizzle all over with the oil. Sprinkle generously with salt and pepper. Gently toss the vegetables, then spread out in a single layer.

Roast the pheasant and the vegetables for 15 minutes.

Add the stock to the pheasant pan. Reduce the heat to 350°F and roast until the juices run clear and an instant-read thermometer inserted into the thickest part of the thigh reads 155°F, about 20 more minutes. Continue to roast the vegetables until tender. Remove from the oven and tent with foil. Remove the pheasants from the skillet and transfer to a platter. Tent loosely with foil.

FOR THE SAUCE: Place a medium skillet over medium-high heat. Add the butter and any juices accumulated from the roasting pan, the thyme, garlic, and shallot to the skillet and cook, stirring, for 3 minutes. Add the port and red wine, scraping up the browned bits from the bottom of the pan, and cook until the liquid is reduced by half, about 10 minutes. Add the stock to the pan and continue to reduce until thickened, 8 to 10 more minutes. Discard the thyme, garlic, and shallot. Stir in the preserves and season with salt and pepper. (This sauce can be used for any roasted meat recipe.)

Carve the pheasants and serve with the vegetables and sauce.

Tip: Try pairing this recipe with the rich and elegant Cauliflower Puree (page 333).

PHEASANTS

2 young pheasants

1 recipe Enriched Brine (page 311)

2 small lemon wedges

2 small onion wedges (can be taken from the roasted veggies below)

4 sprigs fresh thyme

1 tablespoon olive oil or 2 tablespoons softened butter

Kosher salt

Freshly ground black pepper

1 cup Blonde Game Stock (page 306) or low-sodium chicken broth

VEGETABLES

8 ounces cremini mushrooms, halved, or wild mushrooms, cut into large pieces

8 ounces micro potatoes, scrubbed and patted dry

2 parsnips, cut into 1½- to 2-inch pieces, fatter ends quartered

1 red onion, cut into wedges with the core end intact

¼ cup extra virgin olive oil

Kosher salt

Freshly ground black pepper

SAUCE

1 tablespoon unsalted butter

3 sprigs fresh thyme

1 clove garlic, crushed

1 shallot, halved

½ cup tawny port

½ cup red wine

¾ cup Blonde Game Stock (page 306), Brown Game Stock (page 305), or store-bought low-sodium chicken broth

2 tablespoons red currant or lingonberry preserves or jelly

Kosher salt and freshly ground black pepper

WHITE WINE GROUSE OR PHEASANT
WITH BACON AND POTATOES

SERVES 4 TO 6

About 4 pounds grouse or pheasant, separated into legs and breast fillets

Kosher salt

Freshly ground black pepper

3 tablespoons extra virgin olive oil

2 tablespoons unsalted butter

3 medium carrots, sliced into ⅓-inch-thick rounds

1 onion, sliced into thin wedges

1 head garlic, cloves separated, peeled, and smashed

2 sprigs fresh thyme

1 pound waxy baby potatoes (about twelve 1-inch potatoes)

8 ounces mixed wild mushrooms, tough stems trimmed, halved if large

2 pieces thick-cut bacon, halved lengthwise, cut into ¾-inch pieces

¾ cup dry white wine

2 cups Brown Game Stock (page 305) or low-sodium chicken broth

5 sprigs fresh flat-leaf parsley, plus ¼ cup chopped, for serving

1 tablespoon fresh lemon juice

Crusty bread for serving

This recipe turns pretty much any collection of game birds into a delicious and hearty meal that's perfect for cold winter days. The thing to keep in mind here is that not all game birds were created equal when it comes to tenderness. Here we're calling for an hour of cooking time in addition to the searing process, but for something like the thighs of an older pheasant or the thighs of sage grouse, you might find that it takes up to ninety minutes or so of cooking to get the results you want. The only drawback to a longer cooking time is that your potatoes might get a little too soft while you wait for the bird to become just right. But I'm telling you, I'd rather eat soft taters than tough bird.

ALSO WORKS WITH: Any large, white-fleshed upland game bird will work here. Also a good way to prepare cottontail rabbit or squirrel, though be mindful of cooking times. It might take some extra time to tenderize a rabbit.

Preheat the oven to 375°F.

Sprinkle the grouse well on all sides with salt and pepper.

Heat the oil in a heavy-bottomed low-sided braiser or roasting pan over medium-high heat. Sear the pieces of bird in 3 batches until well browned on all sides, 8 to 10 minutes per batch, reducing the heat slightly if the oil starts to get too brown. Remove the browned pieces to a plate.

Drain and discard all but 2 tablespoons of the oil in the pan, or add more oil to equal 2 tablespoons. Add the butter, carrots, onion, garlic, and thyme and cook, stirring, until the carrots and onion begin to soften and brown, about 5 minutes. Add the potatoes, mushrooms, and bacon pieces and sprinkle with a pinch of salt. Reduce the heat to medium, cook for about 3 minutes, until the bacon starts to render, then cover the pan and cook, stirring occasionally, to crisp the bacon, 8 to 10 minutes.

Pour the wine into the pan, raise the heat to medium-high, scrape the browned bits, and let simmer to reduce by half, 2 to 3 minutes. Return the grouse and any accumulated juices to the pan. Pour in the stock and bring to a boil. Add the parsley sprigs and transfer to the oven. Bake uncovered until the meat is tender and the potatoes are cooked through. It'll take an hour, maybe a bit more, depending on the bird. Halfway through the cooking time, stir to submerge the exposed meat into the sauce. If there isn't enough liquid to come halfway up the sides of the meat, add more stock. When the meat is tender and the potatoes are cooked, remove and discard the thyme and parsley sprigs. Taste the sauce and add more salt or pepper if needed. Finish with the lemon juice.

Transfer to a platter or shallow soup dishes, spoon the sauce and vegetables over the meat, and garnish with the chopped parsley. Serve with crusty bread on the side.

POTPIES AND TURNOVERS

Turn leftovers into mini potpies or turnovers with one batch of the Basic Pie Dough (page 324) or thawed, store-bought puff pastry. To prepare, shred leftover meat and discard the bones. Separate an egg and beat both parts separately with a splash of water. Preheat the oven to 425°F. **For Potpies:** Spoon the shredded meat, vegetables, and sauce into individual ramekins. Roll out the dough and cut rounds 1 inch larger than the diameter of the ramekins. Brush the tops of the ramekins with egg-white wash, top with dough rounds, pinch to adhere, and make a half slit in the dough to release steam. Brush with egg-yolk wash. Bake until golden brown, about 20 minutes. **For Turnovers:** Roll the dough into a large rectangle. Cut into 4 or 6 even squares. Brush two adjacent edges of each square with egg-white wash. Spoon 2 tablespoons of shredded meat, vegetables, and sauce mixture off-center in each square. Fold the dough in half, folding the egg-washed corner over the filling to meet the diagonally opposite corner. Seal with a fork. Make a half slit in the dough to release steam. Brush with egg-yolk wash. Bake on a parchment paper–lined baking sheet until golden brown on top and bottom, about 20 minutes.

05 FRESHWATER FISH

INTRODUCTION

One of my earliest fishing memories is of catching a largemouth bass off my neighbor's dock on Middle Lake in Michigan when I was four years old. I was all alone and unsure how to handle the fish, so I grabbed it by the bottom lip and ran down the beach toward home. We had a holding pen in the water next to our own dock, and I wanted to drop my fish in it and then go find my dad so that he could help me clean it. While I fumbled with the lid of the holding pen, the fish slipped out of my grasp and splashed safely back into the lake. It vanished with a thrust of its tail, and I screamed with all my might. The sense of loss is burned into my memory. I was still crying about it later that night while taking my bath. In an effort to make me feel better, my dad told me that there are anglers who actually catch fish and then let them go on purpose, just for the hell of it. This was the first I'd ever heard about catch-and-release fishing. I am only slightly less suspicious of it now as I was then.

Not that I actually disagree with catch-and-release. In overexploited fisheries, it can be a way for people to continue to enjoy the sport of fishing without having a deleterious effect on the resource. But my personal take is this: why bother catching fish that you don't want to eat when there are so many great-tasting and underutilized fish resources swimming around out there? After all, that's what makes fishing so much better than silly games like golf. Not only is it more fun, it rewards you with dinner.

Of all the classifications of wild game discussed in this book, freshwater fish are the most readily available. In the United States, I don't think it's really possible to be much more than an hour's drive away from some sort of worthwhile freshwater fishing opportu-

nity. I've spent at least six months or more living in Michigan, Rhode Island, New York, Wyoming, Montana, California, Alaska, and Washington, and in each place I've uncovered freshwater fishing opportunities close to home that paid off with more than a few memorable meals. That several of these places lie just outside of New York City—one of them is actually *in* New York City—testifies to just how abundant the resources really are. As for proximity, I once rented a house where I could catch American eels from my living room couch. That's not a joke.

As a nomadic and food-obsessed freshwater angler, I've adopted the strategies of a generalist. While some guys have a passion for a specific species of fish, say smallmouth bass or even carp, I have a passion for catching the best-tasting fish that happens to be most catchable at the moment. If that turns out to be giant eight-pound walleyes that would make the cover of a fishing magazine, that's great. If it happens to be some dinky five-inch bluegills that most anglers wouldn't even be bothered to bait a hook for, that's also great. My openness has rewarded me with a vast amount of food experiences. So far I've caught and eaten more than sixty species of freshwater fish in the United States alone. I'm happy to be passing along so much of what I've learned.

Some fishermen might be surprised or outraged to see that I've included salmon here in the freshwater section. There are a few reasons for this. First off, Atlantic salmon and several species of Pacific salmon have been established to varying degrees of success in entirely freshwater ecosystems such as the Great Lakes. There are also populations of salmon that have become separated from the ocean through naturally occurring events, and they manage quite nicely without ever touching the sea. What's more, the ocean-based populations of salmon cannot complete their life cycles without freshwater. They might build their bodies through the utilization of marine resources, but they begin their lives in freshwater and they end their lives in freshwater. Thinking of that, I can't help but see

parallels with my own life. I was born on the freshwater of Middle Lake, but nowadays I can look out my bedroom window and see the Pacific. If I were to grow old and die back where I started, on that same beach where I caught and accidentally released my first bass, I'd feel pretty damn good about things.

THE NATURE OF THE BEAST

Salmon

King salmon, or **chinook,** are the most highly prized of all salmon. They are big fish with excellent fat and beautiful red flesh that flakes easily. They can be used for any salmon recipe, including sushi, and are perfect for grilling. As with all salmon, kings that live their entire life cycle in freshwater, such as those from the Great Lakes, are not nearly as good as saltwater specimens. They are colored more like trout, are less fatty, and have a flatter, weaker taste.

Sockeye salmon, or **reds,** are excellent. Their flesh is firm and deep red. They can be quite fatty ahead of their spawning runs, especially populations that spawn in large rivers where they need to fuel a long migratory journey with stored fat reserves. They are good for any salmon preparation, though not nearly as popular as king salmon for sushi. They are widely used as a canning fish, which is a reflection of their abundance.

Coho salmon, or **silvers,** are comparable to kings; they are smaller and a bit dryer (less fatty) but still excellent. Use them for anything you'd use a king for, though they're not widely utilized for sushi. As with all salmon, the roe is excellent.

Pink salmon, or **humpies,** are not nearly as popular among anglers as kings, sockeyes, or silvers. Their flesh is not as firm, it doesn't flake quite the same way, and the color is more pinkish than red. They also have a reputation for turning mushy in the freezer. Because they generally spawn close to the coast, they do not pack on as much fat as the long-range migrators. Despite all that, pink salmon are still good. If you like trout, you'll love pinks. They're great for frying, smoking, and canning, and fresh fish are perfectly good when baked or on the grill.

Chum salmon, or **dog salmon,** have the lowest reputation of them all. The flesh is less vibrantly colored and they have low fat reserves. An exception would be chum salmon from Alaska's Yukon River, which have a better reputation thanks to a higher fat content. They're great for smoking, but don't be afraid to throw one on the grill to see what you think. There are plenty of people who love eating chums.

Wild **Atlantic salmon** are hard to come by (the stuff in stores comes from aquaculture facilities), but they are excellent. They're good for everything, including raw preparations.

Catfish

Channel catfish are the most widely eaten catfish. They are readily available to anglers and are raised in great abundance by aquaculture facilities. They are as good as anything that swims in freshwater.

Flathead catfish are also excellent. People who are most familiar with the fish sometimes prefer it over channel catfish. The belly meat on flatheads is highly prized; it has a denser texture than the rest of the fish. With flatheads, careful trimming is essential. The fat has to go.

While rare, **blue catfish** are regarded by some as the best of all catfish. Their flesh is beautifully white, firm, and very mild. Get rid of all the fat; it has an off-putting flavor.

The various **bullheads** (**brown, black,** and **yellow**) are generally smaller than catfish but all of them are good when trimmed.

Trout

The ubiquitous **rainbow trout** is the benchmark that all other trout are compared to. It's not that they're the best tasting, it's just that they're the most familiar. The best specimens are around fourteen inches or under; they can be used for any trout preparation. Bigger fish can be filleted and smoked.

Steelhead are an anadromous species of rainbow trout. Saltwater specimens are excellent, on par with good salmon.

Cutthroat trout are excellent, comparable to rainbow trout.

Brown trout have the weakest reputation as food. The flavor can be flatter and muddier, and the texture is a bit mushier. Still, small specimens can be used for anything that you do with trout. Smoke the bigger ones, though it certainly won't hurt you to bake or grill them.

Brook trout (actually a species of char) have beautiful pink flesh and are quite good. Many anglers regard them as the best trout. They are good for anything that can be done with trout.

Lake trout, another species of char, are not universally appreciated. They are an oily fish, but the oil is not as good as salmon oil. The flesh has a pale color, and the meat may strike you as tasting "fishy" or with a subtle hint of fish oil. However, they should be treated seriously by cooks. They are excellent when smoked; the finished product is similar to smoked salmon. They are also good when baked, especially with sauces and a good squeeze of lemon. **Arctic grayling** have delicate white flesh that is prone to quick spoilage. Fish should be chilled upon catching and eaten as fresh as possible. They do not freeze well.

Whitefish are closely related to trout and they have many similar attributes. Like trout, their flesh is mild, a bit oily (in a good way), and flakes easily. **Lake whitefish** are the best, hands down. They can be baked, broiled, grilled, you name it. They are truly exceptional. **Sheefish** are not widely available, but they are also superb. **Mountain whitefish** and **round whitefish** are not as versatile but still deserve respect. They are great when smoked. Same with **bloater chubs,** which are actually a small species of whitefish. When smoked, these fish are extremely popular and demand a high price in commercial markets.

Panfish

Many panfish, including **yellow perch, crappies,** and the various **sunfish (bluegills, pumpkinseeds, redears, redbreasts,** and so on) can all be treated pretty much the same way. They are excellent. The fillets are boneless, and the white flesh is mild and flakes easily. Scale them rather than skin them, as much of their flavor lies in the skin. Soak for a few hours in ice water and then fillet.

Rock bass are a less desirable type of panfish. Still edible, but their flesh tends to be mushy and the flavor isn't as good.

While not aligned through taxonomy, there are a number of large, popular game fish with fairly similar flesh that can be used in similar ways—with a few caveats.

Pike, Bass, and Walleye

Walleye are one of the best freshwater fish. Mild, firm, and with white flesh, they can be used for almost everything and rival many saltwater fish in quality. **Sauger,** a close relative to the walleye, are a bit mushier. They are still good, but not as good as walleye.

Northern pike and **pickerel** have excellent flesh—white, firm, and well-flavored. The problem is the bones, which can be dealt with through careful filleting, or you can get rid of the bones by pickling or canning the fish.

Smallmouth bass, especially smaller fish in the range of twelve to fifteen inches, are as good as walleye when pulled from cold water. **Largemouth bass** are not nearly as good as smallmouth bass. They taste muddier, some call it "weedy," and the flesh isn't as firm. It helps if you soak the skinned fillets overnight in milk.

Sturgeon and Paddlefish

Paddlefish and sturgeon have enough similarities in life history and food quality that they can be treated almost interchangeably by a cook. **White sturgeon** of the western United States and **lake sturgeon** from the eastern half of the country are both highly regarded. Thanks to its dense, meaty quality, sturgeon steaks are often described as a combination of pork chops and fish. Their caviar is highly prized.

Shovelnose sturgeon are smaller, with a lower yield per pound of body weight. The meat is good, though it has to be carefully trimmed. Use a small, sharp fillet knife to trim away all fat and red tissue. You want the glistening white meat and nothing else.

Paddlefish can be compared to sturgeon; their flesh is firm, white, and meaty, though it must be carefully trimmed of fat and red tissue. The caviar is superb. Sturgeon and paddlefish can all be smoked.

Rough Fish

Rough fish is a big, broad category. Sometimes known as non-game fish, these are all species that are commonly hunted with bowfishing equipment.

Common carp are more or less despised by American sportsman, though in other countries they are a staple source of protein. It all depends on what you're used to. If you're used to bluegills and walleye, carp aren't that good. They are edible, however, and maybe even decent, if properly handled. Try pickling and smoking them, or better, make fish cakes.

The many species of suckers commonly encountered by anglers and bowfishers—**longnose, white,** the various **redhorse** and **buffalo** species—are all decent. The trouble is that they're bony, so you have to deal with that. The best specimens come from cold water during the winter and spring months.

Gar are one of the best rough fish. **Shortnose gar** are too small to mess with, but **longnose gar** are worth the effort. You need a pair of tinsnips to get through the skin; the backstraps hold all the meat. **Alligator gar,** which grow to enormous sizes, are a popular food item when prepared as a type of fish cake known as a gar balls.

While **bowfin,** or **dogfish,** are edible, it's a challenging meal. They are seldom eaten. The flesh has a strong taste and a poor texture. Folks who can tolerate them claim that they have to be eaten immediately after they die, as the flesh turns to mush very quickly.

Baitfish

Herrings, shads, smelts, and mooneyes can justifiably be lumped together thanks to their collective status as "baitfish" that can also be eaten. The rainbow smelt is extremely popular everywhere it can be found. It can be fried whole and eaten, bones and all. Same with longfin smelt. Candlefish, or eulachons (sometimes spelled hooligans), are a much oilier species of smelt; their flesh is less firm and has hints of fish oil. It's best if you render them out before eating.

The **American shad** and **hickory shad** are both edible, and both are very bony. The American shad has a much better reputation, because it's a bigger, meatier fish and it's easier to deal with the bones. The roe of an American shad is a true delicacy.

Mooneyes and **goldeyes** are both good smoked, though they are bony and a bit mushy. Mooneyes, being a bit bigger, are better.

Eels and Eel-like fish

Despite appearances that might be unappetizing to many people, the eels and eel-like freshwater fish are actually very good. The **American eel** is phenomenal as a smoked fish; there's a thriving commercial market for the product. It's also good pickled.

Burbot, or **lawyer,** are one of the finest freshwater fish. People call them poor man's lobster, as a popular preparation is to boil the fish and eat it with drawn butter. The **snakehead,** a nonnative species in the United States, is also highly esteemed. The flesh is firm, white, and mild.

SCALING AND FILLETING PANFISH

The term *panfish* encompasses a wide range of small freshwater fish such as yellow perch, crappie, and various sunfish species. They're usually easy to catch, bag limits are liberal, and there's no better choice for a fish fry. All panfish can be scaled using the same method. You can skip the scaling step if you'd rather remove the skin, but the skin contains much of the fish's flavor and it crisps nicely when cooked.

1. Commercially produced fish scalers work well, as do homemade scalers made from bottle caps or spoons with a hand-sharpened edge.

2. Scale both sides of the fish with a scraping motion from the tail to the gill plate. Move the tool in the opposite direction of the scales on the fish, so they are lifted from the fish's skin. Thorough scaling makes for a more palatable meal.

3. Fillet panfish as you would any other round fish, using a small fillet knife with a flexible blade. (See coho salmon on page 190 or mahimahi on page 228.) Use the carcass and head (minus the gills) for fish stock (page 309).

FILLETING SALMON

1

2

3

4

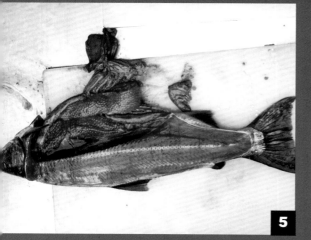

5

6

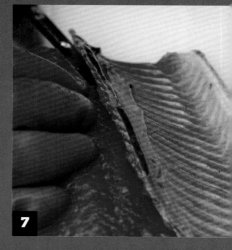

7

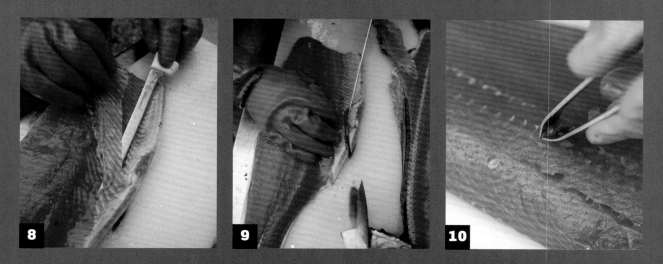

Coho, or silver salmon, spend most of their lives in the ocean, but they begin and end their lives in freshwater, just like all species of Pacific salmon. The process of filleting any salmon is the same for trout, walleye, and many other species of freshwater and saltwater fish. You'll be cutting through skin, bone, and flesh, so use a sharp fillet knife.

1. Start by making an incision through the belly from the anal vent up to the gills.

2. Next, make a cut behind the head and around the pectoral fin that meets your first incision through the belly. The depth of this cut should reach, but not sever, the spine.

3. At the cut behind the head, orient your knife blade toward the tail. Hold the head with one hand, and with the other, begin removing the fillet. Keep your knife running along the spine and just above the centerline of the back and dorsal fin.

4. Continue this cut all the way to the tail until the fillet is removed.

5. With one fillet removed, the guts can now be pulled out of the way. Consider saving the eggs, or roe, for making salt-cured salmon caviar. Now, flip the fish over and remove the second fillet.

6. With both fillets removed, there is very little meat left on the carcass. You can use the carcass for stock and save the collars on large salmon. See how to remove fish collars on page 231.

7. The rib bones in the belly portion of each fillet need to be removed. In the thick, middle part of the fillet, slide your fillet knife just under the ribs.

8. Make very shallow cuts downward toward the belly of the fillet to slice the ribs free.

9. Cut away the ventral fin on the belly of each fillet.

10. Next, you'll need to remove the line of pin bones. They are hard to see, but you can find them by running your fingers over the upper half of the fillet. Pull them free with fish tweezers or needle-nose pliers. Rinse and leave the skin on the fillets. The skin adds a layer of protection in the freezer and holds the fillet together on the grill.

FILLETING AND TRIMMING CATFISH

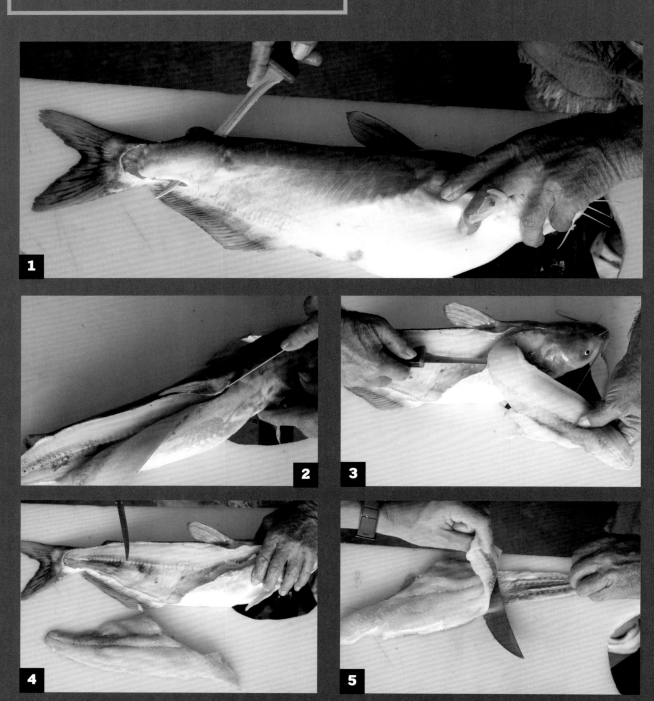

From one-pound bullheads to five-pound channels to blues and flatheads weighing well over fifty pounds, catfish are available to just about every fisherman in the country. They are also a universal favorite when it comes to fried fish platters. When dealing with catfish, it's absolutely necessary to remove dark meat and fat from your fillets.

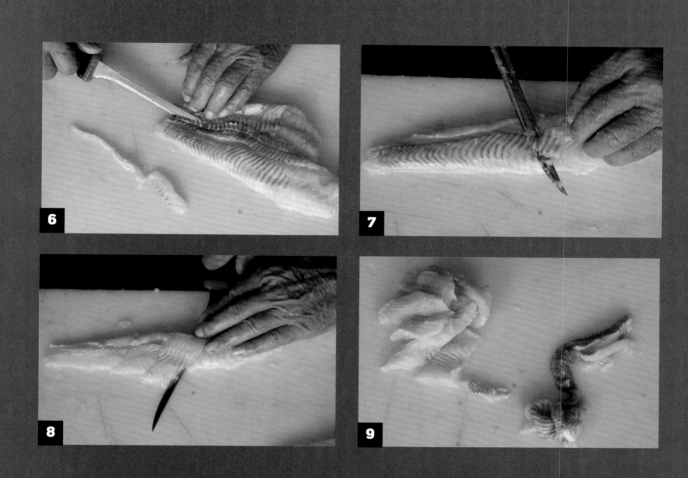

1. Start at the tail and cut the back half of the fillet free to the anal vent.

2. At the halfway point, cut the top of the fillet free along the back up to the head.

3. The belly area is bony, fatty, and has little meat. From the anal vent, angle your cut up and forward around the rib cage and gut cavity.

4. Once the fillet is removed, it should be almost triangular in shape.

5. To remove the tough, thick skin from catfish fillets, start at the tail and cut between the skin and the flesh. A pair of catfish skinning pliers gives you a good grip and makes this job much easier.

6. The side of the fillet that was attached to the skin will have a lot of dark, fatty flesh on the surface. This can give catfish a muddy, fishy taste. Take the time to trim this away from the fillet.

7. Cut each fillet in half at the line that separates the upper and lower muscle groups. Continue to trim each halved fillet until you are left with just firm white meat.

8. Now cut the fillets into nugget-size chunks that are suitable for the deep fryer. Small catfish fillets can be left whole.

9. Discard the trimmings and thoroughly rinse the fish in cold water.

GUTTING A TROUT

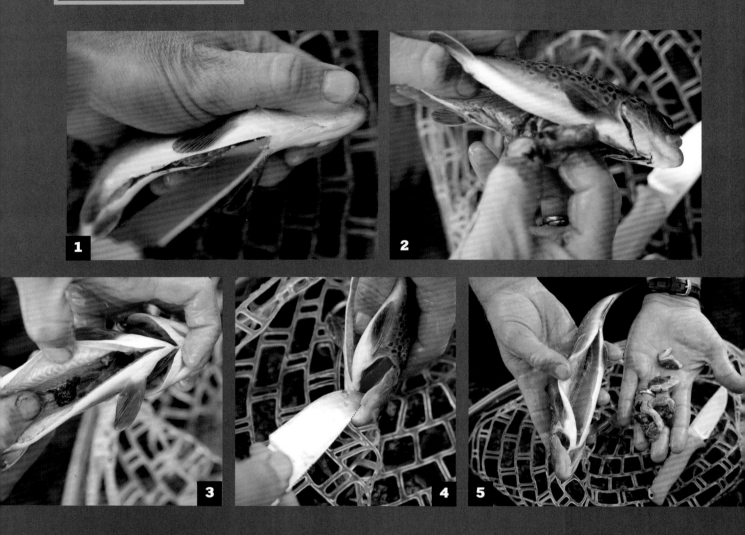

Cooking a freshly caught trout over a campfire is one of life's great pleasures. But first, you'll need to gut it. Gutting fish is fast and simple, and the process is the same on just about every species of fish. This process is similar for many species of fish, though you'll want to scale fish that have large scales. See page 189 on scaling panfish.

1. Start by making a gutting incision from the anal vent up to the gills.

2. Now pull the guts forward toward the gills. They should pull free by hand on smaller fish, but you may need to cut them free at the gills on large fish.

3. Most fish have a dark bloodline that runs the length of the spine. Use your thumb to scrape this away.

4. Now make a cut behind the lower jaw to loosen up the gills. Pull the gills free.

5. Give the fish a quick rinse, inside and out.

SCORING FISH

Tip: Score fish by making vertical cuts in the fillets. Cut through the skin and into the meat without cutting completely through the fillet. Scoring is a smart move if you're going to be grilling or frying whole fish. The seasonings will penetrate the fillet better and the fish will cook more evenly without curling up.

SALMON GRAVLAX

SERVES 4 TO 6

I love smoked salmon as much as the next fisherman, but it's a shame that more anglers don't experiment with other forms of cured salmon. Gravlax is a great place to start, because it's easier than making smoked salmon and the end product is entirely different. While smoked salmon can make you feel like you need to rinse with a glug of mouthwash, this gravlax tastes clean and lively. The key here is to use absolutely fresh salmon, not frozen. Pull it from the water, bleed it, put it on ice, and start making gravlax.

ALSO WORKS WITH: First choice would be either king salmon, sockeye salmon, coho salmon, or Atlantic salmon—the latter only on the condition that it's wild. Pink salmon have a different texture and don't flake as nicely as other salmon, but you can still make a good product with a fresh pink.

Mix together the salt, sugar, cumin seeds, chiles, and lime zest. Cover a baking sheet with a few layers of plastic wrap that are twice as long as the baking sheet. Arrange one of the bunches of cilantro on the plastic in roughly the space the fillet will take up. Rub the salt cure over all the fillet, flesh and skin, and place on the cilantro. Cover with the second bunch. Drizzle the tequila over the top. Fold over the plastic and tightly wrap the salmon, using more wrap if necessary. Place a casserole dish with cans (or some other weight) on top of the fish and refrigerate.

After 24 hours, remove the weight, flip the salmon, and put the weight back on again. Refrigerate for another 24 hours and repeat. Refrigerate for an additional 24 hours, then remove the plastic and herbs. Gently scrape the seeds off the flesh. Thinly slice and serve.

½ cup kosher salt

2 tablespoons sugar

4 teaspoons toasted cumin seeds

2 serrano chiles, halved, seeded, and thinly sliced

Zest of 2 limes

2 bunches fresh cilantro

1 (2-pound) salmon fillet, skin on, pinbones removed

2 tablespoons tequila

SERVE WITH

Cilantro sprigs

Crème fraîche or sour cream

Finely chopped red onion

Toasted rye bread or other variety

HOT SMOKED TROUT

SERVES 6 TO 12 AS AN APPETIZER

¾ cup kosher salt

½ cup granulated sugar

¼ cup packed brown sugar

¼ cup honey

8 cups lukewarm water

6 whole trout, up to 13 inches long, gutted, gills removed

ALSO WORKS WITH: Mountain white-fish, American eels, lake chubs, or any other small, fatty fish

---

SPECIAL EQUIPMENT NEEDED:
Smoker or grill outfitted for smoking. If using a chamber smoker with adequate space to hang the fish, you'll need 1 (8-inch) length of cotton kitchen twine for each fish. Tie each length of twine into a loop.

SMOKED TROUT SPREAD

(See photo, page 199.) A fun and delicious preparation that uses smoked fish, especially leftover bits, is in a dip or a spread. Stir together ½ cup flaked fish (picked over to remove bones), ½ cup sour cream, 1 table-spoon minced shallot or scallion, 1 table-spoon chopped chives, dill, or other herb, the zest and juice of ½ lemon, and salt and pepper to taste. Serve with saltines.

This is by far my favorite way to prepare small trout and mountain whitefish. I've also done it successfully with a variety of other fish ranging from American eels to redhorse suckers. When I make a batch of fish like this, I eat the first few (or the whole batch) right off the bone within a day or two of smoking them. That's when they are best. If I have more than I can eat within that timeframe, I like to share them with friends or neighbors because they are so tasty and beautiful. With leftover fish, you can debone the meat and use it for smoked fish dips, mix it into omelets, or sprinkle it over a bagel that's been spread with cream cheese. A friend of mine, Chef Eduardo Garcia, uses it to fill his homemade empanadas.

FOR THE BRINE: In a nonmetallic container big enough to hold the fish, combine the salt, both sugars, the honey, and lukewarm water and whisk vigorously to dissolve the ingredients. Chill the brine. Thoroughly rinse the trout and submerge them in the brine, using a plate to weight them down beneath the surface. Brine for 6 to 8 hours in the fridge.

Discard the brine and rinse the trout again. Pat the fish dry with paper towels and place them on a wire rack in the fridge until they feel tacky to the touch. Two or 3 hours should do it.

If using a chamber smoker with adequate space, consider suspending the trout. For each fish, place the belly of a loop of twine across the back of its neck and pass the sides of the loop under the fish's gill covers and then push the knotted end out of the fish's mouth.

Prepare your smoker and preheat to a temperature of approximately 170°F. Fruit woods such as apple or cherry are ideal. If possible, suspend the trout in the smoker at least 10 inches above the heat source. If not, place them on wire racks so there's plenty of room between the fish. Begin checking the fish at around 3 hours. When done, the ends of the tail and other fins will have turned dry and crispy. The skin should peel away easily. It should seem that the flesh might easily slip away from the ribs and spine, leaving bare bones. Remove the fish from the smoker and allow to cool enough that they can be handled comfortably. These trout are best when served within a day or two, though you can wrap them in foil and store in a fridge for a week or so. For freezing, chill the fish thoroughly and vacuum seal.

PICKLED PIKE (OR SUCKER)

SERVES 6 AS AN APPETIZER

Growing up, my brothers and I fished for northern pike on the lake in front of our house. We caught them through the ice after the lake froze over, and we caught even more in the summer by trolling deep-diving crankbaits behind a rowboat powered by an ancient 10-horse Johnson outboard. Being kids, we didn't always do the best job of filleting and deboning our northerns. We each spent a fair bit of time lying on our backs on the kitchen table while our dad shined a flashlight into our mouths as he tried to remove the dastardly little Y-bones from our throats. So my family's discovery of pickled pike, with its acidic vinegar brine, was as much a medical breakthrough as a culinary one. With this recipe, it's no longer necessary to remove the bones from your northerns (or from suckers) because the bones rapidly soften and dissolve to a degree that they're no longer an issue. If that's not enough of a selling point, a jar of pickled fish is a beautifully rustic way to decorate a table with edible goods when you're having friends over for holidays or other celebrations.

Dissolve the salt in 3 cups of the warm water in a large glass or ceramic bowl. Place the brine in the fridge or over a bed of ice to cool.

Slice the fillets into 1-inch by 1½-inch chunks. There is no need to remove the Y-bones. When the brine is cold, submerge the fish pieces and weight them down with a plate. Leave in the fridge for 24 hours.

Pour the brine out of the bowl, then cover the fish with 3 cups of the white vinegar and let rest in the fridge for another 12 hours.

Meanwhile, make the pickling solution by combining the remaining 1 cup vinegar, the remaining ½ cup warm water, the sugar, both mustard seeds, the peppercorns, and the allspice berries in a medium saucepan. Bring to a low simmer, stir to dissolve the sugar, and then chill.

Drain the fish pieces in a colander, but do not rinse. In a clean 1-quart canning jar, layer the fish pieces, garlic, onion slices, lemon slices, chiles, and bay leaves. Leave 1 inch of empty headspace. Pour in the chilled pickling solution, making sure to get all of the peppercorns and mustard seeds into the jar even if you don't have enough space for all of the liquid. Dislodge any air bubbles by tapping the jar gently on the counter. Cap the jar and store in the fridge for a few days before eating. Enjoy over the next few weeks.

½ cup kosher salt

3½ cups warm water

Roughly 1 pound skinless northern pike fillets or other white-fleshed bony fish

4 cups distilled white vinegar

½ cup sugar

1 teaspoon brown mustard seeds

1 teaspoon yellow mustard seeds

1 teaspoon multicolored peppercorns

6 allspice berries

6 cloves garlic, peeled

1 medium red onion, sliced

3 lemon slices

2 to 3 jalapeño or dried red chiles

2 large bay leaves

ALSO WORKS WITH: The fish here doesn't necessarily *have* to be a bony variety such as pike or suckers, though the brine's ability to dissolve pesky bones is part of what makes it such an appealing preparation. I've even pickled some delicious jars of shovelnose sturgeon using this recipe—being cartilaginous, they don't have any bones at all.

SPECIAL EQUIPMENT NEEDED:

1-quart canning jar

Tip: For more information canning fish or processing at high altitudes, go to the USDA home canning website, http://nchfp.usa.edu/, and search for the guide on preparing and canning.

PINK SALMON NUGGETS
WITH THAI SWEET CHILE DIPPING SAUCE

SERVES 4 (MAKES ABOUT 32 PIECES)

DIPPING SAUCE

5 tablespoons sugar

¼ cup rice vinegar

3 tablespoons water

1 tablespoon fresh lime juice

1 teaspoon red chile flakes

1 teaspoon chile-garlic sauce or sriracha (optional)

1 teaspoon fish sauce

2 cloves garlic, minced or grated

1 tablespoon cornstarch

Kosher salt

SALMON

½ cup cornstarch or all-purpose flour

3 large eggs, lightly beaten

2 cups panko breadcrumbs

1 pound boneless, skinless salmon fillet, patted dry, cut into 1½- to 2-inch pieces

Kosher salt

Freshly ground black pepper

About 2 cups vegetable oil

Pink salmon have a reputation as a low-grade fish, which is completely unwarranted. My brother likes to conduct blind taste tests with his fishing buddies and pinks score just as high as coho salmon. They're good grilled, they're good broiled, and they're extra-special-good when my buddy Chef Andrew Radzialowski uses them to make his revered salmon nugget recipe up at our remote fishing shack in southeast Alaska. Here's how he does it.

ALSO WORKS WITH: Any salmon. Or, really, pretty much any fish that you can get a boneless fillet from.

FOR THE DIPPING SAUCE: Combine the sugar, vinegar, 2 tablespoons of the water, the lime juice, red chile flakes, chile-garlic sauce, if using, fish sauce, and garlic in a small saucepan. Bring to a boil over medium-high heat, stirring until the sugar dissolves, about 3 minutes. Reduce the heat to medium to maintain a simmer. Mix the cornstarch with the remaining 1 tablespoon water in a small bowl until smooth. Add the slurry to the sauce and stir until it thickens, about 30 seconds. Season with salt. Transfer to a bowl and let cool.

FOR THE SALMON: Put the cornstarch, eggs, and panko in 3 separate wide shallow bowls. Sprinkle the salmon generously with salt and pepper. Working with a couple of pieces of salmon at a time, dredge in the cornstarch, shaking off any extra. Dip in the egg, then roll in the panko until evenly coated. Transfer to a baking sheet in a single layer as done.

Pour oil to a depth of 2 inches in a Dutch oven or other wide, heavy pot and heat over medium-high heat until a deep-fry thermometer reads 375°F. Place a wire rack inside a foil-lined baking sheet and set aside. Working in batches, fry the salmon, stirring gently once or twice, until golden and crisp, 1½ to 2 minutes per batch. Allow the oil to return to 375°F between batches. Transfer the fish to the wire rack as done and season with salt while still hot.

Serve the salmon with the dipping sauce.

SUCKER BALLS
WITH MAGIC SAUCE

SERVES 7 FOR APPETIZERS (MAKES 15 BALLS)

The edibility of rough fish, particularly carp and sucker species, is one of those things that fishermen never get tired of arguing about. Most everyone has an opinion about it, though most of those opinions are based on very little actual experience. Bring up the subject and you'll hear about how so-and-so heard that suckers aren't any good, or so-and-so watched his neighbor cook up some carp, and even though he didn't actually taste it himself, it sure didn't look very appealing. As someone who has a lot of experience eating a wide variety of rough fish from a handful of continents, I'd like to weigh in on the debate in a measured, reasonable way: rough fish can be good. Definitely not the best thing you ever ate, but certainly not the worst. The flesh generally *tastes* perfectly fine, but it can be mushy and, most annoyingly, full of small bones. There are plenty of things to do with rough fish, including canning and pickling, that will render the bones harmless. But fish cakes happen to be my favorite preparation. In this recipe, you bake the fillets until they're ready to fall apart. Then you debone the flesh and work up some cakes and some herbed mayonnaise. No mushiness. No bones. Just good eats.

ALSO WORKS WITH: Freshwater drum, aka sheepshead, plus gar, buffalo, common carp, silver carp, and bighead carp. This also makes an excellent crab cake, using picked crab meat. Also great for northern pike, which are bony as hell, or pretty much any leftover fish that can be crumbled up in your fingers.

FOR THE HERBED MAYONNAISE: Whisk the mayonnaise, mustard, vinegar, salt, pepper, chives, basil, garlic, and lemon zest and juice in a medium bowl until smooth. (This makes about 2 cups.)

FOR THE FISH: Preheat the oven to 375°F. Butter a baking dish. Sprinkle the fish fillets with salt and add to the baking dish. Pour the milk over the fish. Bake the fillets until the fish is cooked through and flakes, about 12 minutes. Pick the bones from the fillets. Once cooled, shred the fish.

FOR THE FISH CAKES: Line a baking sheet with parchment paper. Mix the fish flakes, breadcrumbs, scallions, garlic, salt, pepper, bell peppers, and onion in a large bowl until uniformly mixed. Add ½ cup of the herbed mayonnaise and the eggs and gently combine until the mixture becomes wet and sticky. Form ¼ cup of the mixture at a time into a ball. Place the balls on the prepared baking sheet, leaving space between them. Bake until the cakes turn golden brown, 18 to 20 minutes. Serve with the remaining herbed mayonnaise.

HERBED MAYONNAISE (MAGIC SAUCE)

2 cups mayonnaise

2 tablespoons Dijon mustard

2 tablespoons white wine vinegar

1 teaspoon kosher salt

1 teaspoon freshly ground black pepper

6 tablespoons chopped fresh chives

6 to 8 leaves fresh basil, chopped

4 cloves garlic, minced

Zest and juice of 2 lemons

FISH

Unsalted butter, for the pan

1 pound skinless rough fish fillets (such as carp or suckers)

Pinch of kosher salt

½ cup milk

FISH CAKES

2 cups fresh breadcrumbs

½ cup thinly sliced scallions

1 teaspoon minced garlic

1½ teaspoons kosher salt

½ teaspoon freshly ground black pepper

½ red bell pepper, finely diced

½ yellow bell pepper, finely diced

¼ red onion, finely diced

2 large eggs, lightly beaten

MIDWEST-STYLE FRIDAY NIGHT FISH FRY
WITH PANFISH OR SMELT

SERVES 4

PANFISH OR SMELT

About 2 pounds scaled perch, bluegill, crappie fillets, or gutted smelt, heads removed

BREADING (PANFISH OR SMELT)

1½ cups fine-ground cornmeal

2 cups all-purpose flour

3 tablespoons Creole Seasoning (page 312), or use store-bought

Peanut oil, for frying

FOR SERVING PANFISH

Lemon wedges

1 recipe Herbed Tartar Sauce (page 318)

FOR SERVING SMELT

1 bunch fresh flat-leaf parsley

Lemon wedges

Cocktail sauce

ALSO WORKS WITH: This recipe works with just about any small fish or small pieces of fish. Any boneless freshwater fish fillets, or almost any white-fleshed saltwater fish fillets, cut into panfish-size pieces will work well with this recipe. If you're working with the type of smelt known as a eulachon (sometimes spelled as hooligan, and otherwise known as candlefish), there's an added step. Before you start frying eulachons, preheat your oven to 350°F. When you remove the fish from the frying oil, lay them out on an oven-safe cooling rack and set the rack over a baking dish. Place the fish in the oven and bake for an additional 30 minutes. The oil will render out and collect in the dish. From there, pick things up from the smelt serving step.

Ever since I moved to the Pacific Northwest, where salmon and trout are king, I've suffered endless ribbing from buddies who can't believe that I spend so much time fishing for panfish that are so small that a salmon could swallow them in a single gulp. I've tried explaining by telling them of the cultural importance of panfish to the Midwesterners I grew up around, but that doesn't do much good. What does work, I've found, is inviting them to a Midwest-style fish fry. There's something about a basket containing fifty or sixty golden brown nuggets of perch, bluegill, and crappie that makes a salmon snob question their ways. With their first bite, they're curious about panfish. With their second bite, they're asking for details about where I caught them. With the third bite, they're begging me to take them out on the water. As for smelt, we always cook them the same way that we cook our panfish, except that we eat smelt bones and all.

Rinse the fillets (or whole smelt) in cold water, shake them dry, then lay them out in a single layer on top of paper towels. Pat the surface dry with additional paper towels.

Mix the cornmeal, flour, and Creole Seasoning in a shallow dish. Fill a Dutch oven with several inches of peanut oil, or a deep-fryer to the recommended fill level. Heat the oil over medium-high heat to 375°F.

Working in batches of around a dozen fillets (or whole fish), toss them in the breading mixture so they are thoroughly coated on all sides. Shake off the excess breading and drop them into the oil. The fillets will bubble aggressively when they hit the oil. Fry for just 2 to 3 minutes, until the fillets (or whole fish) float to the surface and the bubbling has slowed significantly. Remove the fillets with a slotted spoon or strainer and place on paper towels inside a Dutch oven or other heavy pot with a tight-fitting lid to keep them warm while you move on to the next batch.

TO SERVE THE PANFISH: Serve with lemon wedges and herbed tartar sauce.

TO SERVE THE SMELT: Before serving, separate a sprig or two of parsley for each serving of smelt and drop them into the hot oil. Fry the parsley just 30 seconds and use it as a garnish. Serve the smelt with a couple of wedges of the lemon and a nice dollop of cocktail sauce.

THE PERFECT FRIED CATFISH SANDWICH

SERVES 4

Every spring, I take my kids fishing for channel catfish along the lower Yellowstone River of eastern Montana. It's one of the highlights of our year. There's usually plenty of action, and catfish are a forgiving quarry. You don't need a ton of finesse to hook one, and they tend to stay on the hook once you do. It's a great way to get kids interested in fishing, and also a great way to get kids interested in eating fish. We trim the fillets of fat in order to get rid of any "muddy" flavors, and then fry up big batches of them. The kids devour the fillets as finger food (backed up by plenty of sliced pickles), while the grown-ups assemble these catfish sandwiches. I love them. The only thing better than the taste is the joy of seeing a kid take pride in the fact that he caught his family's dinner.

ALSO WORKS WITH: Smallmouth and largemouth bass, walleye, big perch, and crappie, or just about any freshwater fish with a boneless fillet that can be trimmed down or stacked up to fill a bun.

Mix the mayonnaise and sriracha together in a small bowl.

Put the flour, egg whites, and cornmeal in 3 separate shallow dishes and sprinkle each with some salt. Add enough oil to an 11-inch cast-iron skillet to be 1 inch deep. Heat the oil and bacon fat in the skillet over medium heat until about 350°F.

Sprinkle each fillet with some salt and pepper. Dredge first in the flour, then the egg whites, and then the cornmeal. Working with 2 or 3 fillets at a time, slip the fillets into the oil and fry until the cornmeal browns nicely, 3 to 4 minutes. Flip and fry on the other side until nicely browned, 3 to 4 more minutes. The crust should be crispy and the fillet should feel firm, not mushy. Remove to a baking sheet fitted with a wire rack. Repeat with the remaining fillets.

Divide the sriracha mayo among all bun surfaces. Place a piece of lettuce, some onion, fried fish, 1 to 2 pickle slices, and a tomato slice into each bun. Serve with potato chips or coleslaw and a chilled beverage.

½ cup mayonnaise

1 tablespoon sriracha

½ cup all-purpose flour

2 large egg whites, beaten

½ cup cornmeal

Kosher salt

Vegetable oil, for frying

2 tablespoons bacon fat

1½ pounds catfish fillets, or about 6 ounces fish per sandwich (see Note)

Freshly ground black pepper

4 round soft buns, 3½ to 4 inches in diameter, split

Green leaf lettuce leaves, for serving

Red onion rings, for serving

4 dill pickle "stackers," halved

4 large tomato slices, for serving

Potato chips or Coleslaw (page 333), for serving

Note: If you're working with large catfish fillets that are more than 1 inch thick, lay them flat and slice in half horizontally so that you end up with two fillets that are only ½ inch thick. Trim to fit the bun. If using smaller fillets, stack them inside to fill the bun.

PADDLEFISH OR STURGEON STEAKS
WITH TOMATOES, OLIVES, AND CAPERS

SERVES 4

¼ cup extra virgin olive oil

2 pounds paddlefish or sturgeon steaks, 1 inch thick

Kosher salt

Freshly ground black pepper

1 tablespoon white wine or vermouth

1 (14-ounce) can cherry tomatoes, drained

8 kalamata olives, pitted and quartered lengthwise

5 anchovy fillets, chopped

5 large fresh basil leaves, chopped or torn, plus additional for garnish

1 small red onion, thinly sliced

2 teaspoons capers, drained

Crusty bread, for serving

ALSO WORKS WITH: Shark, swordfish, or any other "meaty" fish that can be steaked out. You could even steak out a big catfish for this recipe, though it's essential that you trim away the fish's fat and any reddish-colored flesh.

Very few anglers target paddlefish and sturgeon, in part because of limited availability and in part because of apprehension about how to clean and prepare them. The availability issue is legitimate, though I do believe that most fishermen would be pleasantly surprised to learn just how many opportunities to chase these fish actually exist. Recently, I got a paddlefish with my bowfishing rig along the Kentucky shore of the Ohio River in the summer and then caught a handful of shovelnose sturgeon along the lower Yellowstone River the following spring. If it weren't for an ice storm that canceled a trip, I would have followed that up with a chance at a white sturgeon from Oregon's Columbia River that winter. In between those distant locations, there were plenty of opportunities that I didn't try out. So as you can see, the fish are out there. As far as the problems of handling and preparation go . . . well, that's why you bought this book.

Preheat the oven to 400°F.

Grease a 2-quart baking dish with 2 tablespoons of the oil. Sprinkle the fish with salt and pepper and arrange in a single layer in the baking dish. Drizzle a little more oil and the wine over the top of the fish. Put the canned tomatoes in a bowl and crush with your hands (or use a potato masher). Add the remaining oil, the olives, anchovies, basil, onion, capers, and salt and pepper to taste and mix well. Spread the tomato mixture evenly over the fish. Roast until the fish is cooked through and flakes easily, 20 to 25 minutes.

Serve with crusty bread.

GRILLED SALMON
WITH CLASSIC BASIL PESTO

SERVES 4 TO 6

Grilling a salmon fillet is something that most salmon fishermen can do pretty well, but it's the rare angler who can do it perfectly every time. One of those rare few is my buddy Andrew Radzialowski, a chef from the Pacific Northwest's San Juan Island. He and I have been cooking wild game together since the mid-1990s, when we stuffed a quartered-out roadkill deer into the cavity of a whole pig and roasted it inside a fifty-gallon oil drum. We've done a few things that were a tad more elegant since then, though Andy retains his pragmatic approach to cooking. Here's his take on grilled salmon.

ALSO WORKS WITH: Any salmon or steelhead, or any high-quality fish that is suitable for grilling.

FOR THE PESTO: Pulse the basil, pine nuts, and garlic in a food processor several times, until coarsely chopped. Add 2 tablespoons of the oil and the lemon juice and process until smooth. Add the salt and pepper and, with the processor running, slowly pour in the remaining oil. Add the cheese and pulse a few more times to incorporate. (This makes 1 cup.)

FOR THE SALMON: Prepare a grill to high heat (500°F). Rinse the fish with cold running water to remove any slime or loose scales. Gently pat dry with paper towels and place on a clean plate or baking sheet skin-side down. Evenly drizzle the oil over the fish and sprinkle the salt, pepper, and lemon zest on top. Carefully oil the grill with a pair of tongs and a paper towel dipped in oil. This will help keep the fish from sticking. Once the grill is hot, carefully place the fish flesh-side down in the center of the grill. Close the lid and cook until the sides of the fillet begin to curl upward, 3 to 5 minutes. Don't move the fish until this happens or it will stick to the grill. Once a nice crust has formed on the flesh and it curls and frees from the grates, carefully flip it onto the skin side and continue cooking with the lid closed. The time will vary depending on the thickness of your fish. A good way to check for doneness is to carefully "open" the flesh by inserting the tip of the knife between the flakes on the thickest part of the fillet. Once you see the raw pink color slightly turn to light pink, remove the fillet from the grill onto a clean platter and allow the heat in the flesh to finish cooking the fish, another 3 to 4 minutes. Serve the salmon immediately with the pesto on the side or drizzled on top.

CLASSIC BASIL PESTO

2 cups packed fresh basil leaves

⅓ cup pine nuts

1 clove garlic

¾ cup extra virgin olive oil

2 tablespoons fresh lemon juice

1½ teaspoons kosher salt

1 teaspoon freshly ground black pepper

½ cup grated Parmigiano-Reggiano cheese

SALMON

2 pounds salmon fillets, skin on with the pinbones removed

3 tablespoons olive oil

1 tablespoon kosher salt

1 teaspoon freshly ground black pepper

Zest of 1 lemon

SPECIAL EQUIPMENT NEEDED:

food processor

SKEWERED FIRE-ROASTED TROUT

SEE BELOW FOR YIELD

1 or 2 trout per person (depending on the size of the fish and the appetite of the angler; it works best with trout ranging from 8 to 14 inches)

Kosher salt

Freshly ground black pepper

Chermoula (page 321)

SPECIAL EQUIPMENT NEEDED:
food processor; skewers of green wood, 2 to 3 feet long and ½ inch thick at the thin end; campfire

I've cooked many trout like this over the years while on river trips and mountain hikes. It fills you with backwoods pride to see a fish that you caught from the river cooking on a stick that you cut from the riverbank over a fire made from the river's own driftwood. A pinch of salt or Creole Seasoning (page 312) is all that it takes to make it pretty damn good; Chermoula, a tangy Moroccan herb sauce that is commonly paired with fish, is all that it takes to make it perfect.

ALSO WORKS WITH: Try it with other kinds of fish, especially if you're in a pinch, but it's best with trout.

Build a campfire. For each fish, find a skewer of green wood, 2 to 3 feet long and ⅓ inch thick at the thin end. The skewers need to be thin enough to go through the mouth of the fish without ripping it apart but sturdy enough to bear the fish's weight. Strip clean of leaves and smaller branches and sharpen the thin end. Also using green wood, whittle 3 or 4 pins for each fish that are about as thick as a pencil, 3 inches long, and sharp at both ends.

Sprinkle the fish with salt and pepper, inside and out, and rub it in. Run the sharpened end of the skewer into the fish's mouth and pass the end through the body cavity and then into the flesh at the base of the tail. Secure the fish to the skewer by passing the pins through the sides of the fish, crosswise to the skewer, so that the skewer is pinched between the pins and the fish's spine. Gently roast the fish over the fire, rotating every couple of minutes. You can use rocks to support the skewer in place so that you don't need to hold it the entire time. If the trout starts to curl aggressively or the fins turn black and burn, it's too close to the fire. The trout is done when the skin can easily be peeled away and the meat can be separated from the bones. Remove the fish from the skewer and serve with the Chermoula.

COCONUT CURRY FISH FILLET PACKETS

SERVES 4 (MAKES 2 FISH)

Grilling freshwater fish fillets over a fire can be tricky. A lot of the species have small fillets with lean flesh and delicate textures. It's all too easy to dry them out or have them crumble between the grates. You can solve those problems by using foil pouches and a bit of sauce—in this case, a coconut curry sauce—which make your fillets far more impervious to overcooking or other harm. This recipe is especially good for shore lunches over a campfire, but it also works well on a backyard propane or charcoal grill, or right in your kitchen's oven.

TO GRILL OVER A FIRE: Build a fire, preferably with hardwoods, that can accommodate a cooking grate and let the wood cook down to a bed of hot embers. While your fire burns down, prepare the fish.

If using a household grill, preheat a gas grill to medium-high heat.

Rinse the fillets and pat them dry. Stir the curry paste, coconut milk, and oil in a small bowl until smooth.

Cross two 12- by 24-inch pieces of foil. Place the fillets in the center, smear them with the curry paste, and layer them with the basil, cilantro, and lemongrass. Fold the foil around the fish and crimp to create a pouch.

Carefully lay the cooking grate 6 to 8 inches over the bed of embers. Your hand should be able to withstand only 4 seconds of time hovering over the fire. If you can hold your hand longer, add a little more fuel to the fire.

Place the packages of fish on the grates. Grill, covered, for 4 minutes; you should be able to hear the liquid inside the foil sizzling. Carefully flip the package and grill the other side, covered, for another 4 minutes, or longer for fillets that are more than ¾ inch thick. Transfer to a tray or platter and carefully open the package. Serve the fish with coconut rice.

2 pounds fish fillets, boneless if possible (with freshwater fish, either scale them or remove the skin)

¼ cup green curry paste

¼ cup coconut milk, water, or Fish Stock (page 309)

¼ cup vegetable oil

4 sprigs fresh Thai basil

4 sprigs fresh cilantro

1 stalk fresh lemongrass, outer leaves discarded, halved, smashed with the back of a knife

Coconut Rice (page 330)

ALSO WORKS WITH: Stick with white-fleshed fillets that can be easily deboned, such as walleye, smallmouth bass, large-mouth bass, or lake whitefish. Northern pike are great like this, but be careful of those bones! It's also great with many saltwater species ranging from flounder to rockfish to snapper. (*The photograph on the opposite page features the fillets of a small saltwater flatfish.*)

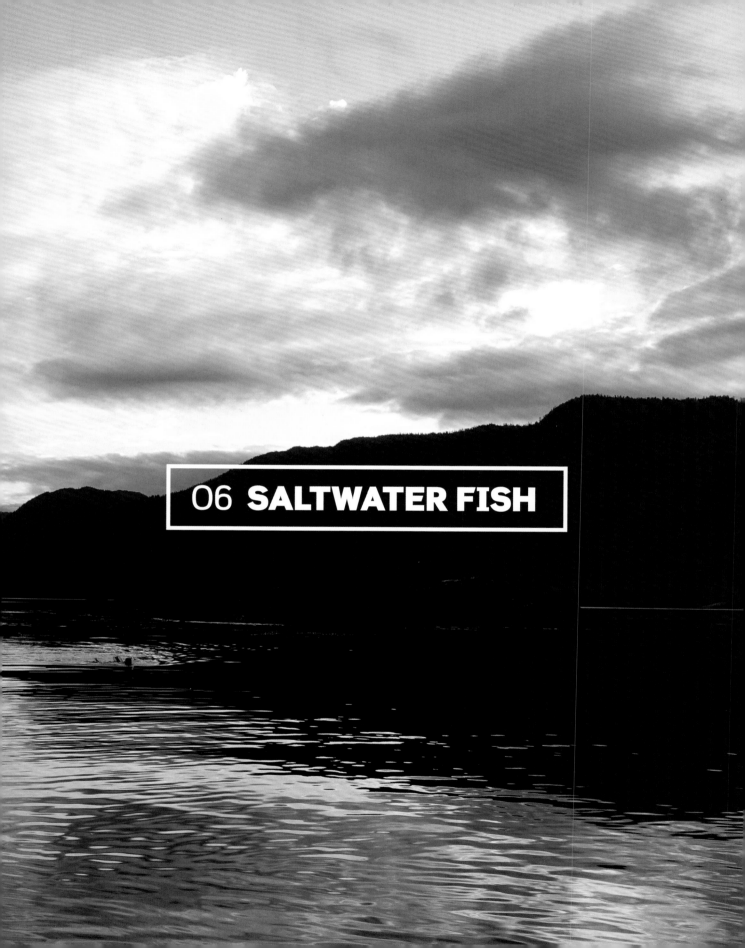

06 **SALTWATER FISH**

INTRODUCTION

The world's oceans, which are all connected and cover 70 percent of the Earth's surface, hold about twenty thousand species of fish. Only a fraction of those are commonly eaten, and an even smaller fraction are available to American anglers, but it's still a dizzying array of tastes and textures swimming around out there. Florida alone has a whopping ninety species that are regarded by the state's fish and game agency as "commonly caught," with plenty more that appear less regularly on the end of an angler's line. These numbers are always on my mind when I take my fishing rod and stroll down to my favorite stretch of Florida beach, which sits on the Gulf Coast side not far from Fort Myers.

My preferred setup is designed to be as appealing as possible to the greatest number of species. I use an eight-foot surf rod paired with a spinning reel that's loaded with a twenty-pound braided line. I slip a plumb sinker onto the main line and then tie on a small barrel swivel to hold it in place. To the barrel swivel I attach about thirty inches of fluorocarbon leader, and to the leader I attach a razor-sharp stainless steel hook that's big enough to hold a single live shrimp.

With that rig in one hand and a bucket of shrimp in the other, I slowly work my way down the beach as I try to read the water for clues about where the fish might be hanging out. I'm looking at a lot of things all at once, with particular focus on identifying the depths and contours of the "trough" that lies between the beach and the submerged sandbars that might sit anywhere from fifty to two hundred yards out there. This trough is like a highway for fish traffic as they travel up and down the surf in search of food.

Sunshine is helpful for reading the water, as the deeper and fishier holes inside the trough will appear to be a shade or two darker than the water around it. But even on a cloudy day you can still figure things out by watching how the waves break, which can be translated into a mental picture of the ocean's floor. Additional information can be picked up by observing the actions of seagulls and pelicans, which will betray the presence of baitfish, or by analyzing any splashes, wakes, or ripples that might be created by baitfish themselves or by bigger things that might be pursuing the bait.

All of this information, or the lack of it, goes into my head and gets processed into impulses that tell me to cast over here or cast over there. When the shrimp hits the water, I know that just about anything could happen, that there's a dozen or more kinds of fish that could take that shrimp in a gulp and then bolt for deeper water as I struggle to keep my head together and do everything necessary to keep the line from breaking. I get so pumped up with high hopes that a mermaid coming up to pluck the shrimp from the hook wouldn't be too far outside of my expectations. While I've yet to see that happen, I've seen just about everything else. To make a list of all the fish that I've ever caught from my Florida beach would be a daunting task thanks to the vagaries of memory, but I think you'll get the picture from a list of things that my buddy and I once caught there in a single long day: a southern stingray, a bunch of gulf kingfish, a redfish, a sheepshead, two spotted sea trout, a Spanish mackerel, a black drum, and several blue runners. Walking up from the beach that night, with a large cooler full of fish and ice, we had a greater assortment of tastes and textures in our personal possession than you're likely to find at even a well-stocked seafood counter in one of your local supermarkets.

No matter where you live on the nation's coasts, the saltwater world represents a nearly infinite frontier of wild game cooking that would be impossible for a single person to fully explore in a lifetime. The wild array of fishes is what excites me so much about saltwater angling. The only thing more exciting than trying to catch them is trying to cook them. Each species presents its own challenges and rewards to an adventurous cook. Sure, there really aren't any deep secrets left regarding restaurant favorites such as halibut, mahimahi, and red snapper, which are widely known thanks to their ready commercial availability and unassailable quality. But no matter how many restaurants you've been to, it's unlikely that you've ever encountered a menu featuring sea robins, monkeyface prickleback, unicorn fish, Irish lord, or the eloquently named ratfish—all of which are edible and easily obtained by a nominally outfitted angler who's willing to put in the time.

The methods and recipes in this chapter are geared toward those commonly caught species that generalist anglers are likely to encounter, but the information can be applied to just about any fish in the sea. Experienced anglers, especially the ones who know how to cook, will tell you that what happens right after you catch your fish is perhaps more important than what happens after you bring them into your kitchen. In general, I find that saltwater fish are more vulnerable to spoilage than freshwater fish. Keeping them in good condition requires constant vigilance. After catching a

fish, make sure to bleed it by cutting open its gills while it's still alive. This is especially important with fish that have lots of anaerobic muscle, such as pelagic species. You can stun the fish with a blow to the head before bleeding it; the heart will still beat for a couple of minutes.

It's smart to gut your fish. This slows down decay. Whether you gut them or not, you have to chill them as quickly as possible. Crushed ice works best, but anything is better than nothing. I've chilled a lot of fish by pouring a few gallons of seawater over a bunch of fro-zen gel packs to create an ice-cold bath. It's not as good as ice, but it works. If you don't have a way of icing your fish, cover it with a wet towel or even a wet jacket to protect it from the sun. As it chills, your fish will stiffen up as it enters rigor mortis. Don't overhandle the fish, and don't try bending it back straight again. That will damage the flesh and turn it to mush. Instead, let the fish relax before you fillet it. If you do all that, and then you follow the methods and recipes below, you'll be well on your way to some delicious meals. Now go. There are plenty of fish in the sea.

THE NATURE OF THE BEAST

The following is a breakdown of some of the most commonly caught saltwater fish in five regions of the United States, including some favorite and not-so-favorite species.

Northeast

Striped bass are an absolute favorite. They are big, meaty fish with white, somewhat translucent flesh that flakes beautifully. And they are highly versatile. While often caught in tandem with striped bass, **bluefish** are far more polarizing than stripers. Their flesh is dark and somewhat oily, with a stronger flavor, but they are superb if you know how to cook them. They need to be bled and chilled immediately upon catching and preferably are eaten fresh. They are great as a smoked fish. **Porgies,** or **scup,** are a smaller species with excellent flesh that is good baked, broiled, fried, grilled, or cooked in a salt crust. Some chefs compare it to red snapper. If anything, **Atlantic cod** could be criticized for being too mild, but it is a good-tasting and versatile fish with white flesh that is suitable for people who say they "normally don't like fish." It's great for making salted cod, a fun and interesting preparation. The various flatfish species are all good, with **summer flounder,** or **fluke,** being a favorite species with a decent yield of meat. It has soft, delicate flesh with mild flavors. **Atlantic black sea bass** is firm and lean with a mild, delicate flavor—another great choice for people who are finicky when it comes to fish. **Sea robins** are much maligned by anglers targeting striped bass and other surf species, but there's no need to toss them. They make wonderful fish tacos. See also: Southeast.

Southeast

Redfish, or **red drum,** are excellent. They are a highly versatile white-fleshed fish that flakes beautifully. **Speckled sea trout** and **gray trout, or weakfish,** are mild, delicate, and widely appreciated as a versatile fish, but they need to be handled very carefully. Chill immediately and keep cold. **Sheepshead** are also excellent. They have firm, moist flesh that is great when pan-fried, baked, broiled, and grilled. **Both gulf and southern kingfish** deserve more credit than they get. When properly chilled and handled, they are excellent frying fish that are easy and fun to catch. Like most flounders, the **southern flounder** has delicate, flaky white meat. The yield is good relative to many other small flatfish. The **spot** fish is small but fun to catch and good to eat; it is the panfish of the Atlantic. See also: Northeast and Gulf Coast.

Gulf Coast

A lot of anglers aren't crazy about them, but **Spanish mackerel** are dark, oily, and very good—they are a full-flavored fish suitable for everything from ceviche to broiling. **Snook** are one of the best fish in the ocean—they are white-fleshed and highly versatile. The various jack species, including **jack crevalle,** are often criticized as being strong-flavored and too dark, but they're good when you trim away the darkest blood-colored meat. In Mexico, they are popular for fish tacos. The **southern stingray** is a common bycatch for shore fishermen, and it's not widely utilized. Prepare according to skate recipes; a classic preparation is to serve them in browned butter with capers. Comparisons to scallops are not far off. **Pompano** are superb and flavorful with pearly white flesh and a delicious skin. **Cobia** are excellent, with a flesh that is comparable to mahimahi, a restaurant staple. They are good for sashimi. **Ladyfish** are a common annoyance to shore anglers. Their flesh is bony and mushy and hard to put to good use. There's little that needs to be said about **red snapper**. Widely regarded as one of the finest fish, they are good for just about anything that can be done with fish, including raw preparations. **Tarpon** are a popular food fish in Jamaica, but eating them in the United States is a no-no. **Tripletail** are outstanding, among the very best of all fish in the ocean. If you encounter a **lionfish** in the more southerly water, the meat is excellent—it's great for ceviche. But be careful, stings from the fish are excruciating. See also: Northeast, West Coast, and Hawaii.

a favorite, though **rubberlip, barred,** and **calico** are all good. The flesh is soft and delicate, similar to small flounder. They are great for grilling or steaming. The fillets are good when brushed with olive oil and baked in an oven until the edges begin to crisp. **White sea bass** have a firm, meaty texture with large flakes. They are similar to halibut. There are a lot of spirited debates around the food qualities of various sharks. **Blue shark** is generally unpopular and can have a strong urine flavor. **Thresher shark** and **shortfin mako** are regarded as excellent and are similar to swordfish. **Yellowtail** are one of the best fish in the ocean, with a buttery texture that is perfect for raw preparations. See also: Gulf Coast, Hawaii, and Pacific Northwest/Alaska. If you're looking for information on salmon, go to Nature of the Beast: Freshwater, on page 182.

West Coast

There is boundless misinformation surrounding the edibility of **barracuda**. The meat is white and flaky and perfectly usable, though larger specimens should be avoided due to accumulations of ciguatera toxin. There are dozens of species of **rockfish**. Fisheries managers sometimes categorize them as pelagic and non-pelagic. All are excellent, with firm white flesh. Smaller specimens have a delicate flesh, while some larger rockfish have a very dense, almost "meaty" flesh. **Kelp bass,** or **calico bass,** have a mild white flesh similar to rockfish. They are very versatile. The larger species of surfperch are all fairly similar, though each species has its peculiarities. The **redtail surfperch** is

Hawaii

While killing **bonefish (o'io)** is generally frowned upon by American anglers, they are eaten in Hawaii. **Unicornfish (kala)** are excellent when grilled whole. Cook until the skin begins to crack and can be peeled away. The flesh is dense and meaty. **Striped mullet ('ama'ama)** and **sharp-nose mullet (uouoa)** are slightly oily fish that can be grilled, steamed, or smoked whole. The fillets can be pan-fried or served in raw preparations. **Mahimahi** are superb, an almost universally appreciated fish that is good for just about everything, including raw preparations. **Wahoo (ono)** are sweet-tasting and highly regarded; they have low fat content with large flakes. In Hawaiian, ono means "good to eat." **Blue line snapper** are a nonnative fish in Hawaii that are readily available in shallow waters. They are not as highly regarded as many other snapper species but are still good. **Hogfish (a'awa)** are rich and sweet-tasting—an excellent fish. **Gray snapper (uku)** have slightly pinkish flesh, similar to many other snapper species. The flavor is very good, and the fish is suitable for many applications. **Goatfish (kumu)** are a flaky, buttery fish that is excellent. **Yellowfin tuna (ahi)** is perhaps the most widely recognized and appreciated tuna species, and also one of the best. See also: Gulf Coast and West Coast.

Pacific Northwest/Alaska

Kelp greenling have mild, very delicate flesh that is excellent. They must be handled carefully and kept on ice. **Yelloweye rockfish** have a white flesh that is very dense, especially on older specimens. They are excellent. Their collars invite comparisons to chicken. **Pacific halibut** are widely loved, with white, mild flesh and large flakes. Specimens in the fifty-pound range and smaller are better than larger halibut, which can be mealy and chewy. **Black cod,** or **sablefish,** are one of the best fish in the ocean from a fish lover's perspective. Its rich, oily flesh is suitable for light smoking. **Spiny dogfish** are edible and can be good, despite their rather poor reputation and sometimes off-putting odor. They need to be gutted and iced immediately. **Ling cod** are superb, far better than halibut in the opinion of many anglers. They have white, almost translucent flesh with large flakes and are highly versatile. **Pacific cod** are similar to Atlantic cod. Their mild, delicate flesh needs to be handled carefully and iced quickly. See also: West Coast. If you're looking for information on salmon, go to Nature of the Beast: Freshwater, on page 182.

FILLETING HALIBUT

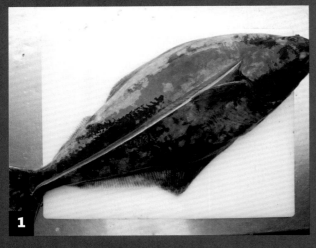

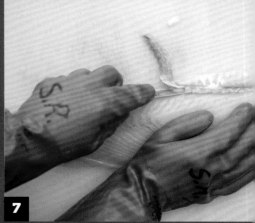

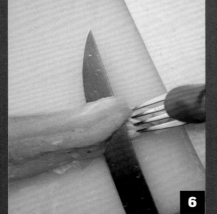

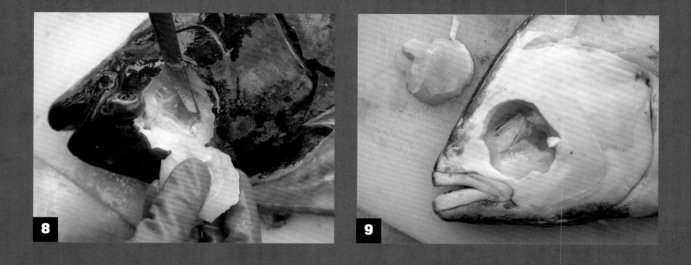

Pictured here is a Pacific halibut, which can grow to over four hundred pounds. The process used to fillet a halibut, often known as "quartering," can be used on pretty much any flatfish including fluke, flounder, and sole.

1. All flatfish have four quarters that need to be removed separately. Each side of the fish is divided into two boneless fillets, or quarters, found on either side of the spine. Start with dark side of the fish. Make an incision along the lateral line from the gill plate to the tail. Cut through the skin down to the rib cage, using the spine as a guide.

2. Along the first incision, follow the ribs outward with your knife to cut the upper quarter free from the carcass. You want to cleanly remove the entire upper fillet from the head to the tail. Use the same technique to remove the second, lower quarter on the dark side of the halibut.

3. Remove any skin from the gut cavity that is still attached to the flesh of the lower quarter.

4. The lower quarter will be shorter because you'll want to stop cutting at the beginning of the gut cavity behind the head.

5. Flip the fish over to the light side. Repeat the quartering process on this side.

6. Anchor the tail end of a fillet on the cutting board with a fork. Now, slide your knife between the skin and the flesh to cut the skin free from the fillet.

7. Take the time to remove any dark, bloody meat and interior skin from the surface of each fillet. This prevents strong, off-putting flavors and ensures better-tasting meals later.

8. Halibut have a tasty, boneless chunk of scallop-shaped cheek meat that shouldn't be wasted. Find it by feeling for the muscle behind the jaw, then make a circular cut around the cheek to remove it.

9. Flip the fish over and remove the second cheek. On large flatfish you'll also want to remove the collars. See page 231.

FILLETING MAHIMAHI

Mahimahi, whose name means "strong" in Hawaiian, are also called dorado or dolphin fish. From a butchering perspective, mahimahi fall into the general category of round fish. A similar filleting technique can be used for a wide variety of other saltwater species ranging from lingcod to redfish.

1. Make the first incision from the top of the head, down to the gill plate, and around the pectoral fin. Notice how this initial cut takes in the meat at the top of the head.

2. Where the first downward cut atop the head began, start cutting the upper portion of the fillet lengthwise toward the tail. Cut alongside the dorsal fin, following the spine, for the correct depth.

3. Following your original cut behind the gill plate and pectoral fin, continue cutting down to the belly. At the belly, you can now begin cutting back toward the tail.

4. The backbone that runs down the center of the fish is a good guide for your knife. Cut along it and continue to work toward the tail until the fillet is completely removed.

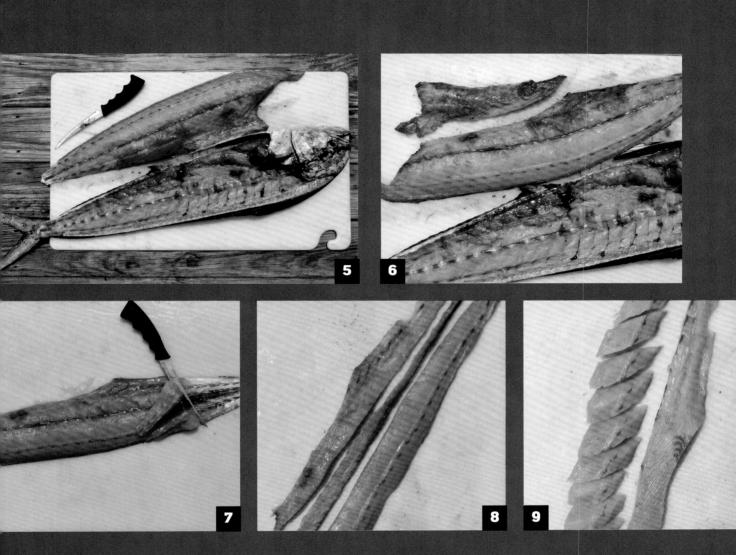

5. Now flip the fish over and repeat the process.

6. You should be able to see and feel the rib bones on the belly of each fillet. Slice the rib bones away.

7. Next, separate the skin from the fillets.

8. Here's where the process differs from many other species of fish. Mahimahi have a bloodline that separates the upper and lower muscles of the fillet. Make a lengthwise cut just above and below this line to remove the strip of dark, bloody, off-tasting meat. If you're filleting a fish that lacks this bloodline, skip this step.

9. You'll be left with two clean pieces of meat, a thick upper loin fillet and a flat, thin lower fillet. On large fillets, slice into steaks for frying, grilling, or baking.

1

2

3

4

5

6

7

8

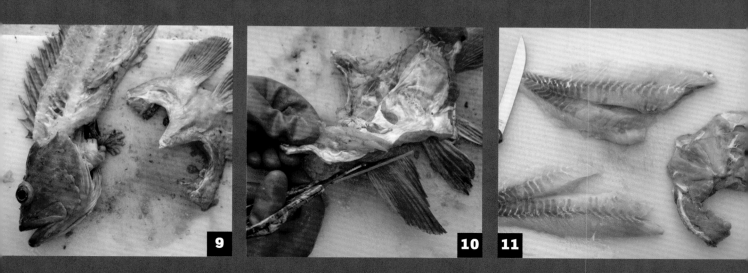

You'll need to remove the pinbones when filleting rockfish species like this yelloweye rockfish. You'll also want to save the collars on large rockfish, striped bass, salmon, and other sizable gamefish. Most anglers don't bother removing collars, but this firm meat holds together very well on the grill and breaded, fried fish collars are the seafood version of fried chicken.

1. Make the first incision from the top of the head, working down around the gill plate to the pectoral fin.

2. Next, cut the fillet free from the back down to the belly, using the spine and dorsal fin as a guide for the correct cutting depth.

3. Cut the fillet free at the belly.

4. Flip the fish over and remove the second fillet.

5. Remove the skin from each fillet.

6. Once the fillet has been skinned, rockfish, small-mouth bass, snapper, and other fish have a line of small pinbones that need to be removed. These pinbones aren't easy to see, but you'll find them by running your fingers over the center of the thickest part of the fillet. Cut away the thin strip of meat that contains the bones.

7. After you've filleted your fish, begin removing the collar by using a pair of game shears to cut through

the skin and bones on the upper portion of the collar behind the gill plate. Do this on both sides of the fish.

8. Now hold the gill plate out of the way and use your fillet knife to begin cutting the collar free from the carcass where you made the initial cut with the game shears.

9. Cut the collar down and around the head. Flip the fish over and continue cutting to remove the collar in one piece. You may need to use the game shears to completely sever the collar from the bony gill and throat area.

10. Use the game shears to clip off the fins.

11. Here, you have the collar and two fillets with the pinbones removed ready to be rinsed and cooked.

MAHIMAHI CRUDO

SERVES 2

This preparation makes me think back to a simplified version that my wife and I prepared on a small island off Puerto Rico. After we polished off our catch, we waded into the water for a swim and a school of juvenile palometa attacked our fingertips to get at the fish oils. My wife had to retreat back up to the beach. I think of that experience as testament to the freshness of our meal, and also to the primal quality of eating raw fish. Here, the experience is elevated with some simple ingredients that add a zesty kick to the already lively flavors of the ocean.

ALSO WORKS WITH: Pretty much any fish that's suitable for sushi or sashimi.

Very thinly slice the mahimahi on a 45-degree angle. Arrange on one or two serving plates. Drizzle the oil and orange juice over the slices. Sprinkle the fennel seeds, chile, parsley, and salt over the top. Grate the orange zest over the fish.

8 ounces fresh raw mahimahi, skin removed

2 tablespoons extra virgin olive oil

4 teaspoons fresh orange juice

½ teaspoon fennel seeds, toasted and lightly crushed

½ small serrano chile, thinly sliced

2 tablespoons small fresh flat-leaf parsley leaves, torn

½ teaspoon flaky sea salt, such as Maldon

Zest of ½ orange

CEVICHE

SERVES 6 (MAKES 3 CUPS)

1 pound firm white-fleshed saltwater fish, cut into ½-inch cubes

Juice of 5 to 6 limes (1 to 1½ cups)

1 medium sweet yellow onion, finely chopped (¼ inch)

3 Roma tomatoes, seeded and finely chopped (¼ inch)

2 scallions, cut into ⅓-inch slices

1 avocado, cut into ⅓-inch cubes

1 small clove garlic, minced

1 roasted poblano chile, seeded and cut into ⅓-inch cubes (see below)

½ jalapeño chile, minced

2 tablespoons chopped fresh cilantro

¼ teaspoon kosher salt

¼ teaspoon freshly ground black pepper

Tortilla chips, for serving

Ceviche is one of my favorite preparations for saltwater fish. It's especially good as a mixed-bag dish that features a handful of different species. I've made this everywhere from a spearfishing trip in the Bahamas (grouper, snapper, lionfish, grunt) to bottom-fishing trips in southeast Alaska (rockfish, lingcod, halibut). You'll be shocked by how quickly a bowl of fish will disappear when you make this, so plan accordingly. And make sure to trim your fish, ridding it of any bones or bloodlines.

ALSO WORKS WITH: It's best with firm, white-fleshed ocean fish such as grouper, rockfish, snapper, sea bass, striped bass, and mahimahi. It can be done with select freshwater fishes, such as walleye. You can also try slightly darker and oilier fish, such as mackerel, which have a bit stronger flavor but are still excellent.

Combine the fish, lime juice, and onion in a bowl. Cover and refrigerate for 2 to 4 hours, stirring 3 or 4 times.

Remove from the fridge and drain off most of the liquid, leaving just enough to keep the fish wet. Add the tomatoes, scallions, avocado, garlic, poblano and jalapeño chiles, the cilantro, salt, and pepper and gently toss together. Serve the ceviche with your favorite tortilla chips.

TO ROAST POBLANO CHILES

Set the chiles directly on an open flame—this could be a gas stovetop, grill, or outdoor pot burner. Char the skin, turning the chiles so that all sides get directly exposed to the flame, until the entire chile is black. Place the hot chiles in a bowl and cover tightly with plastic wrap. Let the chiles steam for at least 30 minutes. Then carefully remove all the charred skin with your fingers, discarding the black flakes. Open up the chiles and remove all the seeds. This is easiest if you lay the chiles open and use the back of a knife to carefully scrape and remove the seeds. Do not rinse the chiles; it's OK if you have a few seeds and charred skin in the mix, but rinsing the chiles will remove some of the flavor. Clean your cutting board of any remaining seeds. Dice the chiles and cool.

FISH CHOWDER

SERVES 4 TO 6

I tend to think of chowder and gumbo in the same way. It's not that they taste similar, but rather they share in common an ability to accommodate a wide variety of perhaps imperfect ingredients. Just as you can make a great gumbo with the mixed odds and ends found in your freezer, such as a squirrel or two, some rabbits, a pair of duck breasts, and so on, you can make a wonderful chowder with a mixed collection of fish that might not be suitable in taste, or adequate in size, for other preparations. To put it another way, I would never take a fresh piece of striped bass or halibut and whack it up for chowder. But let's say I had a few small flounder in the freezer along with the leftover tail section of a striper fillet? In that case, bust out the salt pork and fish stock. This is a Maine style fish chowder.

ALSO WORKS WITH: Virtually any white-fleshed fish, including freshwater fish. We used to make some great chowders using freshwater rock bass, which are not well-regarded as tablefare.

2 ounces salt pork, finely chopped

2 teaspoons vegetable oil

1 medium onion, chopped

1 tablespoon unsalted butter, plus more for serving (optional)

2 russet potatoes (1 to 1½ pounds), peeled and cut into ½-inch cubes

2½ cups Fish Stock (page 309)

1 teaspoon kosher salt

4 cups whole milk

2 pounds white-fleshed fish fillets (boneless, skinless, and trimmed of bloodlines; if using whole fillets, cut them down to 8-ounce portions)

Chopped fresh chives, for garnish

Oyster crackers, for serving

Put the salt pork in a large saucepan with the oil and turn the heat to medium-low. Cook until the fat renders and the bits are lightly crisped, 8 to 10 minutes. Add the onion and butter, raise the heat to medium, and cook until the onion is softened, about 5 minutes. Add the potatoes, fish stock, and ½ teaspoon of the salt, bring to a low boil, then reduce the heat and cook until the potatoes are tender, about 10 minutes. Pour in the milk and the remaining ½ teaspoon salt, raise the heat to medium-high, and bring just to a low simmer. Slip in the whole fish fillets, making sure they're covered with the milk, reduce the heat to maintain a gentle simmer, and simmer without stirring until the fish flakes easily, about 7 minutes. Remove from the heat, garnish with chives, dab a pat of butter on top, if desired, and serve with oyster crackers.

SAFFRON FISH STEW

SERVES 4

In a perfect world, you'd be able to put this stew together in a game-rich environment where it's possible to harvest your own clams and mussels and catch your own fish. I've spent some time in a number of such locations, and believe me, it's deeply rewarding. But don't worry if it's not possible for you. As long as you're starting with either your own shellfish or fish, you're well on your way to a satisfying meal that you can still call your own. So don't be ashamed if you need to round out your ingredients at a local fish shop or supermarket. Likewise, don't be ashamed if you need to cut an ingredient or get creative with substitutions. No one will be upset if your stew is graced with razor clams or quahogs in place of the littlenecks.

Put the clams and cornmeal in a large bowl, cover with 1 inch of cold water plus some ice cubes, and let soak for 30 minutes. Scrub the clams and drain well.

Heat 1 tablespoon of the oil in a large Dutch oven (or other pot with a lid) over medium heat. Add the garlic and one-quarter of the leek and fennel and cook, stirring occasionally, until softened but not browned, about 5 minutes. Raise the heat to medium-high. Add 1 cup of the wine and boil until reduced to half, about 5 minutes. Add the clams and water, cover, and let steam for 4 minutes. Add the mussels and continue to steam until the shells open, about 6 more minutes. Remove the clams and mussels to a bowl, discarding any unopened shells. Strain the broth through a fine-mesh sieve into another bowl or large glass measuring cup. Discard the garlic, leek, and fennel. Add the fish stock and enough water to the strained broth to yield 8 cups.

Melt the butter with the remaining 2 tablespoons oil in a large saucepan over medium heat. Add the remaining leek and fennel, the shallot, and the bay leaves and sweat until softened, about 8 minutes. Raise the heat to medium-high, add the Calvados, and simmer until just glazing the bottom of the pot, about 1 minute. Add the remaining 1 cup wine and reduce by half, about 5 minutes. Add the stock mixture, the saffron, and the cayenne. Bring the soup to a boil, then reduce the heat to maintain a simmer and simmer until it thickens slightly and can just coat the back of a spoon. Raise the heat to medium. Sprinkle the fish generously with salt and pepper and gently slide it into the broth. Cover and poach until the fish is cooked through, 5 to 6 minutes. Discard the bay leaves.

Carefully transfer the fish to 4 bowls. Whisk the crème fraîche into the soup and adjust the seasonings. Return the clams and mussels to the soup to reheat. Then divide the clams, mussels, and soup among the bowls. Garnish with chives and serve with toasted baguette.

12 littleneck clams

1 tablespoon cornmeal

3 tablespoons olive oil

2 cloves garlic, smashed

1 large leek, white and light green parts, thinly sliced

1 fennel bulb, cored and thinly sliced, fronds reserved

2 cups dry white wine or vermouth

2 cups water, plus more as needed

1 pound mussels, scrubbed and debearded

4 cups Fish Stock (page 309) or store-bought clam juice

1 tablespoon unsalted butter

1 large shallot, thinly sliced

2 bay leaves

½ cup Calvados or brandy

½ teaspoon saffron threads

Pinch of cayenne pepper

4 (3- to 4-ounce) pieces of firm, white-fleshed saltwater fish

Kosher salt

Freshly ground black pepper

½ cup crème fraîche

Toasted baguette, for serving

Chopped chives, for serving (optional)

SALT-CRUSTED WHOLE FISH

SERVES 4

5 cups fine sea salt (see Tip below), plus more for finishing

1 (2-pound) or 2 (1-pound) whole fish, scaled and fins removed

Freshly ground black pepper

2 lemons, sliced

1 bunch fresh dill

6 cloves garlic, smashed

2 tablespoons coriander seeds, toasted, cooled, and ground

6 bay leaves, crumbled

2 tablespoons fennel seeds, toasted, cooled, and ground

6 large egg whites, lightly beaten

Olive oil, for drizzling

Lemon wedges, for serving

ALSO WORKS WITH: A wide array of fish can be used here: lake whitefish, snapper, sea bass, porgy, rockfish, black cod, large surfperch—you get the point. It's best to work with fish in the range of 1 to 4 pounds, with 2- to 3-pound fish being particularly nice.

SPECIAL EQUIPMENT NEEDED:

spice grinder

Tip: Salt flavor matters. You can use kosher salt or another salt for this recipe if it's more convenient than fine sea salt, but keep in mind that the fish is essentially steaming inside the hard salt oven—so any flavor the salt carries, the fish will take on. For this reason, I don't recommend using iodized salt, as it's got a bit of a metallic aftertaste, but it would work if it's all you've got and could be disguised with some chopped rosemary or thyme mixed in with the eggs.

This process yields a tasty result and a dramatic presentation for your guests. Cracking into the crusted shell of salt to reveal a perfectly cooked fish is almost as fun as fishing. The key is to get the fish, or fishes, completely buried in the salt mixture. If your fish is larger than a couple of pounds, you might have to mix another half batch or a double batch of the salt mixture to cover it completely. Additionally, you can choose to add herbs and aromatic flavorings to the salt, or not. It adds an extra layer of complexity to your final dish if you do. I'm using lemon and dill here, but you could just as easily use orange and fresh rosemary or lemon and fresh thyme, whatever citrus/fresh herb combination makes you happy. In the end, it's the fish and the fisherman that star in this preparation.

Preheat the oven to 400°F.

Fit a baking sheet with parchment paper and sprinkle a pinch of salt onto the surface of the pan.

Sprinkle the inside of the fish well with salt and pepper. Arrange the lemon slices, dill, and smashed garlic inside the cavity (or cavities if making two fish) as evenly as possible.

Combine the remaining salt, toasted coriander, the crumbled bay leaves, toasted fennel seeds, and beaten egg whites in a medium bowl and mix well with a rubber spatula or your hands. The salt mixture should be the consistency of wet sand.

Drizzle some oil onto the parchment paper. Lay the fish down in the center of the paper. Drizzle the fish lightly with oil. Bury the fish completely in the salt mixture, covering it from head to tail. You are essentially creating a snug oven in which the fish will be happily steamed.

Bake until the salt mixture browns on the outside, about 25 minutes. Remove and let rest for 5 minutes. Then crack the hardened salt crust with a metal spoon to reveal the fish inside. Gently peel away the layer of salt and discard it. Fillet the fish as you would normally, using a knife and spoon to carefully lift the whole fillet from the spine, and transfer to a plate. Lift the head with the spine and discard to reveal the bottom fillet. (Repeat with the remaining fish if cooking more than one.) Serve with lemon wedges and finish with some sea salt.

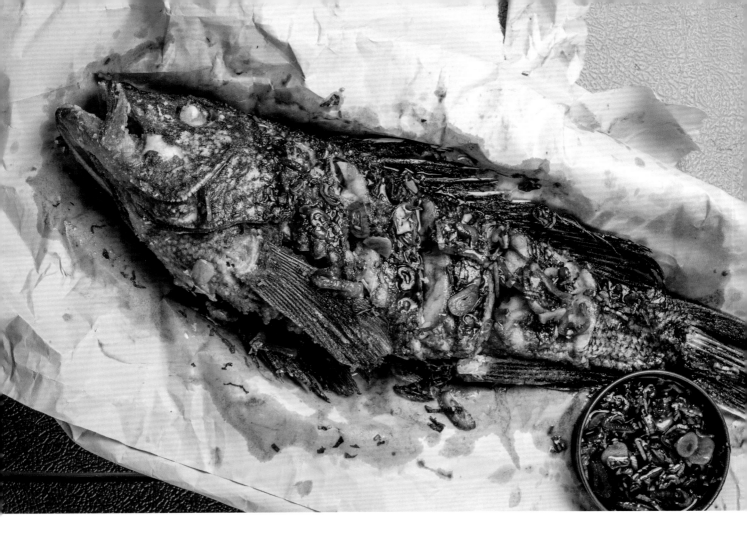

CRISPY WHOLE THAI FISH

SERVES 2 TO 4

This is an all-time favorite of mine that I associate with beachfront vacations where I'm spending a lot of time fishing and cooking with friends and family. When you lay out a freshly caught whole fried fish on the table, you're signaling to everyone that this is a special meal that matters. While pretty much any fish is going to taste good when cooked like this, keep in mind the importance of a positive user experience. Fish that are too bony, or that yield a skimpy amount of meat, should be saved for other purposes. For this dish, you want meaty fish with stout bones that can easily be picked clean.

FOR THE FISH AND MARINADE: Score the sides of the fish diagonally, leaving about 1 inch between each cut.

Pick the basil, cilantro, and mint leaves from their sprigs, reserving them for the dipping sauce, and place the sprigs in a blender. Add the lemongrass, ginger, garlic, shallot, scallions, green chile, water, lime juice, palm sugar, and salt. Pulse rapidly for 30 seconds. Transfer the marinade to a container and let rest for 5 minutes.

Strain the marinade into a measuring cup and discard the solids. Place the fish in a large resealable bag and pour the marinade in the bag. Seal and refrigerate for at least 1 hour and up to 2 hours.

Remove the fish from the marinade and pat dry. Sprinkle each fish with ½ teaspoon salt. Pour the rice flour out onto a large plate. Dredge the fish in the flour, covering the entire surface, including between the score marks and the fins.

Heat the oil in a heavy pot large enough to hold one fish until the oil reaches 325°F.

Meanwhile, make the dipping sauce.

FOR THE DIPPING SAUCE: Slice 6 of the shallots and the garlic into thin rounds. Heat the oil in a medium skillet until hot. Fry the garlic and shallots until golden brown, 30 seconds to 1 minute. Drain on a paper towel. Finely chop the reserved herbs from the marinade and slice the remaining shallot. Add them to a medium bowl along with the scallions. Add the fried shallots, fried garlic, tamarind concentrate, fish sauce, soy sauce, lime juice, and palm sugar. Whisk in the warm water until the dipping sauce is smooth. Stir in the sliced chile. Transfer to a serving bowl.

FOR THE FISH: Fry one fish at a time on each side until golden brown and crispy, 6 to 7 minutes, lifting the fish occasionally with a spatula or spider to ensure it doesn't stick to the bottom of the pot. Carefully transfer the fish to a wire rack to drain excess oil. Repeat with the remaining fish.

Serve family-style with steamed rice and tamarind sauce on the side.

FISH AND MARINADE

Whole fish (Note: Ideally you'll have a fish per person, ranging in size from 1 to 2 pounds according to appetites. Larger fish can be divided at the table for two people. Fish should be scaled, gutted, and de-gilled, with the fins and head intact.)

½ cup fresh Thai basil sprigs with leaves (or substitute Italian basil)

½ cup fresh cilantro sprigs with leaves

½ cup fresh mint sprigs with leaves

1 (3-inch) piece fresh lemongrass

1 (1-inch) piece fresh ginger

6 cloves garlic

1 shallot

2 scallions, sliced

1 Thai green chile (or substitute ½ serrano chile)

3 cups water

2 tablespoons fresh lime juice

1 teaspoon palm sugar (or substitute raw sugar)

1 teaspoon fine sea salt, plus more as needed

⅔ cup white rice flour

3 quarts peanut oil

TAMARIND DIPPING SAUCE

7 shallots

14 cloves garlic

1 tablespoon peanut oil

2 scallions, thinly sliced

1½ tablespoons tamarind concentrate

1 tablespoon fish sauce

1 tablespoon soy sauce

2 tablespoons fresh lime juice

2 tablespoons palm sugar (or substitute raw sugar)

⅓ cup warm water

1 Thai green chile, sliced into rounds (or substitute ½ serrano chile)

Steamed rice, for serving

PAN-SEARED FILLETS
WITH ZUCCHINI AND SHIITAKES

SERVES 4

SAUCE

5 tablespoons unsalted butter, cut into 1-tablespoon pats

1 small shallot, finely chopped

1 clove garlic, smashed

Kosher salt

Freshly ground black pepper

1 cup dry white wine

3 tablespoons fresh lemon juice

1 tablespoon chopped fresh flat-leaf parsley

VEGETABLES AND FISH

2 tablespoons unsalted butter

¼ cup olive oil

1 clove garlic, smashed

2 small zucchini, cut into 2-inch-long baton wedges

Kosher salt

Freshly ground black pepper

4 ounces shiitake mushrooms, stemmed, halved or quartered if large

4 (5½- to 6-ounce) bluefish fillets, patted dry, skin scored 3 or 4 times on a diagonal

ALSO WORKS WITH: Perfect for bluefish, but can work with a wide array of fish that yield a nice thick fillet that flakes easily, such as halibut, lingcod, or striped bass.

Here's a recipe that's perfect for flavorful, dark-fleshed fish like bluefish or mackerel, but it's versatile enough that you can use it for just about any fish that yields nice thick fillets. It's convenient, too, because the addition of zucchini and shiitakes makes it a well-rounded dish that only needs some crusty bread to soak up the sauce and maybe some roasted potatoes on the side. With heavily scaled fish such as striped bass, you'll want to either remove the scales or remove the skin altogether. But with bluefish or halibut, you're better off scoring the skin and leaving it intact. Once the skin's nice and crispy, that can be the best part of the dish.

FOR THE SAUCE: Melt 1 tablespoon of the butter in a small saucepan over medium heat. Add the shallot and garlic and season with salt and pepper. Cook, stirring often, until the shallot is soft and light golden, about 5 minutes. Add the wine and lemon juice and cook until the liquid reduces by half, 6 to 8 minutes. Remove the pot from the heat and keep warm. When ready to serve, reheat until hot. Then remove from the heat and whisk in the remaining butter, one pat at a time, until the sauce thickens. Stir in the parsley and adjust the seasonings.

FOR THE VEGETABLES AND FISH: Add 1 tablespoon of the butter, 1 tablespoon of the oil, and the garlic to a large skillet over medium-high heat and cook until the butter melts and the garlic browns lightly. Add the zucchini and toss to coat well. Cook undisturbed until light golden. Stir and continue to cook until crisp-tender. Season with salt and pepper. Transfer the zucchini to a plate. Melt another tablespoon of the butter in another tablespoon of the oil in the pan. Remove the garlic and discard. Add the shiitakes and toss to coat well. Cook undisturbed for 2 to 3 minutes. Stir and continue to cook until light golden. Season with salt and pepper. Return the zucchini to the pan and toss together. Adjust the seasonings. Transfer to a plate, cover, and keep warm.

Sprinkle the fillets with salt and pepper. Heat the remaining 2 tablespoons oil in the pan. Working in batches if necessary, sear the fish skin-side down, pressing down with a spatula if they buckle up, until the skin is crisp and golden, about 5 minutes. Flip the fillets, then cook until desired doneness.

Divide the vegetables and fish among 4 plates. Serve with the sauce.

BROILED FILLET AND ASPARAGUS
WITH SAUCE VERTE

SERVES 4

An angler should regard his or her broiler as their second-best friend, next only to the tackle that they use to catch fish. I use mine for everything from walleye to salmon. It's convenient, extremely quick, and helps you get a nice crust on the fish's surface while leaving the inner flesh moist and flaky. The important thing is to stay close and pay careful attention when you're broiling fish. It's much touchier than baking fish, and you can annihilate a fillet if you let it go just a few minutes too long. During the cooking process, go ahead and crack open the oven door to keep an eye on it. While this particular recipe is tailored for halibut, which are beautiful when broiled, you can handle a wide array of fish in a similar manner.

ALSO WORKS WITH: You can broil an almost unlimited variety of fish in this manner. Any fish that could be baked or grilled would be fine to cook under a broiler. Think walleye, trout, salmon, snapper, grouper, halibut, rockfish, swordfish, and everything in between.

FOR THE SAUCE VERTE: With the motor of a food processor running, drop the garlic into the food chute and process until finely chopped. Scrape down the sides. Add the parsley, chives, anchovies, and capers and process until finely chopped. With the motor running, add the lemon juice, water, and oil. Process until the liquid is incorporated. Season with salt and pepper. Transfer to a small bowl. (This makes ⅔ cup.)

FOR THE FISH AND ASPARAGUS: Preheat the broiler. Line a baking sheet with foil. Arrange the asparagus in a single layer on the pan and drizzle with 1 tablespoon of the oil. Season with salt and pepper and roll around until well coated. Broil until the asparagus are bright green and crisp tender, 3 to 4 minutes. Transfer the asparagus to a large plate, sprinkle with the cheese, if using, and cover to keep warm.

Rinse the fish under cold running water and pat dry. Place the fish skin-side down in a single layer on the same pan. Drizzle with the remaining oil and the lemon juice and sprinkle with salt and pepper. Broil until the fish is just opaque in the center, about 8 minutes for a fillet that's 1 inch thick.

Serve the fish with the sauce and asparagus.

SAUCE VERTE (PARSLEY, CHIVE, AND CAPER SAUCE)

1 clove garlic

1 cup packed fresh flat-leaf parsley leaves

¾ cup coarsely chopped fresh chives

4 anchovies, coarsely chopped

3 tablespoons capers, drained

2 tablespoons fresh lemon juice

2 tablespoons water

¼ cup olive oil

Kosher salt

Freshly ground black pepper

FISH AND ASPARAGUS

1 (1-pound) bunch asparagus, ends trimmed

4 tablespoons olive oil

Kosher salt

Freshly ground black pepper

Grated Parmigiano-Reggiano cheese (optional)

4 (6-ounce) fish fillets, 1 to 1½ inches thick

1 tablespoon fresh lemon juice

07 REPTILES & AMPHIBIANS

INTRODUCTION

Tastes like chicken. Most hunters and anglers have heard or said that so many times it's more of a joke than an actual observation. When it is applied in a serious way, it's usually used to describe the tastes and textures of reptiles and amphibians. I'm guessing that the reason for this has more to do with the novelty of eating such things as frogs, alligators, or turtles than it does with the actual tastes of those creatures. Whoever's serving the dish might draw the comparison as a way of wooing his guests into giving such an exotic food a try. Either that or the person who's eating it for the first time is so far outside of their comfort zone that they feel the need to bring the experience around to something safer and more recognizable.

I've never been tempted to use this line myself, mostly because I love the unconventionality of wild game and I'm not inclined to make it seem any tamer than it is. Years ago, I was sitting on a riverbank with a buddy of mine trimming some deer steaks for the fire and tossing the scraps out into the water. In the morning we caught a big softshell turtle down the river and decided to have it for our evening meal. When we butchered the turtle we were surprised to find our own venison scraps inside its stomach. That meal always sticks in my head as an example of just how wild and weird the out-of-doors can be, and just how much I like it that way. Another story of another turtle occurred thousands of miles away from there, down in the jungles of South America. I was traveling with some men from the Makushi tribe when they came into camp with a turtle so big that you could fit a large American snapping turtle inside of its shell and the snapper would have room to walk around. They removed the turtle's head with a machete and then ran a long, slender stick down the inside of its spinal column in order to relax the nerves and tenderize the meat. After butchering the turtle, they placed its empty shell directly over a large bed of embers and began building a turtle stew using the same river water that the turtle was hauled out of. That was truly one of the best meals I've ever had. And yes, the turtle's meat was white. And yes, it was tender and mild. And yes, the leg bones were finger thick and you could hold them up to your mouth and gnaw off the goodness. But equating that meal to eating chicken would be like seeing the Rolling Stones in 1970 and then describing the event as being similar to your buddy's karaoke performance of "Satisfaction."

As much as I like to extol the pleasures and rewards of this esoteric category of wild game, I do so with the realization that there are firm limits to how much we can exploit the resources. Reptiles and amphibians are environmentally sensitive creatures that suffer acutely from habitat destruction and environmental pollution. In certain times and places, they have been commercially overexploited. The American alligator rebounded from such abuses in a stunning way, to the point that it went from being an almost vanished rarity to an ever-present nuisance across much of its range. The American bullfrog is actually expanding its range and is now thriving as a nonnative species in states (and even on continents) where it was historically absent. But other species have a less certain future. The diamond terrapin, a small turtle native to the coastal marshes of the eastern and southern United States, was a highly sought delicacy in the fine-dining establishments of America's large cities in the late 1800s and early 1900s. Commercial terrapin collectors, unfettered by regulations, were removing tens of thousands of pounds of

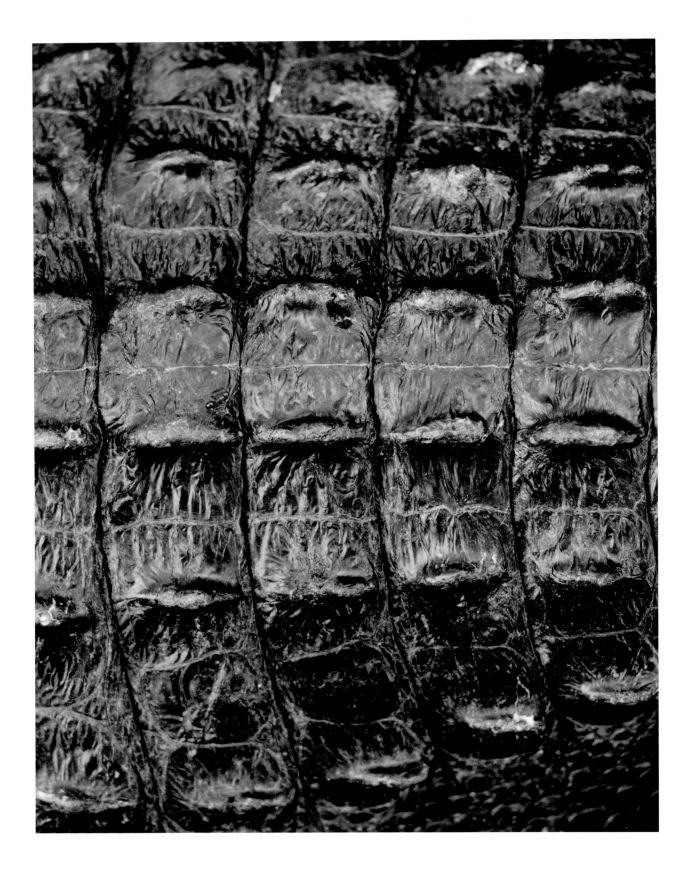

these creatures from Chesapeake Bay every year. Nowadays, the diamondback terrapin is protected across much of its range. There is no allowable harvest in Chesapeake Bay, and there are no diamondback terrapin recipes in this book.

That's not to say that the harvest of reptiles and amphibians is incompatible with long-term sustainability. Quite the opposite—small-scale recreational harvest is good for the resources. License fees from hunters and fishermen fund conservation efforts as well as the wildlife agents who enforce regulations. Plus, environmental advocacy from consumptive user groups is paramount to protecting fragile habitats. But it is important that we exercise restraint with our harvesting practices and stay well within the limits of the law when it comes to harvesting methods and bag limits. You don't need to take the maximum allowable limit of a species just because you can. Instead, take just enough to enjoy the experience and leave enough behind that you can keep coming back, year after year.

NATURE OF THE BEAST

Turtles

The **common snapping turtle** has both light and dark meat. Its meat is excellent, but it can be tough. Many people prefer to slow-cook turtle meat on the bone and then pick the meat before applying it to recipes ranging from fried turtle to turtle soup. The light meat is more tender, and on smaller turtles it can be used without slow-cooking. **Softshell turtles** (spiny and smooth) are even better than snapping turtles. The meat is more tender, though the yield isn't as high.

Frogs

Bullfrog legs are superb, with white, almost translucent flesh that is mild and very tender. It should be prepared simply in order to showcase the delicate flavor. While legal to harvest in many regions, **green frogs** are borderline too small to bother with.

Alligators

The meat from the **American alligator** is popular enough to support a thriving commercial market. The best parts are the two "tenderloins," found on the inside of the tail. The remainder of the tail is well-regarded, and there is usable meat from the legs and body as well.

Snakes

The **western diamondback rattlesnake** is the most commonly eaten snake. Specimens much smaller than 3½ feet aren't really worth messing with, because the yield of meat is minuscule. The flesh is light-colored and a tad stringy. The flavor is mild and delicate. Fried rattlesnake is by far the most common preparation.

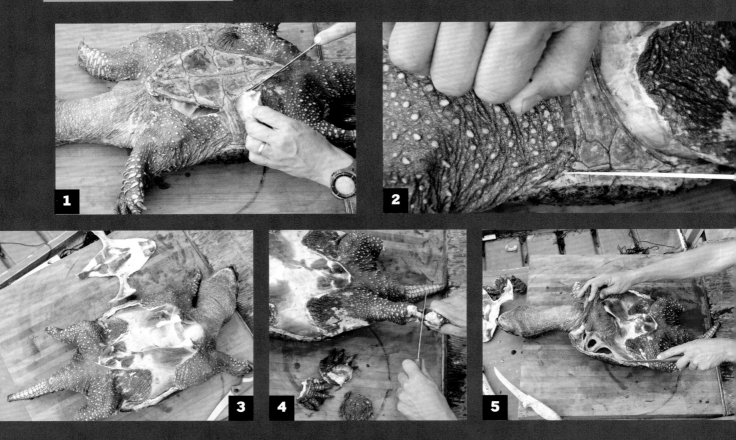

Very few hunters or anglers target turtles, despite the fact that snapping turtles and softshell turtles are common in lakes, ponds, and slow-moving rivers throughout most of the eastern half of the country, and in some areas of the West. Both species offer excellent eating for those willing to put in the work necessary to catch and butcher them. When dealing with trapped, hand-caught, and line-caught turtles, it's necessary to kill the turtle by chopping off its head with a hatchet. This turtle's head is still in place because it was killed with the arrow of a bowfishing rig. The head was later removed during the butchering process.

1. You'll need a very sharp, sturdy fillet knife and shears to cut through a turtle's tough hide, bones, and shell. With the turtle lying on its back, start cutting through the skin around the edge of the plastron, or bottom shell. Continue until the shell is completely separated from the skin.

2. Next, separate the soft abdominal shell from the hard, bony carapace by making a cut through the seam where the two shells are joined. You may need to use game shears.

3. Now you can fillet the lower shell free from the abdominal area.

4. Next, remove all four feet at the ankle joint.

5. Where the lower shell has been removed, cut the carcass free from the upper shell.

6. Make a lengthwise cut through the bottom of the tail. Now skin the turtle's tail, belly, and legs.

7. Remove the head with a hatchet, and then skin the lower neck. The entire underside of the turtle should now be free of skin.

8. Next, open up the abdomen and remove the entrails.

9. Remove the skinned front legs and shoulders by cutting them free from the interior of the carapace. Do the same with the back legs and tail.

10. The backstraps remain hidden between the ribs and the shell. Use game shears to remove the ribs.

11. Now fillet the backstraps away from the shell. Make sure to dry the shell and save it. When lacquered, they make beautiful gifts.

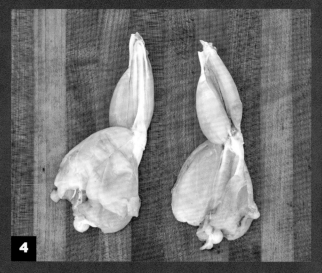

Bullfrogs are America's largest frog species and they are found in many areas throughout the country. The availability of the frogs continues to increase as they spread into ecosystems outside of their native range thanks to ill-advised humans who turn them loose where they don't belong. In some places, introduced populations of bullfrogs have had substantial negative impacts on native amphibians. If you live in one of these areas, eat as many as you can.

1. You'll need a sharp fillet knife and a pair of catfish pliers to clean a bullfrog. Even on large bullfrogs, it's really only worth removing the muscular hind legs.

2. First, make a cut through the skin across the back, above the hips. Next, use your pliers to peel the skin downward off the hind legs.

3. Remove the feet and ankles at the second joint down the leg.

4. Now remove the hind legs at the hip.

5. Although it is not necessary, removing the femur makes eating frog legs easier. Slice the thigh muscle open and cut the bone free from the upper leg.

6. Now you've got two meaty, semi-boneless hind legs. Rinse well in cold water before cooking.

BULLFROG LEGS
WITH BUTTER AND WINE

SERVES 6 TO 8 AS APPETIZERS

Frog legs were a rare treat when I was a kid. We ate them once or twice a year, always cooked in the same way. My dad would bread 'em and fry 'em, just like he did with the vast majority of freshwater fish that we caught. There are plenty of other options for frog legs, with some of the best recipes coming from the culinary traditions of France, China, and the American South. The following recipe is a variation on a classic Louisiana preparation, though it would not be out of place in a contemporary French kitchen. This recipe is hardly elaborate, though you can simplify it by just sprinkling your frog legs with a little salt and pepper and frying them in hot butter for 4 or 5 minutes for a quick and easy appetizer. Likewise, you don't need to do anything special if you're having a fish fry with friends and someone has a few frog legs mixed in with their fish fillets. Just bread them like fish and give them a quick dip in 350°F peanut oil. You really can't go wrong, unless you overcook them to the point that they dry out.

ALSO WORKS WITH: The legs of green frogs are much smaller than the legs of bullfrogs, but if that's all you've got (and it's legal in your state to harvest them), go ahead and give it a try.

1 pound bullfrog legs

1 tablespoon Creole Seasoning (page 312)

1 cup all-purpose flour

⅓ cup unsalted butter

¼ cup minced onion

1 tablespoon minced garlic

2 tablespoons minced fresh flat-leaf parsley, plus more for serving

Kosher salt

⅓ cup white wine

Lemon halves, for serving

Work with single legs, so if your frog legs are in pairs, cut them in half. Rinse them in cold water and pat dry with paper towels. Sprinkle each leg with a small pinch of the Creole Seasoning. Add the remainder of the Creole Seasoning to the flour.

Melt the butter in a pan that's large enough to accommodate all the legs in a single layer. Use medium heat, and be careful not to burn the butter. Working in batches so that you don't overcrowd your pan, dust the legs in the seasoned flour and then add them to the melted butter. Flip the legs after 2 minutes, for a total cook time of 4 minutes per leg. Remove the legs to a plate. Add the onion, garlic, and parsley to the butter. Cook for 1 minute, then return the legs to the pan. Sprinkle the legs with salt. Add the wine and simmer until the legs are fork tender, 5 to 6 minutes. Serve with the halved lemons and additional parsley.

TURTLE SOUP

SERVES 8 TO 10 (MAKES 10 CUPS)

TURTLE MEAT AND STOCK

2 tablespoons olive oil

1½ pounds turtle meat, cut into large pieces

2 cups water, plus more as needed

1 large carrot, cut into large chunks

1 rib celery, cut into large chunks

½ yellow onion, cut into large chunks

4 cups Blonde Game Stock (page 306) or low-sodium chicken broth

TURTLE SOUP

½ cup (1 stick) unsalted butter

1 cup all-purpose flour

1 small yellow onion, chopped

1 small green bell pepper, chopped

2 ribs celery, chopped

2 tablespoons minced garlic

½ cup Worcestershire sauce

⅓ cup dry sherry

3 tablespoons fresh lemon juice

1½ tablespoons kosher salt

1 tablespoon freshly ground black pepper

½ teaspoon cayenne pepper

¼ cup fresh flat-leaf parsley leaves, chopped

½ cup heavy cream

4 hard-boiled eggs, chopped

¼ cup chopped scallion

Buttery crackers, for serving

ALSO WORKS WITH: Try this with alligator or squirrel. Or use any other critter that might prompt people to declare that classic (and somewhat annoying) assessment: "Tastes like chicken!"

For reasons I don't fully understand, turtle meat has long been associated with soup. It seems to be an almost universal phenomenon. French master-chef Auguste Escoffier's 1903 magnum opus, *Le Guide Culinaire*, included a handful of variations on turtle soup. During the American Revolution, frontiersmen who raided an Indian village that was allied with the British reported finding a large kettle of broth with a boiled turtle lying in the bottom. It's also a staple of traditional Southern cooking, which is where this recipe finds its roots. Here, the turtle meat is simmered until it's tender enough to be deboned, and then it's added into a creamy, roux-thickened broth alongside seasonings, bell pepper, and chopped eggs.

FOR THE TURTLE MEAT AND STOCK: Heat the oil in a large skillet over medium-high heat. Brown the turtle meat on all sides, about 8 minutes. Transfer the browned meat to a stockpot and pour in the water, making sure the meat is covered (add more water if needed). Add the carrot, celery, and onion chunks. Bring to a boil. Skim any foam or scum that rises to the surface and discard. Reduce the heat and simmer until the turtle is very tender, about 1 hour.

Remove the turtle meat from the liquid with a slotted spoon, debone the meat, and chop it into a rough medium dice. Strain the simmering liquid into a stockpot, add the stock, and keep at a simmer until needed.

FOR THE TURTLE SOUP: Melt the butter in a heavy soup pot over low heat, and then whisk in the flour, creating a roux. Cook, stirring occasionally, until it has developed a dark brown color and a nutty aroma, 15 to 20 minutes. Add the diced onion, bell pepper, and celery and cook for 4 minutes, stirring often. Add the garlic and chopped, boneless turtle meat and cook for another 4 minutes. Slowly pour in the turtle stock and whisk until incorporated. Add the Worcestershire sauce, sherry, lemon juice, salt, pepper, and cayenne and stir. Bring the soup to a boil, then reduce the heat and simmer for about 1 hour until the flavors meld.

Add the parsley, cream, half of the chopped egg, and half of the chopped scallion. Let simmer for another 15 minutes. Serve the soup hot, with buttery crackers, garnished with the remaining chopped egg and scallion.

FRIED ALLIGATOR
WITH TARTAR SAUCE

SERVES 4

There are currently around 1.3 million American alligators in Florida alone, up from a population of just thousands in the late 1960s. Louisiana has an alligator population approaching 2 million animals. Right now, clearly, we're living in the golden age of alligator hunting. Opportunities abound, especially for hunters who aren't too particular about whether or not they kill a gargantuan specimen. The yield on an alligator is impressive, too. Processors typically get 40 percent of the live weight in usable meat. Considering that alligators in the range of a couple hundred pounds are perfectly common, you can see why alligator hunting—and alligator meat—is growing in popularity.

ALSO WORKS WITH: Honestly, just about anything that walks, swims, or crawls.

FOR THE TARTAR SAUCE: Stir together the mayonnaise, pickle, and hot sauce in a small bowl. Refrigerate until needed.

FOR THE ALLIGATOR: Stir together the buttermilk and hot sauce. Add the alligator, cover, and refrigerate for at least 1 hour or up to 8 hours.

If using an electric deep-fryer, fill it to the maximum fill level with oil and preheat to 350°F. If not, heat 2 inches of oil in a Dutch oven or heavy 10-inch sauté pan over medium heat to 350°F. Put the flour and cornmeal in separate shallow dishes and sprinkle each with salt.

Pull out a few pieces of alligator and dredge in the flour, dip back in the buttermilk, and then dredge in the cornmeal. Slip the meat into the oil and fry, stirring once or twice, until golden brown and the chunks float, about 4 minutes. Repeat with the remaining meat, allowing the oil to come back up to temperature, for 2 to 3 batches total. Drain on a baking sheet fitted with a wire rack that's covered with paper towels. Serve with the tartar sauce for dipping.

TARTAR SAUCE

1 cup mayonnaise

⅔ cup chopped dill pickle

2 tablespoons hot sauce

ALLIGATOR

1 cup buttermilk

2 tablespoons hot sauce

1 pound alligator tenderloin, cut into ¾-inch chunks

About 5 cups vegetable oil or peanut oil (more if you're using an electric deep-fryer)

1 cup all-purpose flour

1 cup cornmeal

Kosher salt

08 SHELLFISH & CRUSTACEANS

INTRODUCTION

I can't say that everything I know about harvesting shellfish and crustaceans comes from my beloved friend Ron Leighton, though I am comfortable saying that everything I know has been *informed* by Ron. He's a lifelong resident of southeast Alaska with deep experience as both a commercial and recreational fisherman. Ron spends so much time in his boat that he looks slightly confused and out of place whenever he's walking on a surface that isn't undulating beneath him. Ron likes to express his opinions about shellfish and crustaceans in a forceful, almost pugnacious way. If you challenge his convictions about the best way to trap a Dungeness crab, he reacts similarly to how someone might respond to having their beliefs about the afterlife called into question. Some of his viewpoints are hard for me to take at face value, as they are colored by things that strike me as being borderline anthropomorphic. For instance, he's a firm believer that halibut heads are inappropriate as crab bait, owing to the fact that halibut will readily eat crabs. In Ron's assessment, the crabs hold a grudge.

"Let's just say that a crab actually watched a halibut swoop in and eat his friend," I once said to Ron. "Do you really think he's going to draw the connection between that experience and a butchered and bloody halibut head lying on the bottom of the ocean?" Ron just looked at me as though I'd never understand anything. Later that summer we were out pulling some of my crab traps and up came a trap that was loaded with Dungeness crabs packed around a halibut head that I'd wired inside for bait. Ron was so annoyed by this that his fist clenched up enough to crinkle his beer can. Gesturing to the crabs, I commented on the fact that he's clearly wrong about halibut heads. "All you proved there," he said, "is that you've got a lot of dumb crabs hanging around this place. Imagine how many you would have caught with a salmon head."

Ron does have one area of expertise that I've learned not to challenge, and that's the process of what he calls "putting up" seafood. In his vernacular, that refers to the actions that one needs to take in order to freeze or otherwise store seafood for later consumption. The reason that I maintain fidelity to Ron's guidance on putting up seafood is that I've had poor results every time I've tried to ignore it. Ron spends what used to strike me as an absurd amount of time washing his shrimp tails before bagging them for the freezer. I started taking shortcuts while washing my own shrimp tails and they came back out of the freezer looking off-color and tasting not great. Likewise, Ron insists that you should only half-cook your crab knuckles before you freeze them, and then you should do the second half of the cooking after you thaw them out. One day I decided to experiment with a batch of crab by giving them a full cooking job before freezing them. When I thawed them out, I had crab meat that was watery and difficult to pick from the shells.

"Best practices" is a good term for describing these sorts of tips and tricks, which are based more on objective reality than subjective opinion. That is, people might argue over the best bait for Dungeness crab, but there's not much room for debate when your family is all puking their brains out over some shrimp that were allowed to spoil inside a warm bucket of water left in the sun. Following best practices while dealing with shellfish can have life-and-death implications. It's generally regarded as a best practice to avoid freshwater clams and mussels. That's because bivalves are filter

feeders that accumulate environmental toxins, and freshwater clams tend to have much higher concentrations of pollutants than saltwater clams. It's also regarded as a best practice to never cook and eat a crab that was dead in your trap when you pulled it out of the water. That's because crabs deteriorate with stunning rapidity after they die, and there's no good way to know if it's still safe to eat. Finally, it was traditionally considered a best practice to only harvest bivalves during months that have an "r" in their name. That's because the dinoflagellate algae that causes paralytic shellfish poisoning is most prevalent during the warmer summer months, or the months with no "r." (Paralytic shellfish poisoning, or PSP, has been known to occur at all times of year. To play it safe, you should only harvest clams and mussels in areas where the beaches are monitored by government officials for the presence of harmful toxins.)

An awareness of the troubles that can befall a careless shellfish harvester shouldn't dissuade you from experimenting with wild-caught shellfish and crustaceans. Rather, a working knowledge of the do's and don'ts should embolden you to get out there and have a good time while making great meals without worry.

I've been targeting shellfish and crustaceans since I was a kid, when we used to gather freshwater crayfish from the lakes and rivers around our home in order to do our best Midwestern impression of a Louisiana crawdad boil. Since then, I've done everything from spearfishing lobsters in the Bahamas to "ticklesticking" octopus in Hawaii to diving for sea cucumbers along Alaska's Inside Passage. The memories and life experiences that I've accumulated through those adventures are vast. The ailments and accidents, zero. If you've had a lot of experiences with shellfish and crustaceans, I trust that you'll find some new things in this chapter that will help you improve your game as a wild game chef. If you're just starting out, the information here will get you up and running toward your next culinary adventure.

THE NATURE OF THE BEAST

Abalone

Abalone are one of the finest delicacies that the ocean produces, and are priced accordingly in restaurants; they are similar to clam, but more buttery and with a springier texture. Any abalone preparation should be all about the abalone. Abalone flesh is often pounded gently with a mallet to tenderize it. Not to be used as filler or something that's tossed carelessly into hot oil.

Crabs

Two crab species, **blue crabs** and **Dungeness crabs,** make up the bulk of the recreational crab harvest in American waters. On the Atlantic Coast, which is blue crab country, they'll tell you that the blue crab is the best crab in the world. On the Pacific Coast, it's Dungeness. Blue crabs are the smaller of the two. Soft-shell crabs, which are regarded as a delicacy, are simply blue crabs caught while molting. These are excellent, as are hard-shell varieties. There is no soft-shell equivalent with Dungeness crabs, as Dungeness crabs have only small amounts of soggy meat during the molting process.

Squid and Octopus

The **market squid,** *Loligo opalescens,* is the squid most commonly caught by recreational fishermen, and it's also the species that's most typically served as fried calamari in restaurants. It's good for pretty much any squid preparation, as most preparations are intended for this exact same critter. The old adage about cooking for either 2 minutes or 2 hours has some truth to it, as anything in between could yield rubbery results. The **Humboldt squid** is a much larger creature that is targeted seasonally along the Pacific coast. Big specimens need to be tenderized by boiling or braising, similar to octopus.

As for **octopus,** it's astonishing how many shrimp trappers turn them loose because they're intimidated by the cooking process. It's really not hard. You can tenderize smaller specimens by placing them in a bucket with some coarse salt and then literally punching (some folks refer to it as "massaging") the legs as you rotate them around in the bucket. For bigger octopus, boil the legs in heavily salted water for thirty minutes and plunge into an ice-water bath. Peel away the outer skin, then finish according to your particular preparation.

Scallops

Scallop species are commonly divided into three classifications, **bay scallops, sea scallops,** and **rock scallops**. All are excellent. Regardless of the scallop, the edible portion that most people are after is the adductor muscle—that's the round "scallop" that shows up on your plate in restaurants. You can also eat the skirt and roe. Smaller scallops, say an inch or less in diameter, are very fragile and should be handled and cooked delicately. Big scallops can be a bit grainier and chewier. As the name implies, the Pacific rock scallop grows attached to underwater rocks or cliff faces. It has to be pried free. Their adductor muscle has different qualities than you find on bay and sea scallops. They are more watery, and are difficult to sear. They can become chewy, and even tough, from overcooking. Still, they are superb.

Mussels

Blue mussels can be found around the planet at certain latitude bands, and they are raised extensively through aquaculture. Mussels gathered in the wild are no different from commercially produced specimens, but in some areas they can be very gritty. It's a good idea to flush them in clean water (or hang them off a dock inside a mesh sack) in order to rid them of grit.

Sea Cucumber

You wouldn't guess it from looking at a **sea cucumber,** but it has a generous yield of meat inside. Each contains five long bands of muscle that look like big clam strips. It is excellent, and many regard it as preferable to clam. It can be dusted in flour and fried in butter, added to chowders, or used in a wide range of other preparations.

Crayfish and Lobsters

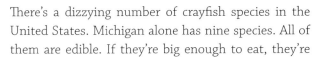

There's a dizzying number of crayfish species in the United States. Michigan alone has nine species. All of them are edible. If they're big enough to eat, they're good. The **red swamp crayfish** or **Louisiana crayfish** is widely available as a commercial crayfish and it's also trapped and gathered extensively by recreational harvesters. The **signal crayfish** is a large species native to the Western United States; it's often compared more closely to lobster than Louisiana crayfish. The **rusty crayfish** is a native species in the United States that has dramatically increased its range due to illegal introductions by humans. They are widely available—nowadays, *too* widely available—and good.

There's little that needs to be said about **Maine lobsters** and **spiny lobsters,** as their reputation as a high-caliber food item is well established. Maine lobster are available to recreational divers and trappers in portions of the Northeast, and various species of spiny lobsters, or rock lobsters, are available in the warmer inshore waters of California, Hawaii, Florida, the Caribbean, and elsewhere.

Clams

There are so many species of clams that it's difficult to keep them straight. Many individual species go by different names according to how big they are. Multiple clam species will sometimes be called the same thing—steamers, for example—because they're commonly cooked the same way. **Manila clams** are not native to the United States, but they're now found on the West Coast. They are sweet-tasting and commonly served either steamed or with pasta. **Hard-shell clams** are called littlenecks, top necks, cherrynecks, and chowders, depending on their size. Smaller specimens are eaten raw or steamed, while larger specimens are used in chowders. Small **soft-shell clams** are also good for

steaming, while larger specimens are used for frying or chowders.

Larger clams that need to be nominally processed before eating include **Atlantic surf clams,** which have a sweet-tasting meat that is highly versatile. They are popular as clam strips but can be used in many other preparations. **Geoducks,** from the West Coast, are one of the biggest clams in the world—wild clams weighing several pounds or more are common. The flesh is springy, even crunchy, like a cross between clam and abalone. The siphon needs to be blanched and then the rough skin can be slipped away. It is often eaten raw, including in ceviche preparations. **Razor clams** are enormously popular in the Pacific Northwest, where harvest is tightly regulated. They are good

sautéed in butter, fried as clam strips, or served in chowder. **Gaper clams,** or horse clams, are another West Coast clam that is very large. The meat is tough and usually needs to be tenderized, either through grinding, mincing, or gently pounding with a mallet for use in raw preparations.

Practice caution when attempting to cook with **freshwater clams** and **freshwater mussels**. As filter feeders, bivalves readily accumulate the industrial and residential pollutants that tend to exist in higher concentrations in freshwater than they do in saltwater. They can also contain harmful bacteria. Always check your state fishing and shellfishing regulations before attempting to collect freshwater clams and mussels because many states prohibit their harvest.

KNUCKLING A CRAB

Dungeness crabs are one of the largest, meatiest crabs available to recreational fishermen. They are found in cold Pacific waters from California north to Alaska. Cleaning them is simple and doesn't require any special tools. Blue crabs, a common catch on the East Coast, can be cleaned in a similar fashion.

1. You always want to start with live crabs. Dead crabs deteriorate quickly and can make you very sick. Discard any dead crabs you find in your traps.

2. The edge of a table, the gunwale of a skiff, or the brim of a 5-gallon bucket will work well for breaking the underside of the crab's shell. Holding the crab with both hands, give it a sharp tap in the middle of the underside to crack it open.

3. A crab has a "knuckle" on each side consisting of the legs, the claw, and the interior meat. Remove each knuckle by firmly grasping the legs near the body and pulling them free from the outer shell.

4. Each knuckle should pull free in one piece.

5. Now pull the gills free from the meat and legs. It's important to rinse each knuckle to get rid of any broken bits of shell, grit, or guts.

SCALLOPS

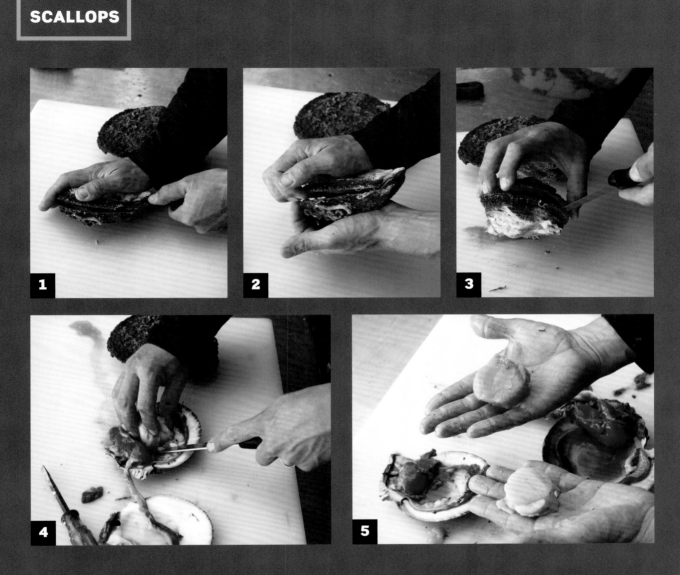

1
2
3
4
5

There are many species of scallops that can be collected recreationally, from small bay scallops along the Eastern seaboard to Pacific rock scallops in southeast Alaska. Cleaning them is a fairly simple process. The scallop here is a rock scallop.

1. Slip a blade or screwdriver between the two shells and pry apart.

2. Slide your knife between the two shells and cut the thin, tough outer ring of muscle that holds them together. Now you can begin opening the scallop by hand.

3. Scallops have a large, circular muscle anchored to the inside center of each half of the shell called the adductor muscle. Slice the adductor muscle free from one of the shells and open the scallop.

4. Slice the opposite end of the adductor muscle free from the other shell.

5. Pictured here are two adductor muscles from a pair of scallops. The bright orange egg sacks, or roe, can be sautéed in butter with the scallops or used to make a sauce. The remaining portions can be used to make stock.

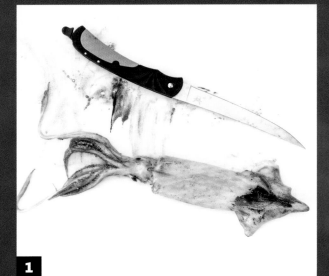

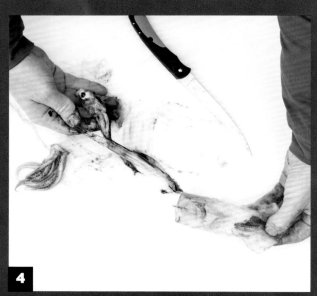

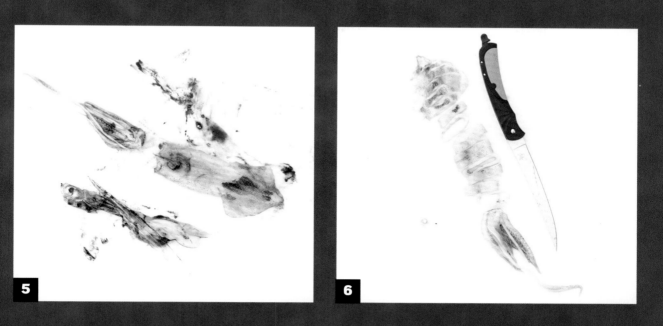

Many saltwater anglers regard squid as bait rather than food, but squid make excellent tablefare and they are easily targeted by anglers on both coasts. Cleaning them is easy, and the yield on a squid is high. Squid ink is used as a coloring agent in several preparations. You can recover ink from the ink sac found inside the mantle.

1. Use a fillet knife to clean squid. The edible meat comes from the arms, tentacles, fins, and the large mantle, or body. (Octopus arms can be removed pretty much the same way as squid arms.)

2. First, remove all the arms and tentacles in one bundle by making a cut just below the eyes. You'll be able to feel the hard beak at the base of the tentacles. Push it back toward the eyes as you cut, so that it stays with the head.

3. Using a fingernail, separate the squid's pen from the lip of the mantle. It looks and feels like a thin plastic blade. With your finger between the pen and mantle, slide your finger down the inside length of the mantle to completely free the pen.

4. Grabbing the top of the pen and the head, pull out the pen and the entrails.

5. The bodies are left whole for many preparations. You may want to remove the outer skin from the mantle of large squids since it can become hard and chewy once cooked. It peels away easily. On small squid it is not necessary to remove the skin.

6. For fried calamari, cut the mantle crosswise into strips. The tentacles and arms are left in a single bundle.

SEAFOOD FRITTATA

SERVES 6 TO 8 (MAKES ONE 10-INCH FRITTATA)

I didn't know what a frittata was until I heard the word on an episode of *The Simpsons* when I was in college. It turned out to be a formative moment in my cooking life, as I've been making these Italian omelets ever since. The beauty of frittatas is that they're pretty hard to mess up. You don't need to worry too much about your ratio of eggs to seafood, just as you don't need to worry too much about your ratio of shrimp to crab or crab to whatever the hell else you're putting in there. So rather than thinking of this recipe as a collection of rules that are chiseled in stone, think of it as a rough guideline on how to build your "egg pies," as my kids like to call them.

Preheat the oven to 400°F.

Whisk the eggs and cream together in a large bowl.

Heat 2 tablespoons of the oil in a 10-inch cast-iron skillet over medium-high heat. Add the potatoes and toss to coat evenly. Season with ½ teaspoon of the Creole Seasoning and salt and pepper to taste. Cook, stirring occasionally, until the potatoes are golden, 3 to 5 minutes. Transfer to a large plate using a slotted spoon.

Reduce the heat to medium. Add 2 tablespoons of the remaining oil to the pan, then add the onion, bell pepper, celery, ½ teaspoon of the remaining Creole Seasoning, and salt and pepper to taste. Cook until the vegetables are softened, about 8 minutes. Transfer to the plate.

Raise the heat to medium-high and add the remaining 2 tablespoons oil to the skillet. Add the shrimp and scallops and toss to coat. Sprinkle with the remaining 2 teaspoons Creole Seasoning and salt and pepper to taste. Cook until the shrimp turns slightly pink but is not opaque. Gently stir in the crab, then return the potatoes and vegetables to the pan and mix well.

Pour the egg mixture over the seafood and vegetables and stir to distribute evenly. Cook until the egg starts to set up a little around the edges of the pan, then place the pan in the oven. Bake until the eggs are puffed up and cooked through, 6 to 8 minutes.

Switch the oven to broil and run under the broiler for a minute or two to brown the top. Remove from the oven, let cool slightly, then cut into wedges and serve.

8 large eggs

3 tablespoons heavy cream

6 tablespoons olive oil

1 (10-ounce) Yukon gold potato, cut into ½-inch dice (about 2 cups)

1 tablespoon Creole Seasoning (page 312)

Kosher salt

Freshly ground black pepper

½ onion, diced (about ½ cup)

½ red bell pepper, diced (about ½ cup)

1 rib celery, diced (about ¼ cup)

6 ounces peeled, deveined shrimp, cut into bite-size pieces

6 small scallops, patted dry and quartered

8 ounces lump crabmeat

ALSO WORKS WITH: Don't feel constrained by the quantities of seafood given here. Just use what you've got. You can also substitute cooked crayfish tails or even a few ounces of cooked leftover fish that's been crumbled up.

SPICY SCALLOP AND CITRUS POKE

SERVES 6 (AS AN APPETIZER) / MAKES 4 CUPS

⅔ cup diced (¼ inch) sweet or red onion

2 scallions, thinly sliced

1 serrano or other chile, thinly sliced

2 tablespoons soy sauce, or to taste

4 teaspoons toasted sesame oil, or to taste

2 teaspoons toasted black sesame seeds

1 pound fresh scallops (the adductor muscles only), cut into ½-inch pieces

2 cups diced grapefruit segments

¼ cup diced lime segments

Cooked rice, for serving, if desired

Oftentimes, the best way to "cook" shellfish is not to actually cook them at all. Fresh shellfish taste as wild and free as the ocean itself, and heat has a way of taming that wildness and turning it into something a bit less inspiring and a bit more rubbery. Scallops are particularly vulnerable to heat. I can't think of ever eating a scallop and wishing it had been cooked longer. That's why scallops are a great choice for making poke, a raw seafood salad whose origins can be traced to Hawaii. Everything here tastes fresh and clean. If I were scallop, this is exactly where I'd want to end up.

ALSO WORKS WITH: Any scallop, regardless of whether it's classified as a sea, bay, or rock species. This is also great with abalone, though you'll want to cut the abalone into ¼-inch slices and tenderize them by hammering them gently with a meat mallet. A host of fish species can be used, in particular oily fish such as salmon and tuna. You want the fish to be fresh and firm-fleshed.

Combine the onion, scallions, chiles, soy sauce, sesame oil, and sesame seeds in a bowl. Add the scallops, grapefruit, and lime and mix well. Adjust the seasonings. Serve with rice, if you like.

Tip: Keep the scallops, grapefruit, and limes well chilled until ready to assemble and serve.

SHRIMP SCAMPI

SERVES 6 (APPETIZER)

My brothers and I do a lot of shrimp trapping near our fishing shack on southeast Alaska's Prince of Wales Island. We mainly get spot shrimp, a big and meaty species that we haul up from a depth of two hundred feet using salmon and halibut heads as bait. When they're ultra fresh I just boil them in salted water for a few minutes and eat them without butter or sauce. They're that good. I also freeze some of the tails in quart-size bags and bring them home. I'll usually handle these frozen tails differently from the fresh tails, mostly because I have more time to cook and easier access to ingredients when I'm home than I do when I'm at our shack. I'll gather up what I need to make scampi; the additional flavors of garlic, parsley, and red chile flakes, plus the crust of toasted breadcrumbs, get me excited about shrimp all over again.

Rinse the shrimp well and pat dry. Sprinkle liberally with salt and pepper.

Heat the oil in a large (14-inch-wide) sauté pan over medium-high heat. (If you don't have a pan this big, divide the ingredients in half and cook in batches.) Add the garlic and red chile flakes and cook until fragrant. Carefully lay the shrimp in the oil using tongs. Add the white wine and lemon zest and bring to a strong simmer. Cook for about 3 minutes, then flip the shrimp with the tongs to cook through; you'll know they're done when the flesh turns pink. Add the butter and swirl it into the sauce. Add the parsley and transfer to a platter. Top with the toasted breadcrumbs, if using. Serve immediately, with lemon wedges.

1 pound shrimp, heads removed

Kosher salt

Freshly ground black pepper

3 tablespoons olive oil

6 cloves garlic, thinly sliced

Pinch of red chile flakes (optional)

1 cup white wine

Zest of 1 lemon, plus wedges for serving

1 tablespoon unsalted butter

1 bunch fresh flat-leaf parsley, finely chopped

½ cup toasted breadcrumbs, optional (see below)

ALSO WORKS WITH: Spot shrimp are my absolute favorite, but they're limited to the Pacific Northwest and southeast Alaska. Substitute any wild-caught shrimp and you'll be happy.

TOASTED BREADCRUMB TOPPING

The *best* way to make seasoned breadcrumbs is to throw semi-stale bread pieces into a food processor and pulse. Then toast the crumbs with a couple of teaspoons of olive oil and a pinch of salt in a large skillet. You can also do the same thing with a cup of panko breadcrumbs.

GRILLED HEAD-ON SHRIMP

SERVES 4 AS AN APPETIZER (MAKES 10 TO 15 SHRIMP)

5 cloves garlic, minced or grated

1 small shallot, minced

3 tablespoons extra virgin olive oil

¼ to ½ teaspoon freshly ground black pepper

Pinch of sugar

1 pound large head-on shrimp, with tails peeled

Kosher salt

Lemon wedges or lemon halves (optional)

Chimichurri Butter (page 323) or

Adobada (page 314) or BBQ Sauce (page 314)

There's not a lot that needs to be said about this recipe beyond what can be ascertained from the title. These are shrimp. They are grilled. They still have their heads on. It's a beautiful and bold way to handle your wild-caught shrimp. Be mindful of freshness here. Well-rinsed shrimp tails can be successfully frozen, but frozen heads lose their magic in a hurry.

ALSO WORKS WITH: Any large shrimp

Soak 4 to 6 wooden skewers in water to cover for at least 30 minutes, or use metal skewers.

Preheat a gas grill to high heat.

Combine the garlic, shallot, oil, pepper, and sugar in a large bowl.

Wash the peeled shrimp and dry well. Add the shrimp to the garlic mixture and toss to coat. Skewer the shrimp snugly on a pair of skewers, using the skewers in a ladder formation so that the shrimp don't rotate when turned. Smear any remaining marinade on the shrimp. Sprinkle the shrimp generously with salt. Place a lemon wedge at the top of each skewer, if using.

Place lemon halves, if using, on a well-oiled grill grate cut-side down. Place the shrimp on the grates, pressing down gently to make sure they're flat. Grill, covered, turning halfway through, until the shells are pink and slightly charred and the shrimp are opaque and just cooked through, about 2 minutes per side. Carefully slide the shrimp from the hot skewers onto a plate or platter. Serve with lemon and the sauce of your choice.

MANHATTAN CLAM CHOWDER

SERVES 4 TO 6

5 to 5½ pounds small live clams (see Tip below for technique to purge clams)

2 bay leaves

1 sprig fresh thyme

2 cups water

2 strips bacon, finely chopped

1 rib celery, finely chopped

1 medium onion, finely chopped

½ teaspoon red chile flakes

¼ teaspoon kosher salt, plus more as needed

1 russet potato (about 1 pound), peeled and cut into ¼-inch cubes

1 (28-ounce) can peeled whole plum tomatoes

Saltine crackers, for serving

ALSO WORKS WITH: The diced meat of sea cucumbers and just about any clam can be put to use in a chowder. When you're dealing with small, live clams such as manila clams or young quahogs, follow the directions below. If you're dealing with larger clam species that are generally processed before cooking, such as geoducks, big razor clams, or gaper clams, plan on using 1 pound of minced clam meat for this recipe. Just sauté it in butter for a couple of minutes before adding to the pot in the final step of the recipe. In place of the 2 cups of cooking liquid that were used to steam the clams, use straight water or homemade or bottled clam juice.

If you're a clamdigger, you probably like to make chowder, and if you like to make chowder, you're probably familiar with the ancient East Coast debate over what color it should be. In New England, chowder is supposed to be creamy and cream-colored; in Manhattan, it's supposed to be thinner and redder. Both of them are good, but if I'm the one going through all the work of digging and cleaning the clams, I tend to prefer the Manhattan-style chowders because you can see and taste the fruits of your labor more clearly when they're not camouflaged by a broth that's about as thick as wood glue. Most chowder recipes take for granted that you're buying a very specific type of clam to make your chowder, but below you'll find some thoughts on how to prepare a great pot of the stuff with just about any clam.

Scrub the clam shells under cool running water. Place in a large saucepan with the bay leaves and thyme. Pour in the water, cover, and turn the heat to high. Once the water boils, reduce the heat to maintain a simmer, give the clams a stir, and continue to steam them until their shells open all the way, about 10 minutes total. Discard any that do not open. Remove open clams to a bowl to cool, while reserving the liquid in the saucepan. Shuck and coarsely chop the meat from the open clams. Line a mesh strainer with a double layer of cheesecloth, put over a bowl, and pour the liquid through the strainer. Reserve the liquid.

Rinse out the pot and return to the stove over medium heat. Add the bacon and cook, stirring, until it's crisp, about 5 minutes. Add the celery, onion, red chile flakes, and salt and cook, stirring, until the vegetables are softened, about 5 minutes. Add the potato, 2 cups of the cooking liquid, and the tomatoes, crushing them as you add them. Rinse out the can with a little water and add to the pot. Bring to a boil, then reduce the heat to maintain a medium boil and cook until the potatoes are tender, about 10 minutes. Add the clams and cook to heat through, about 2 more minutes. Taste and add salt as needed. Ladle into bowls and serve with saltines.

Tip: Purging clams helps to extract any residual sand that is left in your clams. First, tap any open clams on the countertop to be sure they're still alive. They should instantly close. If they don't, toss them. Next, add the clams to a bowl and cover with cold water along with a sprinkle of cornmeal. Let the clams sit for 20 minutes in the bowl; they will spit out the sand while you wait. Remove the clams by lifting them from the potentially sandy water. Scrub before cooking.

GRILLED LOBSTER
WITH COMPOUND BUTTER

SERVES 4

I thought about offering an apology here to wild game cooks who live toward the center of the country, where lobster diving opportunities are geographically prohibitive. My fear was that they'd feel left out. But then I got to thinking that most people will eventually have some sort of travel requirement, vacation or otherwise, that brings them to Florida, California, Hawaii, New England, or one of countless other locales where it's possible to dive for lobster. When that time comes, you'll be glad that you have this book. So no apologies.

4 (1¼- to 1½-pound) live lobsters

Chimichurri Butter (page 323) or Anchovy Butter (page 323)

ALSO WORKS WITH: American lobsters or spiny lobsters. The claws on spiny lobsters are small, with no edible meat, so disregard the below mentions of claws when dealing with those.

Cut each lobster in half lengthwise: Hold a lobster firmly by its back, stomach-side down, using a kitchen towel. Using a very sharp knife, swiftly pierce the base of the head (where it meets the abdomen) to sever the spinal cord, and push the knife down with the heel of your hand to crack the body in half lengthwise. Now continue the cut to cleave the tail in half lengthwise, repeating the pushing technique, then separate the halves. Remove the claws and give a crack in the largest part with the back of the knife. Repeat with the remaining lobsters.

Prepare a charcoal grill for direct heat. Place the claws and lobster halves shell-side down on the grill. Cut off 2 or 3 rounds of butter and put it on the tail flesh. Cover with the lid and cook until the meat is no longer translucent and the shells turn bright red, 10 to 12 minutes. The claws could take a few more minutes. Melt more of the butter and serve for dipping.

CRAB OR CRAYFISH BOIL
WITH WILD GAME SAUSAGE

SERVES 4 TO 6

6 to 8 quarts water

½ to ¾ cup Old Bay Seasoning, to taste

8 medium red, new, or other boiling potatoes

4 wild game andouille sausages, halved crosswise (see page 45)

2 heads garlic, halved crosswise

2 medium onions, peeled and halved

1 lemon, halved

12 blue crabs (3½ to 4 pounds), or 8 to 12 pounds crayfish

4 ears corn, shucked and snapped in half

2 pounds assorted shellfish (clams, mussels, shrimp, crayfish), rinsed or scrubbed if necessary

Large loaf of bread or a couple of baguettes, sliced

Lemon wedges

Bottle of hot sauce

Melted butter

I like anything that brings the woods and waters together, and this recipe does it in a big and dramatic way. It's the ultimate creation for the all-around outdoorsman. For this recipe it's OK to use some wild game andouille from your freezer (visit the chapter on big game for that), but the seafood is going to have to be so fresh that it's still crawling. Don't get overly finicky about the quantities or poundages of your crustaceans on this one. If you come up light on crayfish, or have an extra crab or two, everything will work out fine.

ALSO WORKS WITH: You can use lobster, crayfish, blue crabs, Dungeness crabs, shrimp, or pretty much any other crustacean here.

Combine 6 quarts water and Old Bay Seasoning in a lobster pot and bring to a boil over high heat. Add the potatoes, sausages, garlic, onions, and halved lemon and bring back to a boil. Reduce the heat to medium-low and slow boil until the potatoes are almost done; you should be able to start to pierce them with a fork, but don't let them get soft enough to eat, about 25 minutes.

Raise the heat to high and add the crabs and corn. If you need to add more water at this point, the ratio is 1½ teaspoons Old Bay Seasoning for each cup of water, or to taste. Bring back to a boil and cook until the crabs turn completely red, about 5 minutes. Add the shellfish, bring back to a boil, then remove from the heat and let sit until the shells open or turn completely red, about 3 minutes.

Set a strainer in the sink and pour the seafood in to drain. Spread the seafood and vegetables onto a newspaper-covered table and serve with bread, lemon wedges, hot sauce, and melted butter. No need for plates or forks, just nutcrackers or seafood crackers, maybe a small mallet, and plenty of napkins.

DUNGENESS CRAB
WITH MELTED BUTTER

SERVES 4

My buddy Ron Leighton of southeast Alaska convinced me long ago that it's easier and more efficient to clean your crabs before you cook them, so that you're only boiling the legs, or knuckles, rather than the whole crab. (See page 278 for instructions for knuckling crab.) This approach especially makes sense for a crab trapper, who's likely dealing with a bigger volume of crabs than someone who goes down to the market and buys just one or two live crabs for dinner. Ron feels that the water used for boiling knuckles should be as "salty as the ocean, in order to bring out the sweetness of the crab," and I agree wholeheartedly with his assessment. Boil the knuckles for fifteen minutes. Cooked in such a way, it's easy to save any leftovers for later meals. Just pick the meat from the shells and freeze it in vacuum-sealed bags. It's not quite as good as fresh crab, but it's good enough to make you really happy that you saved some.

3 tablespoons kosher salt, or more as needed

8 knuckles from 4 Dungeness crabs (see page 278)

1 cup (2 sticks) salted butter, melted, for serving

ALSO WORKS WITH: Any crab, but you'll need to adjust cooking times according to the size. As a point of reference, a blue crab should be cooked for about 10 minutes.

Fill a large stockpot with water and add enough salt that it tastes about as salty as seawater. Bring to a boil over high heat, and then add the crab knuckles. Boil for 15 minutes, then remove the crab knuckles and plunge them into a bath of ice water to cool. Allow them to cool to a comfortable handling temperature, then drain in a colander. Serve the knuckles alongside small bowls of melted butter for dipping.

LINGUINE
WITH CLAMS AND CHORIZO

SERVES 6

I'm always finding ways to introduce my crabs, shrimp, and clams into various concoctions that can be stirred into a pot of buttered pasta. Not only does it taste great to grown-ups, but it's a reliable way to open up your kids to the tastes and textures of seafood without camouflaging them so much that you end up hiding the very thing that you're trying to showcase. This particular seafood-and-pasta dish is for clams. I love the springy texture of the clams alongside the softer textures of pasta, and here you're adding some chorizo for a little extra kick. Recipes like this are a good reason to always freeze some of your sausage bulk (uncased, that is) in poly or vacuum-sealed bags. That way, it's quick and simple to add it to dishes without having to undo the laborious task of stuffing your sausage into natural hog casings.

ALSO WORKS WITH: Just about any clam can be put to use here. When you're dealing with small, live clams such as manila clams or littlenecks, follow the directions below. If you're dealing with larger clam species that are generally processed before cooking, such as geoducks, big razor clams, or gaper clams, plan on using a pound or so of minced clam meat for this recipe. It's fine if you're pulling already cleaned clam meat from your freezer. Stir it in after adding the garlic, and never mind the stuff about clam shells. You can also use the diced meat of sea cucumbers here.

3 tablespoons kosher salt

8 ounces Mexican chorizo (about 2 sausage links; see page 44)

¼ cup extra virgin olive oil

6 cloves garlic, minced

3 dozen littleneck or manila clams, purged (12 to 16 ounces of shucked or minced clam meat)—see page 292 for instructions on purging clams

½ teaspoon red chile flakes, or more to taste (optional)

1 cup white wine

1 pound linguine

½ cup Toasted Breadcrumb Topping (page 289)

Leaves from 1 small bunch fresh flat-leaf parsley, finely chopped

Bring a 6-quart pot of water to a boil and add the salt.

Remove the chorizo from its casing if it has one. Heat 1 teaspoon of the oil in a heavy-bottomed pot with a lid over medium heat. Cook the chorizo until it's fully cooked, about 5 minutes. If there is more than 1 tablespoon of grease in the pan, drain the excess grease and discard. Add the remaining olive oil to the pan. Add the garlic and cook for 30 seconds. Add the clams, red chile flakes, and wine. Cover and bring to a simmer over medium-high heat. After 5 minutes, remove any clams that have opened to a bowl. Cover the pot and continue to simmer for another 5 minutes; remove any more opened clams, discarding any unopened ones, as they may be dead. Remove the cooking liquid from the heat and reserve.

Set aside 12 of the clams in a bowl and cover with foil. Shuck the remaining 24 clams onto a grooved cutting board. Chop the clam meat and discard the shells, being careful not to lose any of the clam liquor. Add the chopped clams to the whole clams in the bowl, along with any liquid saved on the cutting board.

Add the linguine to the boiling salted water. Cook according to the package instructions until al dente.

Meanwhile, bring the reserved cooking liquid back up to a simmer. Reserve 1 cup of the pasta water. Drain the linguine. Add the linguine to the simmering cooking liquid, adding the pasta water ½ cup at a time as needed to make a smooth sauce. Add the reserved clams and toss to coat the pasta, adding more pasta water if needed to make a smooth, velvety sauce. Transfer to a serving platter, arranging the 12 whole clams on top. Top with the breadcrumbs and parsley. Serve immediately with additional red chile flakes, if desired.

EXTRAS

BASIC AND NOT-SO-BASIC SAUCES,
SIDES, AND ACCOMPANIMENTS

BROWN GAME STOCK

MAKES 4 TO 6 QUARTS

Brown game stock (roasted game stock) can be used to enrich many of the stews, sauces, and soups in this book. An extraction of flavors housed in bones and vegetables, it's simply a ratio of game bones, aromatics, and water. A good formula to follow is to allow two pounds of bones per gallon of water. And split the ratio of your aromatics into 50 percent onions, 25 percent carrots, and 25 percent celery. In the end, stocks are really more about ratios of ingredients than a specific recipe. This recipe is a good guideline to get started and can be doubled or halved as needed. If you've got a lot of bones, scale up the recipe and use a 12- or 24-quart pot.

Note: Quantities will vary depending on the size of bones or carcasses, but more is better than less. One moose femur is plenty, while several rabbit or small game birds are necessary. A few deer leg bones or a single wild turkey carcass will do the job.

Preheat the oven to 400°F.

Saw the bones into 3-inch pieces or break them with a hatchet or mallet to expose the marrow. This creates a much richer stock. Place the bones on a baking sheet or roasting pan. Drizzle with oil. Roast until well browned and aromatic, about 45 minutes, stirring halfway through. Add the chopped vegetables and roast until just beginning to brown, about 10 minutes. Toss the bones and vegetables with the tomato paste and roast for another 5 minutes.

Fill a stockpot about halfway with water and turn the heat to high. Place the cooked bones with their drippings into the pot and add more water to just cover the bones. Bring to a boil over low heat and skim any foam that rises to the top. Reduce the heat to a bare simmer. Add the garlic, thyme, bay leaves, peppercorns, and half of the parsley stems. Avoid bringing the stock to a boil; a very slow simmer over low heat is best. Cook for at least 4 hours, but 8 to 12 hours is ideal to extract every bit of flavor. Some reduction is expected and intensifies flavors, but if the stock reduces too much (well below the level of the highest bones), add a little water to offset evaporation. In the last 30 minutes of cooking, add the remaining parsley stems.

5 pounds venison or any small or large game bones (see Note)

Olive oil

2 large onions, cut into chunks

2 ribs celery, cut into chunks

1 to 2 large carrots, cut into chunks

4 ounces tomato paste

1 head garlic, top sliced off

6 sprigs fresh thyme

2 bay leaves

2 tablespoons black peppercorns

Stems from ½ bunch parsley

After 4 to 12 hours, remove the stock from the heat, allow to cool slightly, and prepare to strain. It's safest to do the straining process on the floor or at a low table. Set a 6-quart metal pot or heavy-duty plastic container on a baking sheet on the floor or on a low table. Set a fine-mesh strainer (China cap if you have one) or a colander lined with cheesecloth in the pot. Using tongs, carefully transfer the largest solids into the strainer and allow excess liquid to drain into the empty pot. Discard the bones. Strain the remaining stock and discard the solids. If there are still a lot of particles in the stock, you can strain again and be left with a clear liquid.

TO COOL: The fastest way to cool the stock is to place the pot of strained stock in a stopped-up sink and surround the pot with ice. Fill the sink with water. Stir the stock occasionally. When completely cooled, refrigerate. After about 4 hours, the fat will rise to the top of the stock and solidify. Remove the fat and discard. Transfer the stock into quart containers and freeze until ready to use.

BLONDE GAME STOCK

MAKES ABOUT 6 QUARTS

3 to 5 pounds wild turkey or any small game bones (see Note)

2 large onions, cut into chunks

2 ribs celery, cut into chunks

1 to 2 large carrots, cut into chunks

1 head garlic, top sliced off

4 sprigs fresh thyme

2 bay leaves

1 tablespoon black peppercorns

Stems from ¼ bunch parsley

Note: Quantities will vary depending on the size of bones or carcasses, but more is better than less. A single wild turkey carcass will do the job, while several rabbit or small game birds are necessary.

This blonde game stock (called a "white" stock in classic French cuisine) is a stock that is not roasted. Think of it like the chicken broth your grandmother made for soup. It can help enrich lighter-colored stews, soups, and dishes when more subtle flavors are called for. A good formula to follow is to allow two pounds of bones per gallon of water. And split the ratio of your aromatics into 50 percent onions, 25 percent carrots, and 25 percent celery. This recipe is a good guideline to get started and can be doubled or halved as needed. If you've got a lot of bones, scale up the recipe and use a 12- or 24-quart pot.

Saw or break the bones to expose the marrow. This creates a much richer stock.

Fill a stockpot about halfway with water and turn the heat to high. Place the bones in the pot and add more water to just cover the bones. Add the onions, celery, and carrots and bring the liquid just up to a boil. Skim any foam that rises to the top (do this as needed throughout the cooking time). Reduce the heat to a bare simmer. Add the garlic, thyme, bay leaves, peppercorns, and parsley. Avoid bringing the stock to a boil; a very slow simmer over low heat is best. Cook for at least 2 hours and up to

4 hours. Some reduction is expected and intensifies flavors, but if the stock reduces too much (well below the level of the highest bones), add a little water to offset evaporation.

After 2 to 4 hours, remove the stock from the heat, allow to cool slightly, and prepare to strain. It's safest to do the straining process on the floor or at a low table. Set a 6-quart metal pot or heavy-duty plastic container on a baking sheet on the floor or a low table. Set a fine-mesh strainer (or China cap if you have one) or a colander lined with cheesecloth in the pot. Strain the stock and discard the solids. If there are still a lot of particles in the stock, you can strain again and be left with a clear liquid.

TO COOL: The fastest way to cool the stock is to place the pot of strained stock in a stopped-up sink and surround the pot with ice. Fill the sink with water. Stir the stock occasionally. When completely cooled, refrigerate. After about 4 hours, the fat will rise to the top of the stock and solidify. Remove the fat and discard. Transfer the stock into smaller containers and freeze until ready to use.

FISH STOCK (FISH FUMET)

MAKES 1 TO 2 QUARTS

Fish stock makes great use of fish carcasses that can pile up after an afternoon of filleting. Use it to enrich seafood-based stews and soups. It's a surprisingly fast stock to prepare and makes a big difference in the flavor of your dish—it's one of those tasks that's absolutely worth the effort if you're cooking a lot of fish dishes. Traditionally made with white-fleshed fish, it can also be made with salmon; it just won't be as clear. If you enjoy the flavors of dill or tarragon, feel free to add a few sprigs with the parsley.

Chop the fish skeletons and heads into manageable pieces if using large fish skeletons. Fill a bowl with salted water and rinse the fish bones. Drain and rinse well under fresh water.

Fill a stockpot about halfway with water and turn the heat to medium-high. Place the bones in the pot and add more water to just cover the bones. Add the celery, fennel, onions, carrot, and leek and bring up to a fast simmer. Reduce the heat to low and skim and discard any foam that rises to the top. Add the garlic, bay leaf, parsley stems, and peppercorns. Avoid bringing the stock to a boil; a very slow simmer over low heat is best. Cook for 45 minutes. Some reduction is expected and intensifies flavors, but if the stock reduces too much while cooking, you can add a little water to offset evaporation.

Remove from heat and cool slightly before straining. Set a fine-mesh strainer in a large bowl or pot and strain the stock. If there are still a lot of particles in the stock, on the second run, line the strainer with a paper towel. This will filter the stock thoroughly and you'll be left with a clear liquid. Transfer to storage containers and freeze until ready to use.

2 pounds fish bones and heads but not gills

Kosher salt

4 ribs celery, thinly sliced

2 fennel bulbs, thinly sliced

2 medium onions, cut into chunks

1 small carrot, cut into chunks

1 medium leek, white parts only, thinly sliced (optional)

3 cloves garlic, crushed

1 bay leaf

Stems from ¼ bunch parsley

5 black or white peppercorns

BASIC BROWN GRAVY
(AKA HUNTER'S SAUCE)

MAKES ABOUT 1 CUP

Reserved juices from pan-searing game steak or roast

Up to 2 tablespoons unsalted butter, if needed

2 tablespoons chopped shallot or scallion whites

8 ounces mushrooms (button, cremini or other mushroom), sliced

1 sprig fresh rosemary or thyme (optional)

½ teaspoon kosher salt

2 tablespoons all-purpose flour

¼ cup dry white or red wine (see Note)

1 cup Blonde Game Stock (page 306) or low-sodium chicken broth

Kosher salt

Freshly ground black pepper

Splash of Worcestershire sauce

Note: If you're out of wine, ¼ cup beer or a splash of red wine vinegar will work just as well.

This is a simple gravy recipe to make when pan-searing any kind of game steak or roast. It can be embellished with different herbs, flavored with 1 teaspoon of mustard (in with the shallots), or finished with 2 tablespoons cream or crème fraîche for extra richness (best with fowl or small game) or 2 tablespoons rinsed capers or green peppercorns. Once you've seared and cooked your piece of meat and it's safely resting, begin this gravy. It can be doubled or tripled for large roasts.

Discard all but 2 tablespoons of fat from the pan; if less than 2 tablespoons, add up to 2 tablespoons butter to make up the difference. Heat the pan over medium-high heat. When the fat is shimmering, add the shallot, mushrooms, and rosemary and cook until softened, 6 to 8 minutes. Add the salt. Reduce the heat to medium and sprinkle the flour over the mushroom mixture. Cook, stirring constantly, for 1 to 2 minutes to lightly toast the flour; be careful not to burn it or you'll ruin your sauce. Add the wine and deglaze, scraping up any caramelized bits that may have adhered to the bottom of the pan (this is where the flavor lives). Add the stock and any reserved juices released by the resting meat, raise the heat to medium-high, bring to a boil, and whisk briskly to break up any lumps. Season with salt and pepper and a splash of Worcestershire sauce. Remove from the heat.

BASIC BRINE

1 gallon water

1 cup kosher salt

1 cup packed brown sugar

10 black peppercorns

3 bay leaves

8 pounds ice (from 1 gallon water)

Good for waterfowl, upland birds, or wild hogs.

Combine the water, salt, brown sugar, peppercorns, and bay leaves in a large pot and bring to a boil over high heat. Remove from the heat and let cool to close to room temperature. Transfer the liquid to a large container with a tight-fitting lid and add the ice. Add your meat, cover, and refrigerate for the amount of time specified in your recipe.

ENRICHED BRINE

This brine is used in the Roast Pheasant recipe on page 172. It can be used for any waterfowl, upland birds, or wild hogs.

Combine 4 cups of the water, the salt, sugar, juniper berries, bay leaves, and garlic in a large pot and bring to a boil, stirring until the salt and sugar dissolve. Remove from the heat and add the remaining 4 cups water. Set aside to cool completely. Put the meat into a container with a tight-fitting lid and pour the brine over the meat. Cover and refrigerate for the amount of time specified in your recipe.

8 cups water

½ cup kosher salt

2 tablespoons sugar

1 teaspoon juniper berries, crushed

2 bay leaves

2 cloves garlic, crushed

BASIC BRINE FOR SMOKING FISH

This brine is used in the Hot Smoked Trout recipe on page 198, but it will work for just about any fish or small-size bird you plan to smoke.

In a nonmetallic container big enough to hold the fish, combine the salt, both sugars, honey, and water and whisk vigorously to dissolve the ingredients. Chill the brine. Thoroughly rinse the fish and submerge in the brine, using a plate to weight it down beneath the surface. Cover and refrigerate for the amount of time specified in your recipe.

¾ cup kosher salt

½ cup granulated sugar

¼ cup packed brown sugar

¼ cup honey

8 cups lukewarm water

BRINE FOR CURING A HAM

2 gallons water

2½ cups kosher salt

2 cups packed brown sugar

2 teaspoons yellow mustard seeds

20 black peppercorns

8 juniper berries

6 bay leaves

8 cloves garlic

1 tablespoon Prague Powder #1

This brine is used in the Smoked Ham recipe on page 68. It can be used for any large muscle bone-in or bone-out cuts of meat intended for smoking.

Combine the water, salt, brown sugar, mustard seeds, peppercorns, juniper berries, bay leaves, garlic, and Prague Powder #1 in a large pot and bring to a boil over high heat. Remove from the heat and let cool to room temperature, then let it chill in the refrigerator. See the recipe on pages 68–69 for how to inject the brine into a large bone-in roast and the process for brining and smoking.

CREOLE SEASONING

MAKES ABOUT ⅓ CUP

1½ tablespoons paprika

1 tablespoon garlic powder

1 tablespoon onion powder

1 teaspoon freshly ground black pepper

1 teaspoon cayenne pepper

1 teaspoon dried thyme

½ teaspoon dried oregano

This rub can be multiplied and stored for up to six months in a cool, dry place for use on grilled or smoked meats and fish, in stews (see Small Game and Sausage Gumbo on page 98), or as a seasoning for sides like roasted potatoes. Be sure to season with salt along with the rub, as this recipe doesn't include salt.

Combine the paprika, garlic powder, onion powder, black pepper, cayenne, thyme, and oregano in a small bowl. Store in an airtight container.

BBQ RUB

MAKES 3 CUPS

This rub will make just about any grilled roast or steak even tastier. You'll find it in use in the BBQ Smoked Beaver Sandwiches (page 101) and Split and Smoked Turkey with BBQ Sauce (page 169).

Mix the chile powder, salt, brown sugar, cumin, granulated garlic, oregano, Hungarian paprika, powdered mustard, smoked paprika, black pepper, onion powder, and cayenne together in a bowl. Store in an airtight container. The rub will last for up to 6 months in a cool, dry place.

½ cup chili powder

½ cup kosher salt

½ cup packed brown sugar

2 tablespoons ground cumin

2 tablespoons granulated garlic

2 tablespoons dried oregano

2 tablespoons Hungarian paprika

1 tablespoon powdered mustard

1 tablespoon smoked paprika

1 tablespoon freshly ground black pepper

2 teaspoons onion powder

1 teaspoon cayenne pepper

CLAYTON SAUNDERS'S BBQ SOP

MAKES ABOUT 1 QUART

This recipe pairs with Clayton Saunders's South Texas Wild Hog Shoulder (page 64). But this sop is too good to be kept to just one recipe. Use this to baste any game meat you throw on the grill: elk, rabbit, turkey, duck—they'd all benefit from the range of flavors here.

Combine the vinegar, water, butter, ketchup, Worcestershire sauce, lemons, onion, and some salt and pepper in a medium saucepan and bring to a simmer. It is now ready to be applied to the cooking meat. You will need a pastry brush or kitchen rag to apply the sop.

1 cup distilled white vinegar or apple cider vinegar

1 cup water

½ cup (1 stick) unsalted butter

1 cup ketchup

1 cup Worcestershire sauce

2 to 4 lemons, sliced

1 onion, sliced

Kosher salt

Freshly ground black pepper

BBQ SAUCE

MAKES 3 CUPS

2 cups ketchup

½ cup apple cider vinegar

¼ cup BBQ Rub (page 313)

¼ cup packed brown sugar

⅓ cup molasses

2 tablespoons fresh lemon juice

2 tablespoons Worcestershire sauce

1½ tablespoons liquid smoke

1 tablespoon Dijon mustard

1 tablespoon kosher salt

1 tablespoon freshly ground black pepper

Whisk together the ketchup, vinegar, BBQ rub, brown sugar, molasses, lemon juice, Worcestershire sauce, liquid smoke, mustard, salt, and pepper in a bowl. Store in an airtight container in the refrigerator, where it will keep for about 1 week, or longer if you omit the lemon juice.

ADOBADA

MAKES ABOUT 2 CUPS

8 dried guajillo chiles, wiped clean, stems and seeds removed, torn into large pieces

4 dried pasilla chiles, wiped clean, stems and seeds removed, torn into large pieces

12 cloves garlic

4 canned chipotle chiles in adobo sauce

¼ cup honey

¼ cup cider vinegar

2 teaspoons ground cinnamon

2 teaspoons ground cumin

2 teaspoons dried oregano

¼ teaspoon ground cloves

2 tablespoons kosher salt

This deep, spicy sauce is used to braise shanks (see Whole Braised Venison Shank Adobada, page 59) or any other meat from game birds to shoulder roasts. It can also be used as a basting sauce for grilled or roasted meats or seafood.

Heat a large, heavy skillet over medium heat until hot. Working in batches, toast the chiles until they blister slightly and are pliable. Transfer to a large bowl. Pour hot water over the chiles to cover them. Place a small plate on top of the chiles to keep them submerged. Soak until soft, about 1 hour.

Transfer the chiles to a blender with ½ cup of the soaking liquid. Reserve the remaining liquid. Add the garlic, chipotles, honey, vinegar, cinnamon, cumin, oregano, cloves, and salt and blend until a smooth thick paste forms. Add enough of the reserved soaking water to yield 4 cups of marinade (*adobo*) and blend until emulsified.

BASIC VINAIGRETTE

MAKES ABOUT ¼ CUP

This vinaigrette is a standard for any salad. Bump it up with herbs or swap out the vinegar for a different kind. It's one to commit to memory.

Whisk the vinegar (use 1 tablespoon vinegar for a standard vinaigrette, 2 tablespoons if you like yours a little more acidic), salt, pepper, and mustard in a small bowl. Slowly whisk in the oil to emulsify. Taste and adjust the seasonings.

1 to 2 tablespoons red wine vinegar

½ teaspoon kosher salt

½ teaspoon freshly ground black pepper

½ teaspoon Dijon mustard

3 tablespoons extra virgin olive oil

SPICY CITRUS DRESSING

MAKES ABOUT ¼ CUP

This is a more elaborate dressing. It's used on the salad that's paired with the Venison Carpaccio on page 34.

Whisk the orange juice, lemon juice, vinegar, honey, mustard, salt, pepper, and red chile flakes in a medium bowl. Slowly drizzle in the oil while whisking vigorously until the dressing is emulsified.

1 tablespoon fresh orange juice

1 teaspoon fresh lemon juice

1 tablespoon rice wine vinegar

1 teaspoon honey

1 teaspoon Dijon mustard

½ teaspoon kosher salt

½ teaspoon freshly ground black pepper

Pinch of red chile flakes

3 tablespoons extra virgin olive oil

CLASSIC GREMOLATA

MAKES ABOUT ⅓ CUP

Zest of 2 lemons (grated on a Microplane)

2 cloves garlic, grated

⅓ cup finely chopped fresh flat-leaf parsley

2 teaspoons sea salt

Freshly ground black pepper to taste

This is an excellent condiment for wild game and fish. Sometimes I like to use orange zest in place of the lemon zest, and you can play with the herbs too—parsley, mint, oregano, and basil are all possibilities. It's fantastic on Venison Carpaccio (page 34), Osso Bucco (page 60), roasted birds (pages 133, 170, and 172), and even grilled fish (page 209).

In a small bowl, combine all the ingredients. The gremolata is best if used within 24 hours.

BALSAMIC REDUCTION

MAKES ABOUT ½ CUP

1 cup aged balsamic vinegar

This reduction works with simply prepared meats, fish, vegetables, and cheese. It's also paired with the Grilled Venison Loin with Cauliflower Puree (page 40).

Pour the vinegar into a small, wide sauté pan and bring to a boil. Reduce the heat and gently simmer for 15 to 20 minutes, stirring occasionally, until it reduces by half and is thick enough to coat the back of a spoon. Let cool and serve at room temperature.

BLUEBERRY PORT COMPOTE

MAKES 1¼ CUPS

Heat the oil in a small saucepan over medium heat. Add the shallot and cook, stirring often, until softened, 6 to 8 minutes. Add the blueberries, ginger, cinnamon, star anise, sugar, port, both vinegars, the orange zest, salt, and red chile flakes and bring to a simmer. Cook, stirring occasionally, until the blueberries start to burst and give off liquid and then slightly thicken, 8 to 10 minutes. Remove from the heat and set aside to let cool. The compote will thicken more as it cools.

Remove and discard the ginger, cinnamon, and star anise, if you like. Adjust the seasonings. Serve immediately, or transfer to a jar with a tight-fitting lid and store in the refrigerator.

1 tablespoon vegetable oil

1 large shallot, finely chopped

2 cups (1 pint) fresh or frozen blueberries

2 slices fresh ginger, smashed

1 cinnamon stick

1 star anise pod

¼ cup sugar

¼ cup tawny port

2 tablespoons balsamic vinegar

1 tablespoon red wine vinegar

1 teaspoon finely grated orange zest

Generous pinch of kosher salt

Generous pinch of red chile flakes

APPLE, CHERRY, AND SAGE CHUTNEY

MAKES 2¼ CUPS

Combine the apples, apple juice, brown sugar, vinegar, dried cherries, raisins, honey, sage, rosemary, garlic, and lemon juice in a medium saucepan and cook over medium heat until the mixture starts to bubble. Add the salt. Reduce the heat to low and simmer, stirring occasionally to prevent sticking, until the fruit is soft and pulpy, the liquid is mostly absorbed, and the chutney is fairly thick, 35 to 40 minutes. Remove from the pot and let cool. Taste and add more salt if needed. The chutney will keep, covered, in the refrigerator for up to 1 week.

1½ pounds unpeeled Granny Smith or other tart apples, cored and chopped

½ cup apple juice

⅓ cup packed brown sugar

¼ cup apple cider vinegar

½ cup dried cherries

¼ cup golden raisins

2 tablespoons honey

2 tablespoons finely chopped fresh sage

1 tablespoon finely chopped fresh rosemary

1 tablespoon minced garlic

Juice of 1 lemon

Kosher salt

HERBED TARTAR SAUCE

MAKES 2½ CUPS

2 cups mayonnaise

2 tablespoons minced garlic

2 tablespoons chopped fresh chives

1 tablespoon chopped fresh rosemary

1 teaspoon freshly ground black pepper

10 fresh basil leaves, chopped

2 tablespoons chopped capers

10 cornichon pickles, chopped

Zest and juice of 2 lemons

This recipe can be quadrupled if you're feeding a crowd.

Whisk the mayonnaise, garlic, chives, rosemary, pepper, basil, capers, pickles, and lemon zest and juice in a medium bowl until incorporated.

BRANDIED CHERRIES

MAKES 3 CUPS

¾ cup water

¾ cup granulated sugar

2 juniper berries, lightly crushed (optional)

1 cinnamon stick

Pinch of kosher salt

1 cup brandy

1 pound fresh cherries, stemmed and pitted

Combine the water, sugar, juniper berries, if using, the cinnamon, and salt in a medium saucepan. Bring to a simmer over medium-high heat, stirring until the sugar dissolves, about 5 minutes. Add the brandy and cherries and stir to combine. Remove from the heat and set aside to cool. Transfer the cherries and their cooking liquid to a clean jar with a tight-fitting lid and refrigerate at least 2 days before serving. The cherries will keep in the refrigerator for at least 1 to 2 weeks.

SPICY PICKLED RED ONIONS

MAKES 1⅔ CUPS (THE ONIONS THEMSELVES MAKE 1¼ CUPS)

1 cup white wine vinegar

3 cloves garlic, smashed

1 large red onion, thinly sliced into rings

¼ cup sugar

1 teaspoon red chile flakes

1 teaspoon coriander seeds

1 teaspoon yellow mustard seeds (optional)

Generous pinch of kosher salt

Bring the vinegar to a boil in a medium saucepan over high heat. Add the garlic, onion, sugar, red chile flakes, coriander seeds, mustard seeds, if using, and salt. Cook, stirring, until the sugar dissolves and the onion wilts, about 5 minutes Remove the pot from the heat and let cool. Transfer the pickled onions to a clean jar with a tight-fitting lid and chill in the refrigerator for up to 10 days.

WALNUT AND MINT PESTO

MAKES 1½ CUPS

1 cup walnuts, toasted

1 clove garlic, peeled

2 cups packed fresh flat-leaf parsley leaves

1 cup packed baby arugula

1 cup packed fresh mint leaves

Freshly grated zest from 1 lemon

¾ cup extra virgin olive oil, plus more to float on top

½ cup finely grated Parmigiano-Reggiano cheese

Juice of ½ lemon (about 2 tablespoons), or to taste

Kosher salt

Freshly ground black pepper

This recipe can be multiplied and frozen for future use. A pinch of ascorbic acid or a smashed vitamin C tablet will help to preserve the green color of the pesto. This is recommended especially if you're making a large batch.

Put the walnuts and garlic in the food processor and pulse until coarsely chopped. Add the parsley, arugula, mint, and lemon zest and process until coarsely chopped. With the motor running, drizzle in the oil through the hole in the lid. Add the cheese, lemon juice, and salt and pepper to taste and pulse until combined.

Transfer the pesto to a container with a tight-fitting lid and add a thin layer of oil to cover the top of the pesto.. Store in the refrigerator for up to 2 weeks or freezer for up to 3 months.

CLASSIC BASIL PESTO

MAKES 1 CUP

2 cups packed fresh basil leaves

⅓ cup pine nuts

1 clove garlic, peeled

¾ cup extra virgin olive oil, plus more to float on top

2 tablespoons fresh lemon juice

1½ teaspoons kosher salt

1 teaspoon freshly ground black pepper

½ cup grated Parmigiano-Reggiano cheese

This recipe can be multiplied and frozen for future use. A pinch of ascorbic acid or a smashed vitamin C tablet will help to preserve the green color of the pesto. This is recommended especially if you're making a large batch.

Pulse the basil, pine nuts, and garlic in a food processor several times, until coarsely chopped. Add 2 tablespoons of the oil and the lemon juice and process until smooth. Add the salt and pepper and, with the motor running, slowly pour in the remaining oil through the hole in the lid. Add the cheese and pulse a few more times to incorporate.

Transfer the pesto to a container with a tight-fitting lid and add a thin layer of oil to cover the top of the pesto. Store in the refrigerator for up to 2 weeks or freezer for up to 3 months.

CHERMOULA

MAKES 1 CUP

Chermoula is traditionally served with grilled fish in Morocco. But like other sauces of this type (like pesto, chimichurri, and sauce verte), it goes well with just about anything grilled, meat and fowl included.

With the motor of a food processor running, drop in the garlic through the hole in the lid, one clove at a time, until chopped. Scrape down the sides with a spatula. Add the cilantro, parsley, cumin, paprika, salt, lemon zest, coriander, and cayenne and pulse to chop. With the motor running, drizzle in the oil and lemon juice and process until still slightly chunky. Transfer to a small container with a tight-fitting lid and refrigerate until ready to use.

6 cloves garlic

2 cups packed fresh cilantro leaves

2 cups packed fresh flat-leaf parsley leaves

2 teaspoons ground cumin

2 teaspoons paprika, preferably smoked

1½ teaspoons kosher salt

2 teaspoons finely grated lemon zest

1 teaspoon ground coriander

Pinch of cayenne pepper

¾ cup extra virgin olive oil

2 tablespoons fresh lemon juice

SAUCE VERTE
(PARSLEY, CHIVE, AND CAPER SAUCE)

MAKES ⅔ CUP

Versions of this flavorful sauce are called sauce verte in France and salsa verde in Italy. It's used as a sauce for simply prepared fish and meats and as a condiment in sandwiches. The addition of anchovies and capers gives it a briny richness that makes it taste more complex than it really is.

With the motor of a food processor running, drop in the garlic through the hole in the lid to chop it. Scrape down the sides with a spatula. Add the parsley, chives, anchovies, and capers and process until finely chopped. With the motor running, add the lemon juice, water, and oil through the hole in the lid and process until the liquid is incorporated. Season with salt and pepper. Transfer to a small bowl.

1 clove garlic

1 cup packed fresh flat-leaf parsley leaves

¾ cup coarsely chopped fresh chives

4 anchovies, coarsely chopped

3 tablespoons capers, drained

2 tablespoons fresh lemon juice

2 tablespoons water

¼ cup olive oil

Kosher salt

Freshly ground black pepper

ANCHOVY BUTTER

MAKES 2 LOGS

Put the anchovies, garlic, and Worcestershire sauce in a mini food processor and process until finely ground. Break the butter up into chunks and add it to the bowl. Process until smooth. Zest the lemon into the bowl and process again until combined. Scrape onto two pieces of parchment paper, roll into logs, and refrigerate until firm. Store in the refrigerator for up to 1 week or the freezer for up to 3 months.

10 to 12 anchovy fillets

6 cloves garlic, peeled

1 teaspoon Worcestershire sauce

1 cup (2 sticks) unsalted butter, softened

Zest of 1 lemon

CAYENNE BUTTER

MAKES 2 LOGS

Put the garlic in a mini food processor and process until chopped. Break the butter up into chunks and add to the bowl. Add the cayenne, salt, lemon zest, and lemon juice and process until smooth. Scrape onto two pieces of parchment paper, roll into logs, and refrigerate until firm. Store in the refrigerator for up to 1 week or in the freezer for up to 3 months.

2 small cloves garlic, peeled

1 cup (2 sticks) unsalted butter, softened

1½ teaspoons cayenne pepper

¼ teaspoon kosher salt

Zest of 1 small lemon (2 teaspoons)

Juice of ½ small lemon (1 tablespoon)

CHIMICHURRI BUTTER

MAKES 2 LOGS

Put the parsley, garlic, oregano, red chile flakes, salt, and vinegar in a mini food processor and process until finely ground. Break the butter up into chunks and add to the bowl. Process until smooth. Scrape onto two pieces of parchment paper, roll into logs, and refrigerate until firm. Store in the refrigerator for up to 1 week or in the freezer for up to 3 months.

2 cups packed fresh flat-leaf parsley leaves

4 cloves garlic

2 teaspoons fresh oregano leaves

½ teaspoon red chile flakes

½ teaspoon kosher salt

2 tablespoons white wine vinegar

1 cup (2 sticks) unsalted butter, softened

BREADCRUMBS, BISCUITS, AND DOUGHS

HOMEMADE BREADCRUMBS
(USING FILONE BREAD OR OTHER CRUSTY BREAD)

MAKES ABOUT 2½ CUPS

6 ounces filone (or other crusty bread)

Filone is a rustic, crusty Italian bread. Another type of crusty rustic bread may be substituted. These breadcrumbs are used in the Scotch Eggs on page 29 and the Wild Hog Milanese on page 43.

Preheat oven to 300°F.

To make coarse breadcrumbs: Cut the bread into small pieces and pulse in a food processor until they become coarse crumbs. Dry on baking sheets in the oven until dry and firm, about 20 minutes. Allow to cool before using or storing.

To make fine breadcrumbs: Return desired amount of cooled, dry breadcrumbs to the food processor and pulse until fine.

Use as recipe indicates or store in an airtight container in the freezer for up to 6 months.

BASIC PIE DOUGH

MAKES ONE 9-INCH DOUBLE CRUST

2½ cups all-purpose flour

1¼ teaspoons fine salt

1¾ sticks (14 tablespoons) unsalted butter, chilled and cut into ⅓-inch pieces

4 to 6 tablespoons ice water, or more as needed

1 teaspoon vodka or apple cider vinegar

Use this dough to turn any stew into a potpie. This recipe makes a double crust for a standard 9-inch pie dish. If rolled into a rectangle, it will make a crust large enough for a baking dish you'd use for a large potpie or enough dough to cut out a bunch of rounds for individual servings. I like to double the recipe and freeze half for future use.

In a food processor, combine the flour and salt and pulse a few times. Distribute the chilled butter pieces in the flour and toss gently with a spoon to coat each piece in a little flour. Pulse again about 20 times, until the butter pieces look like coarse meal. Remove the top and add 4 tablespoons of ice water and the vodka evenly across the crumbled butter-flour mixture. Return the lid and pulse again 2 to 4 times. Check the texture. If it's not just coming together as a dough when you give it a pinch, add 2 more tablespoons ice water and pulse again. Check the texture again. It should be crumbly but not dry.

Lay a piece of plastic wrap on a cutting board (if you can lay two pieces of plastic wrap side by side, even better). Turn the dough out onto the plastic and pat it down. It will still be crumbly. Carefully fold over the edges of the plastic wrap to make a tightly wrapped parcel, roughly ½ inch thick. Once the dough is wrapped, use a rolling pin to press the dough into a uniform thickness. Chill the dough for at least 1 hour before using. The dough will keep for up to 3 days in the refrigerator and 6 months in the freezer.

CHEDDAR CHIVE BISCUITS

MAKES EIGHT 3-INCH BISCUITS

These biscuits work as a side for just about anything. Split them in the middle, add a slice of leftover game meat, and call it a sandwich.

Preheat the oven to 425°F and line a baking sheet with parchment paper.

Whisk the flour, baking powder, salt, and pepper in a large bowl. Add the cheeses and chives and toss gently with your fingers. Cut in the chilled butter with a pastry blender or two butter knives. When the butter is pea-size and somewhat incorporated, form a well in the shaggy dough and pour the milk in the center. Pull the sides of the well in and knead together lightly until the mixture forms a solid mass.

Sprinkle flour onto a cutting board. Pat the dough into a ½-inch-thick rectangle. Fold the dough into thirds like a letter. Pat the dough out again into a rectangle about 1 inch high. Lightly flour the top; cut biscuits with a 2¾-inch round cutter, pressing the scraps together and patting down to 1 inch, to get about 8 biscuits. Place them on the prepared baking sheet and brush the tops with milk. Bake until lightly browned on the top and bottom, about 14 minutes. Serve warm, with butter.

2 cups all-purpose flour, plus more for dusting

1 tablespoon baking powder

1 teaspoon fine salt

½ teaspoon freshly ground black pepper

⅓ cup finely shredded cheddar cheese (about 1 ounce)

1 tablespoon grated Parmigiano-Reggiano cheese

2 tablespoons chopped fresh chives

½ cup (1 stick) unsalted butter, chilled and cubed

¾ cup milk, plus more for brushing

CORNBREAD

MAKES ONE 8 BY 8-INCH PAN

¼ cup (½ stick) unsalted butter, melted, plus more for the pan

1½ cups yellow fine cornmeal

½ cup all-purpose flour

¼ cup sugar

1½ teaspoons baking powder

½ teaspoon baking soda

1 teaspoon fine salt

2 large eggs

1½ cups milk

This is a versatile cornbread recipe. Feel free to add crumbled bacon, chopped jalapeños, or even corn kernels to jazz it up.

Preheat the oven to 425°F. Grease an 8 x 8-inch baking dish with butter.

Whisk the cornmeal, flour, sugar, baking powder, baking soda, and salt in a large bowl. In another bowl, whisk the eggs, then add the milk and melted butter. Add the wet ingredients to the dry ingredients and mix until a smooth batter forms, whisking out any lumps. Pour the batter into the prepared pan and bake on the middle rack until a toothpick comes out clean when inserted into the center of the cornbread, about 30 minutes. Let cool for 5 minutes before slicing and serving.

CATHEAD BISCUITS

MAKES 5 BISCUITS

These biscuits are intended to accompany Kevin Murphy's Kentucky-Style Squirrel Gravy (page 92). But they'd go well with just about any meal.

Preheat the oven to 425°F.

Mix the flour, salt, and sugar in a large bowl. Rub the lard or shortening (or cut the butter) into the flour. When you're done, the mixture should look like coarse cornmeal.

Pour in the buttermilk and gently mix it into the flour with your hands to where it feels and looks like brick mortar (firm and wet, where it can still flow). Sprinkle in more flour as needed; the dough will be wet and sticky, but not so wet and sticky that it clings to your fingers or won't scrape off the counter. Place on a hard floured surface. Pat out into a rectangle about 7 by 9 inches. Fold into thirds like a letter. Pat the dough out again into a rectangle about 1 inch high. Lightly flour the top; cut 3 biscuits with the mason jar. Then re-form to cut out 1 more, and re-form one more time for the last biscuit. Grease up a 10-inch cast-iron skillet with lard, shortening, or butter. Arrange the biscuits around each other, leaving about a ½-inch gap between them. Brush a little melted butter on top of the biscuits, if desired (it will help with browning).

Bake until puffed and light golden brown on top, 13 to 15 minutes. Turn the oven light on to check the biscuits (don't open the door or you'll lose your heat). All ovens are different, but Kevin's takes about 13 minutes for his biscuits. If you think the bottom of the biscuits are done, you can turn your broiler on for 30 seconds or more to brown the tops.

2 cups self-rising flour, plus more for sprinkling

¼ teaspoon kosher salt

½ to 1 tablespoon sugar (depending on how sweet you like them)

2 tablespoons lard, shortening, or unsalted butter (cut into small pieces), chilled, plus more for the pan

1 cup buttermilk

1 tablespoon unsalted butter, melted (optional)

SPECIAL EQUIPMENT: 1 mason jar (diameter of a cat head, or 3 inches)

POLENTA

MAKES 4 TO 6 SERVINGS

5 cups water

Big pinch of kosher salt

1 cup polenta or yellow coarse cornmeal

½ cup grated Parmigiano-Reggiano cheese

2 tablespoons unsalted butter

Used to accompany both the Osso Bucco (page 60) and the Rabbit Caccia-tore (page 103), this Italian starchy staple would pair well with any other stewy dish, especially the Whole Braised Venison Shank Adobada (page 59). This makes a very soft, creamy polenta. For a firmer polenta, use 1 cup less water for cooking and pour into an oiled 9 x 13-inch pan once cooked. Cool and refrigerate until firm.

Bring the water to a boil in a 4- to 6-quart pot. Add the salt. Whisking constantly to avoid lumps, slowly add the polenta in a thin stream. Reduce the heat to medium-low and continue to stir for 15 to 20 minutes, until the polenta becomes thick and large bubbles form (kind of like a volcano erupting). Remove from the heat and stir in the cheese and the butter until glossy and smooth. Set aside, covered, until ready to serve.

COCONUT RICE

MAKES 6 CUPS

2 cups jasmine rice

1 (13.5-ounce) can full-fat coconut milk, well shaken

½ cup water

1 tablespoon granulated sugar (optional)

1 teaspoon kosher salt

This fragrant, rich rice is a fantastic side for the Coconut Curry Fish Fillet Packets (page 213). It also works as an accompaniment for many other dishes in this book.

Put the rice in a heavy medium saucepan, add water to cover, and swish around with your fingers until the rice becomes cloudy. Drain. Repeat two more times, or until the water runs clear. Drain well. Stir in the coconut milk, water, sugar, if using, and salt and mix well. Bring to a boil. Stir the rice, scraping up any rice sticking to the bottom of the pan. Reduce the heat to low, cover, and cook, undisturbed, until the rice has absorbed the liquid and is tender, about 20 minutes. Remove from the heat and let sit undisturbed for 10 minutes. Fluff and serve.

CAULIFLOWER PUREE

MAKES ABOUT 1½ QUARTS

This recipe makes a decadent puree—great for holidays or other celebratory meals. It can be made less caloric by using solely whole milk, less cheese (6 ounces versus 8), and omitting the butter. Using a high-powered blender like a Vitamix makes the final puree velvety smooth with a texture as rich as the flavor.

Segment and chop the cauliflower into 1-inch pieces. Put the pieces in a large saucepan and add the cream, milk (it won't completely cover the cauliflower—that's OK), and salt. Cover and bring to a gentle simmer over medium heat, being careful not to let the cream mixture boil over. Adjust the heat if necessary and simmer until knife tender, 15 to 20 minutes. Remove the cauliflower from the cream mixture with a slotted spoon, reserving the cream mixture, and put it into a blender (do this in batches if necessary). Keeping the blender lid ajar and covered with a clean kitchen towel, puree the cauliflower while hot, slowly pouring in ¼ cup of the cream mixture, until the puree becomes very smooth. While still very warm, add the cheese and butter and blend. If the mixture is lumpy, blend with a little more cream. Pour the cauliflower puree into a bowl, season with salt and pepper, and stir to fully mix. This can be made up to a day ahead of time (cool, cover, and refrigerate). Gently rewarm in a saucepan over medium-low heat when you are ready to serve.

1 medium head cauliflower, halved and cored

1 cup heavy cream

1 cup whole milk

1 teaspoon kosher salt, plus more for seasoning

8 ounces Gruyère cheese, grated

2 tablespoons unsalted butter

Freshly ground black pepper

COLESLAW

MAKES 4 TO 6 SERVINGS

This slaw accompanies the BBQ Smoked Beaver Sandwiches (page 101), but it's too good to only use when you've hunted down a beaver. Make it a go-to recipe for barbecues and picnics. It makes an excellent side.

Whisk the mayonnaise, vinegar, sugar, mustard, granulated garlic, salt, onion powder, and pepper in a medium bowl until smooth. Slice the cabbage very thinly across the layers and add to a large bowl. Thinly slice the scallions. Shred the carrot on a box grater. Add both to the cabbage. Add the dressing to the cabbage and toss until it is completely incorporated.

½ cup mayonnaise

¼ cup apple cider vinegar

3 tablespoons sugar

1 tablespoon Dijon mustard

1 tablespoon granulated garlic

1 tablespoon kosher salt

1 teaspoon onion powder

1 teaspoon freshly ground black pepper

½ head green cabbage (about 8 ounces), cored

4 scallions

1 carrot

ACKNOWLEDGMENTS

Many hunters, anglers, and wild-game cooks gave freely of their knowledge, recipes, techniques, and ingredients in order to make this book possible. It would be impossible to list them all, but special thanks to Ed Arnett, April Bloomfield, Ron Boehme, Ryan Callaghan, Tim Collins, Doug Duren, Shannon Harper, Jon Heindemause, James Miller, Nick Moe, Kevin Murphy, Andrew Radzialowski, Daniel Rinella, Matthew Rinella, Clayton Saunders, and Tyler Webster. Thanks also to Vivian Jao, Liz Tarpy, Stacy Basko, Jeannie Chen, and Patty Nusser for their help in testing these recipes to ensure their accuracy and ease of use.

The recipe photos in this book (as well as a lot of tweaking and refining of the recipes themselves) are the result of a great collaborative effort that took place in Bozeman, Montana. Thanks to Pancho Gatchalian, Koren Grivson, and Indra Fanuzzi for cooking. Thanks to Brian Hoffman and Jason Roehrig for dozens of other things, ranging from lighting assistance to vacuum sealing. Finally, thanks Rick Gilbert and Liz Saubuste for their work on sourcing props, and to Yeti, Weston, and Camp Chef for an array of high-quality products that made our work possible.

The imagery in this book comes from a variety of sources. Thanks to the talented John Hafner for the recipe photos in addition to a number of other beautiful images. Thanks to Garret Smith for his many contributions to this book, which were often captured under extremely difficult field conditions. Additional photography thanks to Helen Cho, Patrick Durkin, Kyle Johnson, Mahting Putelis, Daniel Rinella, Jennifer Jones, and Brian Grossenbacher. The detailed and beautiful wildlife illustrations are the work of Ryan Frost.

Many of my colleagues at Zero Point Zero Production were instrumental in the making of this book. Thanks to Joe Caterini, Lydia Tenaglia, and Chris Collins for building a company that fosters the creation of quality work. Thanks to Jared Andrukanis, Eliza Comer, Lou Festa, and Matt Gerish for general support, and to the talented team at ZPZ's graphic-design department (Mike Houston, Naoko Saito, and Dan DeGraaf) for conceptual assistance. Lastly, a huge thanks to Annie Raser and Brittany Brothers for their help and support.

Everyone at MeatEater, Inc., jumped in whenever required to make this book as good as possible. Brody Henderson provided valuable insight, research, and writing. Michelle Jorgensen provided both creative and practical support through much of the process. And, as always, Janis Putelis was involved at virtually every level of the project, ranging from photography to in-the-field expertise to core decisions around content and layout.

Thanks to my agent, Marc Gerald, for his continuing support over the last fourteen or so years, and thanks to Cindy Spiegel of Spiegel & Grau for betting on me time and again over much of that period. You guys have proven to be some of the most important people in my life. Many other folks from the S&G and Penguin Random House teams were deeply involved in this project, including Mengfei Chen, Nancy Delia, Debbie Glasserman, Mark Maguire, Greg Mollica, and Leda Scheintaub.

Lastly, thanks to my collaborator, Krista Ruane. As a writer, editor, stylist, thinker, and chef, Krista oversaw this project from inception to completion. Krista, this book is as much yours as it is mine.

ILLUSTRATION AND PHOTO CREDITS

Helen Cho 74, 220, 225, 293

Patrick Durkin 264

Ryan Frost 10,11, 80, 81, 112, 113, 148, 149, 182, 183, 184, 185, 222, 223, 224, 254, 274, 275

John Hafner vi, viii, ix, x, 28, 32, 34, 37, 38, 41, 42, 45, 46, 47, 51, 52, 55, 56, 58, 61, 66, 88, 90, 91, 93, 96, 99, 102, 104, 106, 108, 109, 122, 125, 126, 130, 134, 138, 140, 142, 144, 155, 156, 163, 164, 167, 168, 171, 172, 196, 199, 200, 205, 206, 211, 212, 234, 238, 240, 243, 244, 250, 252, 255, 260, 263, 284, 287, 288, 294, 297, 298, 300, 302, 304, 308, 315, 322, 326, 331, 334, 336, 340

Jon Heindemause 218

Kyle Johnson 191, 268, 280, 281, 282

Jennifer Jones 271, 277

Janis Putelis 216

Mahting Putelis 72, 76

Daniel Rinella 191, 237, 272, 279

Krista Ruane 246

Garret Smith xiii, xiv, 2, 3, 4, 6, 8, 9, 12, 14, 15, 16, 18, 20, 22, 23, 24, 25, 26, 27, 29, 31, 70, 75, 77, 78, 82, 83, 84, 85, 86, 87, 110, 114, 116, 117, 121, 145, 146, 150, 151, 152, 153, 154, 176, 178, 180, 181, 186, 188, 189, 190, 192, 193, 194, 195, 214, 226, 227, 228, 229, 230, 231, 232, 248, 256, 257, 258, 259, 270, 276, 278, 291, 307, 311, 319, 328, 332, 338

Yeti Coolers iv, 219

Yeti Coolers/Brian Grossenbacher 266

INDEX

ABOUT THE AUTHOR

STEVEN RINELLA hosts the TV show *MeatEater* and the MeatEater podcast. He is the author of two volumes of *The Complete Guide to Hunting, Butchering, and Cooking Wild Game; Meat Eater: Adventures from the Life of an American Hunter; American Buffalo: In Search of a Lost Icon;* and *The Scavenger's Guide to Haute Cuisine.* His writing has also appeared in many publications, including *Outside, Field and Stream, The New Yorker, Glamour, The New York Times, Men's Journal, Salon, O: The Oprah Magazine, Bowhunter,* and the anthologies *Best American Travel Writing* and *Best Food Writing.* He was born and raised in Michigan.

stevenrinella.com
Facebook.com/StevenRinellaMeatEater
Twitter: @stevenrinella